Architect's
Essentials of
Cost
Management

Architect's Essentials of Cost Management

Michael D. Dell'Isola, PE, CVS

John Wiley & Sons, Inc.

Library of Congress Cataloging-in-Publication Data:

Dell'Isola, Michael D.
    Architect's essentials of cost management / by Michael D. Dell'Isola.
       p. cm.
    ISBN 0-471-44359-X
    1. Architectural practice—Economic aspects.   I. Title.
    NA1996 .D45 2002
    720'.68'1—dc 21
                                        2002001014

Contents

Foreword

Few things can be more devastating to an architectural practice than a major project cost overrun. A client is probably lost, profits evaporate as the damage is contained and corrected, and the firm's reputation is irreparably damaged for many years to come.

Despite all this, not a lot has been done to improve the profession's capabilities in estimating and managing costs creatively. Certainly there is a lot of product dealing with the estimating of construction costs and extensive published and automated databases, with exhaustive up-to-date cost information, all supplemented by a wide variety of automated estimating programs. But, is this all really useful to the profession?

It has always seemed to me that trying to sell, train, or persuade architects to become construction estimators, was a misdirected effort. Most architects by their nature are more focused on concepts than details. Rather, what is needed is a new approach to dealing with costs during design which is not focused on detail, but on design concepts.

It all comes down to how we actually look at costs. To many, there is only one way they can be viewed—building costs equate to an aggregation of exhaustive detail, beginning with the cost of labor to install, materials required, equipment needed, overheads and profits to be absorbed, and so on. Thus, from this perspective, the only way to estimate costs is to determine the quantities and values of these basic ingredients from the bottom up. Unfortunately, this is not the way a building design evolves. In fact, it is quite the reverse. A written statistical and descriptive program leads to a highly creative translation into a schematic/conceptual design, which is only then followed by the definition of systems, components, and products required to fulfill the concept.

While the seeds of a building's final cost are sowed in the initial program, it is really during the conceptual design that the template is established. It is exactly at this point and the immediate phase of design, that the architect must concentrate his or her efforts in establishing and setting the framework for ongoing cost control.

At long last, a book has been written that will help every architect in this endeavor. It provides background in understanding the fundamentals of building economics, that is, exactly what are the main conceptual drivers of construction cost. For those unfamiliar with the UNIFORMAT, it explains the use of this powerful framework for checking and establishing budgets, preparing conceptual estimates, controlling costs through design and construction, and recycling cost experience for future use creatively on other projects.

It has been my pleasure to have worked with the author, Michael Dell'Isola, during my years at Hanscomb and before. During his career he has done a great deal to promote the concepts of life-cycle costing, value-enhanced design, and responsible cost management to the architectural profession.

I commend this book to you and I trust that it will serve you well.

Brian Bowen
President (retired), Hanscomb Inc.
Atlanta, GA

Acknowledgments

This book presents the subject of cost management with an emphasis on the early planning and design phases of project delivery and with a focus on the importance of integrating cost management into the design process. Building economics and cost estimating are presented as key subjects. The book also includes important subjects integral to cost management including value management/engineering, life-cycle costing, sustainability, risk management, and the impact of new delivery methods on cost management.

I believe that effective cost management and high-quality design are not contradictory subjects. In the long run, effective cost management may in fact benefit the quality of design. This is an important issue for designers and architects alike.

Numerous individuals and organizations participated in the development of material utilized in this book and provided important information and examples. In particular, Hanscomb Inc., my employer for nearly 15 years, generously supported the development of this book, contributed projects from which material was drawn, and provided a positive environment for the book's development.

For many years Hanscomb has actively developed cost management workbooks and seminar material for such organizations as Pennsylvania State University, the American Institute of Architects, and the General Services Administration of the federal government, to name a few. Much of the material contained in this book was originally conceived in these workbooks and seminar materials, with special credit to Brian Bowen, former president of Hanscomb and an industry leader in cost management.

It would not have been possible to prepare this text without the continuing support and encouragement of my family. This includes my brothers, Al and Anthony; my sister, Ann; my sons, Michael, Drew, and John; and especially, my wife of many years, Debbie.

Architect's Essentials of Cost Management

Introduction

Owners are demanding that designers and builders relate more strongly to their financial and economic objectives and demonstrate more effective cost management in the delivery of projects. Regardless of industry, location, or financial situation, owners expect their design and construction team to manage project costs in an accurate and responsive manner. Architects, as leaders and managers of the design process, are also expected to take a leadership role in the cost management process.

Owners expect that an accurately defined budget will be prepared early in a project and, subsequently, that the project will be completed to required scope, quality, and performance, all within that budget. Owners invariably consider cost to be a high-priority issue and often a differentiating aspect of perceived success or failure, regardless of the quality or other attributes of the built facility. Often, meeting a budget is necessary to financially justify a project.

During the past decade, organizations including the American Institute of Architects (AIA), A/E/C Systems, Georgia Institute of Technology, Pennsylvania State University, The Design-Build Institute of America, and the U.S. General Services Administration have supported the development of methodology, seminars, and other educational programs on this subject. Numerous papers, workbooks, and several textbooks have been written on the subject of cost estimating and cost management. Furthermore, organizations including The Construction Specifications Institute, The American Society for Testing and Materials (ASTM), The National Institute of Standards and Technology (NIST), and The National Institute of Building Sciences (NIBS) have cooperated on efforts to define and describe cost-estimating and document-management formats.

This book, *The Architect's Essentials of Cost Management,* reviews, collects, and expands on these efforts to present an organized approach to cost management for architects and designers, in the following format:

- ➤ Chapter 1 introduces the topic.
- ➤ Chapter 2 discusses building economics, which include components that make up construction cost, major factors influencing cost, and new industry trends to consider.
- ➤ Chapter 3 deals with cost-estimating methodology and presents suggested formats, probable cost drivers, basic estimating principles, and recommended estimating methods, as well as advanced techniques associated with life-cycle costing and value management.
- ➤ Chapter 4 summarizes available cost-estimating tools, both in published form and through computer systems; how to develop and maintain cost data files; how to work with cost indexes; and offers some suggestions on dealing with computer-assisted estimating.
- ➤ Chapter 5 suggests a cost management methodology, with a focus on the essentials to be

applied. Subjects include budgeting and cost planning, cost management during design and construction, and the potential impacts of alternate delivery methods on cost management.

What in fact are the essentials of cost management? The methodology is not complex in concept; in practice it is very simple, comprising only three steps:

1. Accurately define scope, user/owner expectations, and budget from the outset.
2. Assure that scope, user/owner expectations, and budget are all in alignment.
3. Maintain a balance and alignment through completion of the project.

Graphically, this relationship is depicted in Figure 1.1.

Experience has clearly shown that projects must start right to have a reasonable chance of finishing right. That said, for numerous reasons, it seems to be extremely difficult to invest the time and effort required to start projects correctly. Typically, this is not one person's fault per se; it is simply a result of the impatience that is common to our industry.

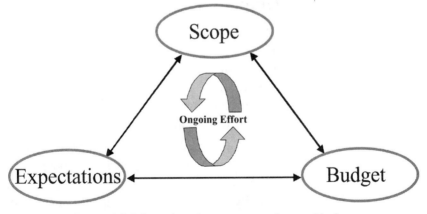

Figure 1.1 Relationship of scope, expectations, and budget.

There is often a rush to get a project started, to commit funds, to gain a leg on the competition, and to commit resources.

Alignment problems are caused by disconnects among scope, expectations, and budget. One lesson we have learned over the past several decades is that it is extremely difficult, time-consuming, and contentious to try to design our way out of alignment problems. The message is simple: *The design process should not be a solution for alignment problems.*

Initial alignment problems usually result from incomplete or ineffective planning and programming, from inconsistencies in requirements, or from significantly flawed conceptual approaches. To solve these problems, planning and programming level solutions are required. When alignment problems surface during the design process, that is the time to recognize that the project will likely require replanning and reprogramming, not just redesign. This is not just semantics, but a clear statement that design should follow adequate planning and programming.

Terminology

In our industry, there are few absolute rights and wrongs in use of terms and accepted standards, and definitions vary considerably. However, to facilitate clear communication it is important to use basic definitions and terminology consistently. To that end, in this book, we will apply the following definitions:

> ▶ *Scope.* Essentially, scope defines the "how much" portion of the process, to include the measurable and quantifiable aspects of the facility: measures of program, building geometry, and facility performance.

▶ *Expectations.* A working definition of this term is difficult to achieve, as it is subject to judgment. That said, essentially, we can define expectations as the "how good" component of the process, the resulting quality and performance the client anticipates. These expectations include aesthetics, quality, systems performance, facility performance, project delivery, and external requirements.

▶ *Budget.* Budget addresses the "what will it cost" portion of the process. A comprehensive budget, especially from the owner's point of view, should include not only the initial procurement, but also the total owning costs of the facility, which are composed of initial costs, future onetime costs, facility annual costs, and functional use costs.

Figure 1.2 assigns these definitions to a hierarchy. Keep in mind that these definitions may vary from project to project and that consistency is more important than precision.

Cost Management Considerations

Implementing a successful cost management methodology requires utilizing appropriate standards, concentrating efforts for maximum effectiveness, and being consistent. Some key considerations in this regard presented in this book are:

▶ *Instituting standard formats.* A standard format is essential to effectively communicate information from project phase to phase and from project to project. The most common format, MasterFormat, is based on trades/crafts and materials, and works well for prescriptive speci-

SCOPE	EXPECTATIONS	BUDGET
• Program ‑ Functional Space Program ‑ Blocking & Stacking ‑ Public Space ‑ Efficiency **• Geometric Drivers** ‑ Wall Area Ratio ‑ Degree of Articulation **• Volume Drivers** ‑ Clear Ceiling Height ‑ Plenum Height ‑ Interstitial Needs ‑ Atria ‑ Light Shelves **• Facility Parameters** ‑ HVAC SF/Ton ‑ Watts/SF ‑ Plumbing Fixtures ‑ Ductwork Poundage ‑ Steel Pounds/SF ‑ Etc.	**• Aesthetics** ‑ Form & Massing ‑ Image ‑ Community Requirements ‑ Design Issues **• Quality** ‑ Systems ‑ Materials ‑ Workmanship **• Project Delivery** ‑ Phasing &Scheduling ‑ Continued Occupancy ‑ Delivery System **• Systems Performance** ‑ Functional Space Elements ‑ Building Management ‑ Maintainability ‑ Energy Consumption ‑ Sustainability **• Facility Performance** ‑ Live Loads ‑ Expandability ‑ Flexibility ‑ Security & Safety ‑ Access & Egress ‑ Adjacencies ‑ Natural Light **• External Requirements** ‑ Codes ‑ Standards & Criteria	**• Initial Costs** ‑ Site Acquisition ‑ Fees ‑ Construction ‑ Inflation and Market Conditions ‑ Contingencies ‑ Other Costs **• Future One-Time Costs** ‑ Replacements ‑ Alterations ‑ Salvage ‑ Other One-Time Costs **• Facility Annual Costs** ‑ Operations ‑ Maintenance ‑ Financing ‑ Taxes ‑ Insurance ‑ Security ‑ Other Annual Costs **• Functional Use Costs** ‑ Staffing ‑ Materials ‑ Denial of Use ‑ Other Functional Use Costs

Figure 1.2 Hierarchy of scope, expectations, and budget.

fications. But MasterFormat is less useful for comparing competing design alternatives and tracking historical data. Instead, UNIFORMAT, a system originally developed in the 1970s and updated in the last few years, is an elemental or systems-based format that is more effective when dealing with the issues of design phase cost management. Therefore, UNIFORMAT is strongly encouraged in this book for use as a primary format. (Chapter 3 presents a detailed discussion of recommended formats.)

➤ *Focusing on cost drivers.* It is critical to concentrate on the true cost drivers for any project; there simply is not enough time to "sweat all the details" from a cost perspective. Often, relatively minor decisions can cause substantial ripple effects or may force other decisions not anticipated. Effective cost management requires having a "big picture" focus, using Pareto's "20 percent – 80 percent" principle of cost distribution, as presented in Figure 1.3. (Vilfredo Pareto, an Italian economist of the late nineteenth and early twentieth centuries, developed the principle of The Maldistribution of Costs, which essentially stated that in any item made up of a large number of components, a very small number would contain the vast majority of cost.) This rule is a common thread in cost management approaches.

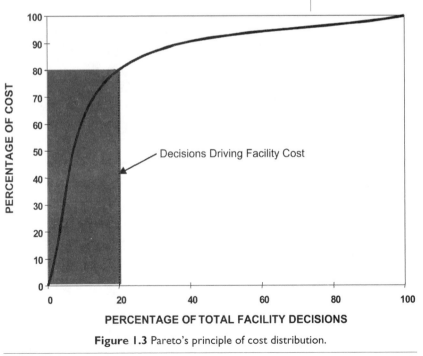

Figure 1.3 Pareto's principle of cost distribution.

▶ *Emphasizing early design process.* Effective cost management requires focusing on the planning, programming, and early design decision-making process where change can usually be accommodated without major disruption to the project. Often, by the design development phase, significant change causes major disruption. This is not to imply that cost management during design development or during the preparation of construction documents is not important, but that the level of focus should be substantially narrowed by design development; otherwise, the cost to implement change will be prohibitive. Figure 1.4 diagrams the relationship between time and change; this will be further emphasized in Chapter 5, where cost management philosophy is discussed.

▶ *Paying attention to the relationship between quality and cost.* The relationship between quality and cost is not linear. If it were, decisions would be much simpler to make, in that increases or decreases in cost would follow comparable increases or decreases in quality: a 25 percent

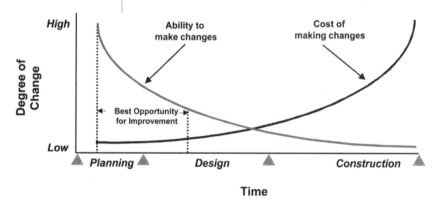

Figure 1.4 Relationship between time and change.

increase in quality or performance would always be accompanied by a 25 percent increase in price. Unfortunately, the fact is that building systems and components can exhibit sharp skews, where modest increases in quality can result in substantial increases in cost. When confronted with these selections, great care should be taken to select an appropriate level of quality. Unnecessary added quality might come at a prohibitive cost.

▶ *Considering life-cycle costs.* Because spending more initially might result in beneficial payback over the life of the project, future cost implications should also be considered. Likewise, an unnecessary investment in quality or performance may have an extremely poor payback. For any system there is probably a "best" life-cycle choice, that is, there likely is a system choice with superior economic performance. This relationship is presented in Figure 1.5. Chapter 3 describes life-cycle costing and value engineering and demonstrates how they can be useful tools in the overall cost management process. Emphasizing life-cycle costs, as opposed to initial costs, is an important aspect of this book.

▶ *Identifying and managing risks.* Every project decision contains risk; but from a cost perspective, some decisions are much riskier than others, requiring sharper focus on contingency planning and identifying alternate approaches that help to mitigate the inherent risk. Figure 1.6 provides a simplistic comparison of how single-point estimates can have significantly different risks. Later, in Chapter 3, risk management is

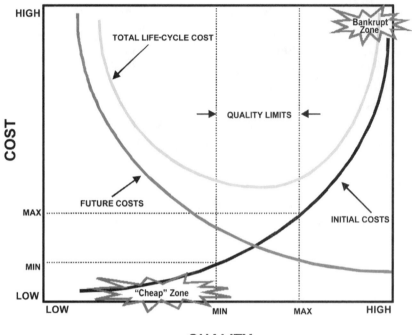

Figure 1.5 Relationship between quality and cost.

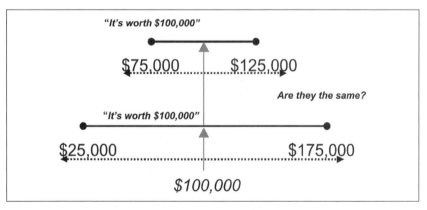

Figure 1.6 Single-point estimate comparisons.

discussed in greater detail, to provide guidance for how to identify significant risks and to determine potential cost implications. Many of the "20–80" decisions are risk-related; therefore, accurate and sensitive cost management should be responsive to risk issues.

► *Using historical cost information wisely.* Historical cost information can be obtained from a variety of sources: experienced staff, published cost data, information from other organizations, and owner-provided cost data. Early cost estimates may be largely based on historical cost, while later estimates may be priced in detail from a complete quantity survey. Regardless of where cost information comes from, great care should be taken to ensure that sources are reliable and that "comparables" are in fact comparable. It is extremely important to clearly understand the technical basis, market conditions, timeframe, and exclusions/inclusions associated with historical cost information. A factor as seemingly straightforward as "method of measurement" can be a source of dramatic error if it is not interpreted in a consistent manner. Though experience proves that establishing budgets and enacting controls solely on the basis of historical costs can lead to severe project problems, there is no rational excuse for not maintaining accurate historical data on "in-house" projects. To help with that endeavor, this book will present methods and techniques for gathering and storing historical project information.

► *Estimating costs effectively.* There is no substitute for sound cost estimating, whether provided from internal sources or outside consultants or constructors. Furthermore, the accuracy of any estimate is only as good as the information on which it is based; this is also true of the assumptions that invariably must be made from those estimates, especially for early-stage estimates. Experience dictates taking these steps to improve the accuracy and validity of estimates: (1) clearly document the estimate; (2) promote a clear understanding among all parties of anticipated level of detail and format; (3) assure buy-in by all parties involved in the estimate; (4) properly evaluate market factors, contingencies, and major risks; and (5) allow adequate time both in terms of the calendar and level of effort required to prepare an accurate estimate. Chapters 3 and 5 describe a methodology and techniques for including estimating into the overall cost management process.

Cost Management Methodology

Cost estimating is a tool; cost management is the application of that tool within an overall project management structure. Effective cost management enables all involved in a project to respond to project challenges and to understand the interrelationships that result from various decisions about costs. Effective cost management is achievable for most organizations if they have a clear objective to align scope, user/owner expectations, and budget from the outset and over time. Here are the basic steps necessary to implement and maintain a cost management process, as differentiated from simple, reactive cost estimating:

1. *Develop the proper budget.* A proper budget is one that is connected to scope and expectations. This requires the conversion of the facility program to a "Cost Plan" prior to initiating design. This effort entails converting program requirements to facility requirements and assuring that user/owner expectations of quality and performance are reflected in specific facility materials and systems assumptions that drive the Cost Plan. The Cost Plan is the basis of a design-to-cost approach and connects the budget to a specific program, user expectations, and scope. This approach may represent a substantial change for designers. Preparing cost plans is discussed in Chapters 3 and 5.

2. *Use the Cost Plan to apportion the overall budget by major components and disciplines.* Ensure that each participant in the design process has a clear understanding of his or her respective budget and the key parameters for measuring the individual's discipline.

3. *During design development, monitor individual technical decisions for their effect on project cost.* Decisions affecting cost typically are made incrementally as the design evolves; therefore, *as these decisions are made,* their consequences (economic and otherwise) should be clearly understood by the designers, builders, and owner/user staff. Update the Cost Plan periodically to reflect these changes between milestone estimates. At major milestones, prepare new estimates and modify the baseline Cost Plan accordingly.

4. *During the process, make intelligent trade-offs as necessary between aspects of scope, quality, and performance to maintain the project within the overall budget.* Track critical measures and parameters

of scope and user/owner expectations as indicators of progress. Deviations from planned amounts may indicate potential cost problems. Adjust contingencies relative to current design development and outstanding risks. As an integral part of the process, select the particular delivery method to be utilized for construction. Continue this process through the design phase, preparing milestone estimates to fully update the Cost Plan.

5. *Use benchmarking as a technique for comparing and contrasting the project with other projects already constructed.*

6. *Use life-cycle costing and economic analysis as tools for determining long-term costs, operations sustainability, and, potentially, functional staffing.* Owners expect their designer, consultants, and builders to be fully aware of economic consequences. These issues are discussed in Chapters 3 and 5.

7. *Consider value management/engineering as another important tool for improving the cost management process.* Too often in the past, value management has been applied too late, and with insufficient sensitivity to issues that drive the project and are important to the owner. Chapters 3 and 5 present techniques that have been successfully applied to formal value management sessions involving the design team, owner staff, constructor staff, and outside expertise as necessary. These sessions, which provide creative input and a comprehensive review of all decisions, become progressively more detailed as the design develops, culminating in a prebid constructibility review.

8. *Throughout construction, review and assess changes, and address potential schedule/cost issues. Once construction is complete, assess the project for performance*

relative to expectations, catalog historical data, and benchmark the project against comparable projects.
Applying these techniques will help to assure that scope, expectations, and budget remain aligned throughout the life of the project and that owner demands for more effective cost management will be satisfied.

Building Economics

What makes buildings cost what they cost? We all understand the cost of buying a suit, an automobile, or even a house. From experience we develop a feel for what something should cost; but unless we ourselves fabricate the item from its component parts most of us can't develop a sense for what *makes it* cost what it costs. Construction projects are complicated entities made up of many materials put in place by workers, assisted by machines. But like the famous $400 toilet seat, a lot more goes into its cost than just the seat itself. The point is, to gain an understanding of how to manage costs, it is first necessary to decipher and differentiate the components of construction cost.

Buildings are complex, from the way they are designed to the way they are constructed, and it is the purpose of this chapter to introduce the concept of building elements as they relate to issues of design. In contrast, the way buildings are specified and constructed tends to relate more to the trades, crafts, and materials of construction, and this topic is covered in Chapter 3.

Breakdown of Construction Costs

Construction costs derive from the materials, labor, and equipment necessary to put those materials in place. A variety of job-site-related overheads contribute to management of the project, while additional markups are applied relative to the "home office" cost of doing business. Figure 2.1 presents these costs as a hierarchy of elements.

Material cost is the most straightforward of all the cost components. The first step is to purchase the material directly at a direct material purchase price. Taxes may be added at both the local and regional levels. Shipping and handling (S&H) costs may be added to cover transportation, warehousing, and, in some cases, security. For stateside contracts, S&H is not usually a substantial burden on top of the initial purchase costs, but in remote areas or in overseas

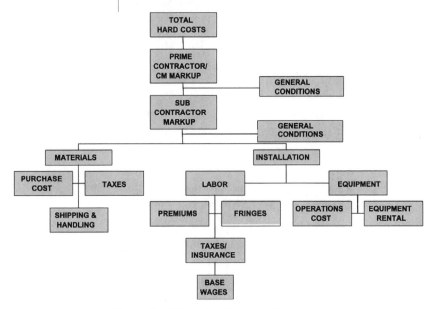

Figure 2.1 Hierarchy of construction costs.

locations, shipping, handling, and other overheads may exceed the direct purchase costs of the material itself.

Installation is made up of labor and equipment costs. Labor consists of direct labor, made up of base wages, plus a variety of taxes and insurance relative to those base wages. There are also so-called fringe costs that consist of a variety of items such as vacation and other benefits. Other premiums may be associated with labor—costs for overtime or, in remote locations, for transportation, housing, and subsistence. Equipment costs are generally considered companion costs to labor in that most equipment is intended to enhance labor's productivity. Of course, there is the direct cost of the equipment itself (whether it is a purchase amortization or a rental), plus the cost of the equipment operator, which includes, in some cases, supporting staff. In other cases, the mobilization and demobilization costs associated with equipment will be included in the direct equipment costs.

Direct costs usually include materials and installation. In some cases, special burdens for shipping and handling on materials or premiums associated with managing labor, such as travel and subsistence, will be carried separately as an extended general conditions cost.

Management costs associated with overseeing the actual in-place process consist of elements usually referred to as *general conditions*. Field-related general conditions consist of the field supervisory staff, additional professional services staff, usually on a part-time basis to handle scheduling, engineering, temporary facilities, small tools, temporary utilities, and a variety of safety and security equipment. Also included in this category, and allocated to the project under this category, are bonds, permits, and insurance costs. As mentioned previously, additional costs such as temporary lodging, travel, and other labor-related costs may be allocated under general conditions. All contractors and subcontractors on-site incur general conditions costs, which sometimes, at a subcontractor level, are rolled up as part of the subcontract costs; on larger projects, general conditions costs for major subcontractors may be rolled in to the overall general contractor or construction manager general conditions. Some facilities and services, such as temporary power, will be shared among all contractors, but their costs can be easily separated for each subcontractor, as they apply, for example, to the job-site trailer and on-site storage.

Additional markups include overheads associated with the main office of each contractor, comprising salaries of home office staff, certain insurance costs, various home office overhead costs (job procurement, marketing, advertising, etc.), and profit. Depending on the degree of risk associated with the project, a contingency may be carried as part of general conditions and/or markup.

Why Costs Vary

The availability of materials and the relative supply and demand against those materials will affect their direct purchase price. Availability may also affect the time required for delivery, which can have a significant impact on the overall installation—for example, necessitating an out-of-phase installation. As already noted, shipping and handling costs, especially in remote areas, can have a major impact on the cost of materials. Special project requirements, such as the

Buy America Act and other procurement-related factors, can substantially drive up cost by limiting competition. A variety of sales taxes, import/export duties, and other special fees indirectly affect the cost of material.

Installation costs vary according to an even more complex series of relationships. Labor productivity is a driving force in the cost of installation. It is not uncommon in areas where labor rates are very low for productivity to also be very low, such that the actual in-place cost per unit may be relatively high in spite of low wages. Taxes and insurance also have the potential to generate a major impact on labor costs. Certain trades, such as demolition, carry very high insurance premiums due to the risks associated with the work. Furthermore, the safety record of the contractor will affect the insurance premium. Work conditions, particularly associated with renovation, will also have a dramatic impact on productivity; factors to consider include access, egress, laydown area, staging area, and general space available to conduct business. Scheduling ramifications can also reduce productivity, hamper access to the work, and may require multiple work activities to be going on at the same place at the same time. Equipment costs have numerous variables, from a direct as well as an indirect cost point of view. For example, all trades may share certain equipment such as cranes, conveyors, and even basic vehicles. How efficiently this equipment sharing is scheduled and managed will have a significant impact on the cost of equipment relative to the installation tasks.

The complexity of the project site, the remoteness of the site, and availability of utility services on the site affect general conditions costs. Security required to control overall access and installation likewise may be a major issue. The owner may dictate site availability, and have dust, dirt, and general job cleanup requirements; all these indirectly affect cost.

Other markups are a function of market competition and project risk. In competitive times, allocations of overhead and profit to a project will tend to be reduced; in less competitive periods, naturally these costs will tend to increase. Risk is always a significant factor, but can be difficult to predict because each contractor may view risk in different ways. Owner bonding requirements indirectly affect risk relative to payment/performance bonds that in fact may cascade up and down from subcontractor to subcontractor. Some owners, who feel that extremely onerous bonding requirements protect them, may be unaware of the price.

Obviously, how well these issues are understood and controlled will have a significant impact on cost. Implementing an effective cost management system to handle these issues involves preparing an initial budget and managing that budget throughout the life of the project. Experience has shown that owners and their representatives will tend to amplify risk control and/or seek to transfer risk in an effort to protect against nonproject risks. The point is, costs and benefits of transferring risk will not always be in proportion.

Cost Components

The previous section subdivided costs as applied to the actual conduct of work. But costs can also be subdivided based on the reasons for spending the money in the first place. Capital costs are normally subdi-

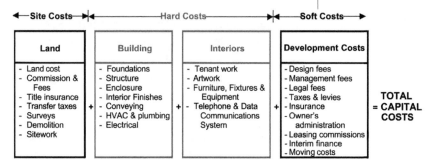

Land	Building	Interiors	Development Costs

- Land cost
- Commission &
  Fees
- Title insurance
- Transfer taxes
- Surveys
- Demolition
- Sitework
	- Foundations
	- Structure
	- Enclosure
	- Interior Finishes
	- Conveying
	- HVAC & plumbing
	- Electrical
		- Tenant work
		- Artwork
		- Furniture, Fixtures &
		  Equipment
		- Telephone & Data
		  Communications
		  System
			- Design fees
			- Management fees
			- Legal fees
			- Taxes & levies
			- Insurance
			- Owner's
			  administration
			- Leasing commissions
			- Interim finance
			- Moving costs

Figure 2.2 Components of capital costs.

vided into three major categories—*site costs, hard costs,* and *soft costs*—all of which are summarized in Figure 2.2.

Site Costs

Site costs normally relate to the initial acquisition and development of the land on which the building is being constructed. Associated with the purchase price of the land are commissions and fees, along with a variety of insurances and taxes. There are also often a series of work-site costs for the initial preparation of the site; these may include surveys, demolition, environmental impact statements, and special studies, as well as developmental costs for roads, utilities, and site amenities. In some situations, these costs may be incurred in advance of the development of the building project. In other cases, many of these costs may be directly associated and allocated to the building project.

Hard Costs

The hard-cost component of the work can be subdivided into two and perhaps three categories, depending on the nature of the project. Building costs include the core and shell development associated with the structure, closure, basic building services, and, in some instances, public space. The building costs may also be subdivided into *shell* and *fit-out* costs, where the fit-out includes interior work for finishes and mechanical electrical services. The other major component of hard costs is a collective comprising furniture, fixtures, equipment (FF&E), and specialized mechanical electrical services. These costs usually are not incurred under the direct construction costs contract, but often are procured directly by the owner.

A relatively recent development in the hard-cost category is the increasing owner emphasis on *building commissioning*. Essentially, building commissioning consists of the initialization of building systems, training of operating staff, and handing over of manuals and building management software. Until recently, building commissioning was an aspect of only very complicated buildings, such as laboratories or wafer fabrication plants, but more owners are becoming interested in securing a separate building commissioning process. Building commissioning may be part of the construction contract for the building and interiors or be procured through a completely separate contractor.

Soft Costs

A variety of soft costs are incurred by the owner: design fees, management and legal fees, taxes, insurance, owner's administration costs, and a number of financing costs. Moving costs and other tenant-related costs may also be included in the soft-cost category.

Collectively, all costs associated with the initial development of a facility are considered *capital costs*.

From a cost management perspective, a sizable portion of capital costs may be entirely beyond the control of the cost manager; experience indicates that few owners allocate costs in exactly the same way, meaning there is a high likelihood that some costs will be included in the wrong category or not included at all. One owner, for example, may spend a great deal of time and effort estimating and budgeting for certain very prominent costs, while spending minimal time and effort budgeting for other less "visible" costs. The message to the cost manager is: Be extremely careful and diligent when budgeting for those items under your direct control, while assuring that other costs are properly budgeted and managed by the owner. If this is not done, once the owner has allocated capital costs, and certain categories prove to be under-budgeted, the owner may be forced to compensate by cutting costs in other categories. The result may be that hard costs will have to compensate for inadequately budgeted soft costs.

Distribution of Hard Costs

Costs are distributed by labor, materials, and equipment in relatively consistent proportions for most building types. This relationship is shown in Figure 2.3. However, the building type will dictate distributions of cost between the major building elements. First, every building type will have a significantly different cost; second, the system requirements for every building will vary substantially. For example, an office building can typically be built for between $80 per square foot and $150 per square foot, depending on quality and performance requirements. In contrast, a laboratory building may cost from $150 per square foot to over $400 per square

TIP

Costs are distributed by labor, materials, and equipment in relatively consistent proportions for most building types.

Component	Basis of Estimating	Approximate Percentage
Materials	Quantities + waste x price	55%
Labor on-site	Hours x rate per hour	30%
Equipment & Tools	Type + length of time required x rate + setup	3%
Site Supervision	Nos. x months	3%
Site Overheads	Type/cost	5%
Office/Co. Overhead	Percentage	1%
Profit	Percentage	3%

Figure 2.3 Approximate distribution of building costs.

foot, again depending on quality and performance requirements. Obviously, the subdivision of costs will vary accordingly. To illustrate this issue, Figure 2.4 compares the cost of an office building and apartment, based on information extracted from an R. S. Means publication (*Square Foot Costs* [2000]). Note that the approximate total cost per square foot of the apartment building and the office building (core and shell only) are quite close, at approximately $90 per square foot. However, the way the costs are distributed among elements vary substantially, with two elements being immediately obvious. One, the superstructure costs of the office building are higher than those of the apartment building because loads are higher and spans are likewise longer. Two, interior construction costs are distributed differently, primarily because the office building represents only shell and core, whereas the interior construction costs are allocated for only public spaces.

Building Element		Apartment Building 15 st – 162,000 SF	Office Building 15 st – 140,000 SF (shell & core)
A.10	Foundations	$ 1.05	$ 1.64
A.20	Basement Construction	—	—
B.10	Superstructure	11.95	16.28
B.20	Exterior Closure	8.89	13.16
B.30	Roofing	0.26	0.39
C.10	Interior Construction	13.94	2.76
C.20	Staircases	1.04	1.44
C.30	Interior Finishes	10.20	10.10
D.10	Conveying	5.64	6.53
D.20	Plumbing	8.06	1.48
D.30	HVAC	9.12	11.64
D.40	Fire Protection	2.01	2.89
D.50	Electrical	6.62	9.27
F.10	Special Construction	1.92	—
Z.	General Conditions	12.11	11.64
	(Sitework Excluded)	$ 92.81/SF	$ 89.22/SF

Source: R. S. Means's *Square Foot Costs* (2000 issue).

Figure 2.4 How the building dollar is spent.

Interestingly, in Figure 2.4, the cost distribution for interior finishes is quite close overall. This is because interior finishes throughout the apartment building are generally modest, and interior finishes of the office building are very high-end but only include the public spaces. This illustrates that even though functional requirements drive costs, care must be taken to account for costs. Other cost-distribution categories, such as plumbing, differ between the two building types because of functional requirements. Apartment buildings have a very dense fixture requirement, whereas office buildings have relatively light fixture requirements.

Even within similar building types the cost per element may vary because of program and/or performance requirements. Laboratory mechanical costs also could exceed $150 per square foot especially when control, filtration, and cleanliness requirements are extreme.

Thus, the cost manager has to be aware of the potential variations that may exist as a cause of functional requirements. If, for example, mechanical costs are expected to represent 40 to 50 percent of overall project costs, the cost manager would have to pay closer attention to initial budgeting and ongoing cost management activities for mechanical elements. Great precision may be required in deciphering project/program requirements in order to manage costs properly.

Factors That Influence Building Costs

In Chapter 1, the concept of *alignment* was presented in the context of the importance of connecting scope, expectations, and budget. The importance of focusing on cost drivers was also introduced, pointing out that 20 percent of the decisions made throughout a project's life will dictate 80 percent of the eventual cost (Pareto's principle). It becomes obvious that effective cost management will result from controlling the major factors that influence building costs.

Scope

The first and most basic issue to deal with is scope. As scope increases, costs almost invariably increase accordingly. Scope is dependent on the facility's space program, certain elements of which require time and attention to prevent their running out of control. For example, a major private building owner commissioned a study in the late 1980s to examine trends and patterns associated with building scope and, specifically, gross area. Approximately 50 projects were selected for review, to compare the initial size of the project as budgeted (gross area) and then as constructed. The average growth in the size of the buildings was 11.5 percent. If the buildings grew by an average of 11.5 percent, it is not surprising that building costs would tend to grow by an approximately comparable amount. Interestingly, many of the budgets for the projects did not increase over their life, indicating that other compromises were required to offset the increase in building size. In many cases these compromises reduced some aspect of building performance.

According to the study, some of the program growth was absolutely necessary to meet the needs placed on the building, but most of the facilities did not have an increase in budget to accommodate growth, necessary or not. Compromise against building performance became necessary to maintain budget, but this was complicated by the fact that the funding mechanism approach the company had adopted made adding budget a very difficult process.

It must be noted, however, that the study did not examine the buildings in great detail, raising this question: Did those compromises affect the long-term operations of the building? For the cost manager, the point is that scope must be managed and accurately tracked. If program requirements increase, or are not correctly reflected in the first place, then scope will necessarily increase. On the other hand, if the resulting compromises will severely impact the building's intended purpose, then this "robbing Peter to pay Paul" approach is probably not a good idea. Clearly, scope management is an essential element of cost management, and it may be necessary to replan and reprogram the facility rather than rely on the design process as a means of correcting what is basically a planning and programming error.

Expectations

Managing quality and performance expectations as they relate to cost is a much more complicated process than managing scope. For convenience, factors affecting the process can be divided into five major areas:

- ▶ Geographical and site factors
- ▶ Design factors
- ▶ Qualitative and performance factors
- ▶ Legal and administrative factors
- ▶ Market and economic influences

Geographical and Site Factors

Factors affecting the cost of developing the site include the location and the condition of the site. The site location will affect labor rates, material costs, and a variety of urban versus rural cost issues. Local climate, too, has a major influence over selection of building materials and in basic approaches to developing the building itself. Site location will also have an immediate impact on access, egress, and utility provisions. Some large site areas, such as campus and military bases, may require extending utility lines great distances to serve the project. The cost of doing so can exceed the rest of the cost of the project.

Site conditions include basic topography, which will tend to dictate the amount of earth that must be moved to allow for site development and for utilities provisioning. Environmental factors, especially if mitigation is required in some way, could have a significant impact, both on direct and indirect costs, in the latter caused by the effects on scheduling. Water retainage and wetlands mitigation likewise can have major impacts on cost and basic site utilization. Obviously, the presence of rock or other difficult soils will directly impact site development costs, as well as eventual choices for foundations for the building itself.

What do these factors mean to the cost manager? Certainly, many of these issues are difficult to predict, manage, and budget. However, experience has clearly shown that paying attention in advance to site issues, conducting the proper surveys, and investing in appropriate geotechnical work can reduce the risks inherent to these factors. It is, unfortunately, all too common for owners to scrimp on front-end services to save a few dollars of up-front costs, which serves only to create downstream cost and scheduling problems. Proper site investigation efforts will invariably pay for themselves several times over. As an alternative, the cost manager might choose to allocate additional contingency for site-related issues, but the owner may not be willing to go along with this approach.

REMINDER!
Proper site investigation efforts will invariably pay for themselves several times over.

Design Factors

Facility designers control directly and indirectly a number of factors that will affect building costs. Some of these factors are obvious, and others are a bit more subtle. The first issue is plan shape, which relates directly to the degree of articulation of the basic plan and form of the building. From a cost perspective, the simplest floorplate is a perfectly square footprint, but from an architectural perspective, a square footprint may be unacceptable and overly simplistic; the designer may want to enhance the appearance of the building by articulating the form.

Figure 2.5 presents a very simple example of the effects of plan shape on cost. The basic rectangular footprint (excluding the notch) represents a 200-foot perimeter. By creating a notch and adding a "bump," the perimeter expands to 220 feet, a 10 percent increase. The floor area remains constant at 2100 square feet. As a consequence of the perimeter being increased by 10 percent, the wall surface area would also increase by 10 percent, thereby increasing the wall cost by 10 percent. In addition, the number of corners increases from four outside corners to six

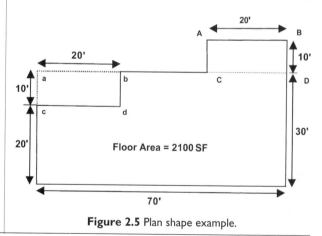

Figure 2.5 Plan shape example.

outside corners, plus two inside corners, for a total of eight. Because, as a general rule, where corners are involved, material utilization is less effective and slightly more labor is required, each corner adds a slight increase in cost. The result is that articulation may be desirable from an aesthetic perspective, but it will cause an increase in cost.

Consequently, plan shape and exterior articulation both require proper budgeting and oversight during the design process. Highly complex forms consisting of shadow lines, notches, and expansions all add benefits to the form but represent concomitant cost increases. This is especially true for buildings that have high-quality skin systems, such as glass or stone, because craftsmanship becomes very important. Another related issue, which will be addressed in later chapters, concerns maintenance and life-cycle performance.

The larger a building becomes, the more the ratio of skin area to enclosed space reduces; hence, certain fixed elements, such as elevators, can be "amortized" over a larger area. It should be obvious that the total building size itself also affects the cost of buildings; the larger a building becomes, the more significant the relationship between external perimeter and enclosed space. This relationship affects many building systems, and the relative proportions of many of the system components will change as the building becomes larger, especially in terms of relative footprint.

Figure 2.6 presents a basic example to illustrate this relationship; it uses a warehouse of simple shape and expands it two bays (loading docks) at a time to double its size. Many of the items in the estimate are related to number of bays, while others are relative to the size

Develop estimates for a warehouse shell of the three different sizes indicated below. For your calculations, use the following composite unit rates:

Wall footing	$ 30.00 LF
Column footings	$250.00 Ea.
Slab on grade	$ 5.00 SF
Structural steel frame and deck	$ 10.00 SF
Exterior siding (15 feet high)	
- front	$ 20.00 SF
- side (load-bearing)	$ 15.00 SF
- rear	$ 10.00 SF
Loading docks	$1,500.00 Ea.
Roofing	$ 5.00 SF
Gravel stops and fascia	$ 3.00 SF

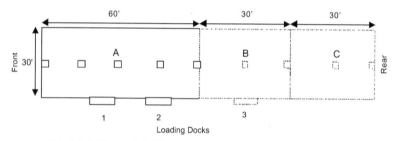

Calculate total cost of shell for (A), (A+B) and (A+B+C), develop unit rate per square foot and plot in graph form.

			A		A + B		A + B + C	
Component	Unit Cost	U/M	Quantity	$	Quantity	$	Quantity	$
Wall Ftg.	30.00	LF	180	5400	240	7200	300	9000
Col. Ftg.	250.00	EA	5	1250	7	1750	9	2250
Slab	5.00	SF	1800	9000	2700	13500	3600	18000
Steel & deck	10.00	SF	1800	18000	2700	27000	3600	36000
Siding-front	20.00	SF	450	9000	450	9000	450	9000
Siding-side	15.00	SF	1800	27000	2700	40500	3600	54000
Siding-rear	10.00	SF	450	4500	450	4500	450	4500
Docks	1500.00	EA	2	3000	3	4500	3	4500
Roofing	5.00	SF	1800	9000	2700	13500	3600	18000
Stops	3.00	LF	180	540	240	720	300	900
				86690		122170		156150
				$48.16		$45.25		$ 43.38

Figure 2.6 Cost effects based on changes in building size.

of the building directly (slab on grade). Referring to the chart in Figure 2.6, it becomes evident that the cost per overall gross square foot will reduce as the building gets larger. The original building at 1800 square feet cost slightly over $48 per square foot; as the building grows, the cost reduces to $45 per foot at 2700 square feet and to just over $43 per foot at 3600 square feet. Once the building doubled in size, the cost reduced by 10 percent. This exact relationship will not necessarily repeat for all buildings and all sizes, but it serves to indicate that as buildings grow their cost per square foot will tend to reduce.

Building height also has an influence on building cost because of the magnitude and scale of the building, because certain costs will increase relative to height (such as structure), and because codes will vary for low- and high-rise construction. Figure 2.7 indicates the general patterns and trends associated with the cost of building elements as the number of floors, and therefore building height, increases. Note that certain elements, such as foundations, roofing, and basement construction, decrease in unit cost because, as building height increases, the relative proportions of these elements decrease and their cost per overall gross square foot likewise decreases. Other elements increase because they become more important as building height increases; superstructure, stairs, and conveying are prime examples. Other items increase because provision of these services, plumbing and HVAC, for example, tends to become somewhat more complex in taller buildings. Exterior closure is another item that will generally go up slightly as building height increases, for the reason that it is slightly more complex to put building closure in place as buildings get taller.

Building Element	As height increases, unit price per SF of gross floor area (GFA) tends to:		
	Increase	Decrease	No Change
A.10 Foundations		✓	
A.20 Basement Construction		✓	
B.10 Superstructure	✓		
B.20 Exterior Closure	✓		
B.30 Roofing		✓	
C.10 Interior Construction			✓
C.20 Staircases	✓		
C.30 Interior Finishes			✓
D.10 Conveying	✓		
D.20 Plumbing	✓		
D.30 HVAC	✓		
D.40 Fire Protection	✓		
D.50 Electrical			✓
F.10 Special Construction			✓
Z. General Conditions	✓		
G. Sitework		✓	

Figure 2.7 Cost effects based on changes in building height.

Certain elements tend not to go up in cost as building height increases because they are more dependent on the interior functions of the building. These include interior construction, interior finishes, and electrical elements—although electrical costs can, to some degree, be affected by building height depending on how power is provided. Generally speaking, sitework will decrease as building height increases because the footprint area is reduced; but this relationship can change if, because of building height, additional requirements are placed on the building site. Where space is limited, underground parking may be required, which obviously would increase the overall building cost. General conditions costs tend to increase because of limitations or constraints over laydown areas, staging areas, access and egress to the site, plus the fact that moving materials is somewhat more complicated to do vertically than horizontally. Thus, the cost manager must factor in building height during the budgeting and overall cost management processes because it has a definite impact on overall building cost.

Space utilization and efficiency are extremely important as well to the overall cost of the building and to the delivered cost of the building per occupant. Whereas direct scope issues discussed previously related primarily to overall gross square foot, space utilization focuses more on net square footage, in particular regarding how the design relates to efficient space utilization. Consider the simple example presented in Figure 2.8. Note that a 5 percent difference in space utilization efficiency yields over 6 percent difference to the cost per net square foot even though the cost per gross square foot is constant. In practice, however, it is always a challenge to accommodate a net program in a particular building form and shape, and buildings tend to grow. Therefore, the cost manager should recognize that it is important to assess actual *delivered* space efficiencies using the delivered efficiencies of comparable buildings to establish this cost.

	GFA	Cost per SF	Net Rentable Floor Area Ratio	Net Rentable Floor Area
Office Building A	140,000 SF	85.00	80%	112,000 SF
Office Building B	140,000 SF	85.00	85%	119,000 SF

What is the cost per SF of rentable area?

A = $106.25
B = $100.00

Figure 2.8 Building efficiency example.

Qualitative and Performance Factors

To repeat, the quality–cost relationship (shown again in Figure 2.9) is not linear; for example, a 10 percent increase in quality is not always accompanied by a 10 percent increase in cost. Understanding this relationship is critical to effective cost management because the selection of materials and systems will have a major impact on cost. In particular, it is extremely important that the owner's requirements be carefully considered both during budgeting and throughout the cost management process. Owners generally set requirements with a bottom threshold, anticipating that delivered quality will meet at least stated minimums. Almost certainly, designers will

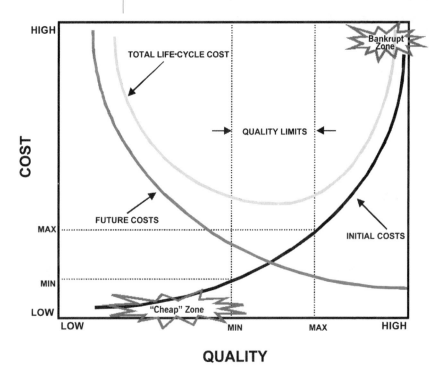

Figure 2.9 Relationship between quality and cost.

meet these minimums and will tend to exceed them because of their desire to provide better quality and performance. If all systems in the building can be ratcheted up by 10 percent and the cost can be contained at or near the original budget, obviously, this will be desirable to the owner. On some projects, this improvement may be possible, but in today's complicated construction environment, if quality and performance are increased by 10 percent, the cost will likely increase by more than 10 percent. Improved quality and performance do not always represent improved value, in that the price paid for this improvement may be disproportionate to the benefit. Raising the level of quality and performance unnecessarily does not equate to good value. This subject will be discussed in more detail in Chapter 3, in the section on value engineering.

It is interesting to note that this phenomenon of increasing quality above owner's needs is evident in many design-bid-build construction projects where the designer does not have a direct risk relationship to the cost outcome other than through a redesign clause. When design-build projects are reviewed, this phenomenon tends to not occur; in fact, there is a tendency for the opposite to happen. For design-build projects to be effective in a cost-driven competition, they should be aligned around the minimum points on most requirements. If the owner emphasizes cost competition, then the design-builders may even slide below that minimum line in an effort to be cost-competitive. This complicated issue is discussed in more detail in Chapter 5, in the section on the impact of delivery methods on cost management.

Figure 2.10 summarizes the factors that influence building element costs, with a principal variable and

System/Element	Principal Variable	Secondary Variables
A.10 Foundations	Footprint area at grade	Soil conditions, site configuration, water table, seismic zone, weight supported, soil disposal, grade slab specs
A.20 Basement Construction	Volume of basement	Soil conditions, soil disposal, water table and flow, depth of basement, type of soil retention, seismic zone
B.10 Superstructure	Area of supported floor & roof	Number of stories, floor-to-floor height, building configuration, loading, span and bay sizes, roof type and openings, seismic zone, MEP integration, type of cladding system
B.20 Exterior Closure	Area of exterior closure	Area and type of fenestration and exterior doors, thermal and sound insulation requirements, seismic zone
B.30 Roofing	Area of roof	Roof configuration and type, number and types of openings, thermal and sound insulation requirements, extent of glazing
C.10 Interior Construction	Gross floor area	Floor-to-ceiling heights, partition/wall density, flexibility required, extent of glazing and special features
C.20 Staircases	Number of flights	Floor-to-floor heights, fire regulations, staircase type
C.30 Interior Finishes	Gross floor area	Floor-to-ceiling height, area of enclosed and finished spaces, type of ceiling, special finish requirements
D.10 Conveying	Number of stories	Capacity and speed required, type of drive system, number of stories, building occupancy
D.20 Plumbing	Density of fixtures	Building occupancy, story heights, roof area, building configuration, special system requirements
D.30 HVAC	Heating/cooling load	Building occupancy and orientation, building area and volume, building configuration, story heights, thermal insulation provided, heat loss & gain, local climate
D.40 Fire Protection	Area protected	Number of stories and story height, fire and insurance regulations, internal configuration
D.50 Electrical	Connected load	Building area, number of stories, building occupancy, standby requirements, lighting levels, power supply and distribution system
F.10 Special Construction	Building function	Special user requirements
Z. General Conditions	Value of construction	Time for construction, temporary utility availability, site access and storage, bonding and insurance requirements, interest rates, market conditions
G. Sitework	Developed area of site	Site configuration and levels, paved areas, special features, demolition required, soil disposal and compaction, soil conditions, exterior lighting and utilities, landscaping extent

Figure 2.10 Factors influencing building element costs.

with a variety of secondary variables. This chart can assist the cost manager in understanding what to examine and what may be the driving factors of cost. Chapter 5 elaborates on these issues.

Legal and Administrative Factors

Legal and administrative factors also affect cost. The delivery method chosen may impact the cost of the project in a number of ways. Whether the choice of delivery method is design-bid-build, design-build, or construction management at risk, and if the owner is utilizing a project manager as an agent, the initial budgeting and the cost management process will be affected. The choice of delivery method one way or another transfers risk to/from the owner, and risk is a prime determinant of cost.

When a construction contract is awarded will also impact budgeting and cost management, as it can occur at almost any point in the procurement process. The primary issue is whether the owner wants to award a construction contract prior to the completion of documents. As a general rule, pricing on the basis of preliminary construction documents requires a negotiated approach, while having final construction documents allows for a lump sum bid.

Locking in a contract price before design work is complete can be accommodated using one of two basic approaches. First, some form of initial design and documentation can be developed, consisting of a preliminary scope and specifications, or the design may be advanced to as much as 65 percent complete. When a contract is solicited in this fashion, it is often referred to as a *guaranteed maximum price* or GMP. If minimal documentation has been developed for the initial GMP, the process will often lead to a final negotiation at some future point to fix a firm price for the contract, or a final GMP. In some circumstances, as a means of finalizing the price, the owner may choose to have individual trade subcontracts openly bid and assigned to the construction manager.

The second approach requires subdividing the project into definable subprojects that can be independently bid and priced as lump sums on the basis of completed documents for that scope of work. These packages can represent sequential elements of work (e.g., sitework, foundations, structure, etc.) or the packages may be trade groupings. In some cases, in certain states and municipalities, the packages may represent complete major trades and subtrades. Regardless, the final cost will not be complete until all subprojects have been bid.

It is obvious that choosing a delivery system is an important task in the cost management process, particularly when some form of the GMP is being provided and negotiated with the owner. The cost manager should carefully consider the form of contract and the overall approach to either negotiation or bidding together with the delivery system during both initial budgeting and subsequent cost management activities. This subject is covered in more detail in Chapter 5.

The cost manager should also be aware of another subtle but very important issue: how the owner views cost management and cost management policies. As Brian Bowen, former president of Hanscomb, Inc., observed, "Buildings cost what they're allowed to cost." That is, if the owner's attitude toward cost management is lax, it is reasonable to assume that costs will increase over time. Conversely, if the owner demonstrates a concern for costs, then they will tend to be contained over time. The owner may view the capital cost of the project as simply a line item in the overall program. Or trade-offs may be going on behind the scenes without the awareness of project designers. Regardless, it is important to educate the owner in cost management issues and to demonstrate a concern for how the owner's money is being spent.

Market and Economic Conditions

In spite of the best efforts of designers, owners, and project/construction managers to control the driving costs of construction, when all is said and done, market and economic conditions may overwhelm all other issues. Market shifts of from 10 to 20 percent can occur, especially during turbulent economic times. The overall economy, in particular the gross domestic product (GDP), will have an effect on construction prices. Figure 2.11 graphs the history of inflation from 1977 to the present, using the consumer price index (CPI) and the construction index, as published by the R. S. Means Company. (Note: These indices are both based on "input" information relating to wages and material costs and therefore do not directly reflect supply- and demand-driven market factors.) These two indices track rather closely, indicating that construction inflation will generally follow that of the general economy.

Likewise, market conditions tend to mimic the overall economy. Figure 2.12 graphs a history of the GDP along with the two previous indices. It becomes apparent that inflationary indices do not

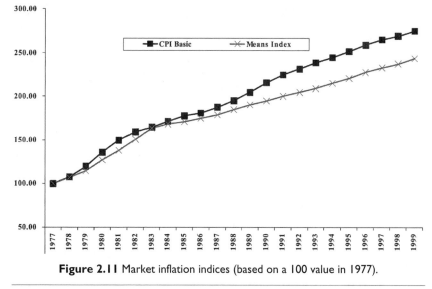

Figure 2.11 Market inflation indices (based on a 100 value in 1977).

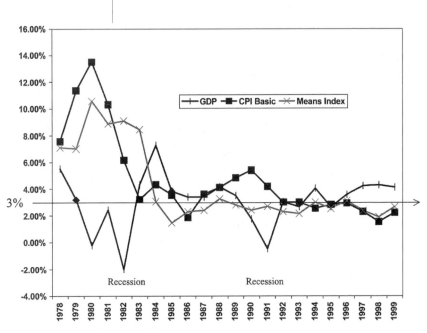

Figure 2.12 Index history (yearly percent change).

necessarily lower when the economy goes down; in some respects, the opposite has tended to happen over time. During a recession or slow economy, prices will tend to drop because demand is down; conversely, during boom times, prices will tend to rise because demand is up. Figure 2.13, which relates bidding response to the number of bidders, provides an analysis of the effect of competition on prices, as originally determined by the U.S. Army Corps of Engineers in the late 1980s, but still current today. The chart demonstrates that, as the number of bidders increased, the price went down; conversely, when the number of bidders was lower, the price went up. At the time of the study, a desirable number of bidders was considered to be seven. The analysis indicates that if only two bidders responded, prices

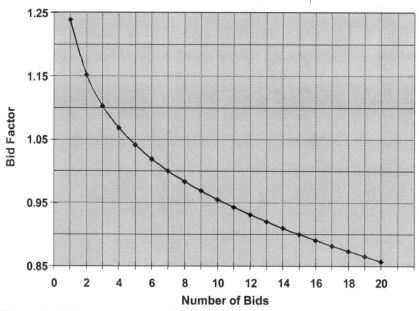

Figure 2.13 Effect of competition on bid prices. Source: *Area Cost Factor Study,* U.S. Army Corps of Engineers.

would increase by approximately 15 percent; if a large number of bidders responded, the price could go down by as much as 10 percent. In bidding to general contractors, these relationships tend to hold true over time. And though this example does not relate precisely to competition in general, it is reasonable to conclude that as competition increases or decreases these relationships will hold.

A recent analysis of the relationship between actual bidding prices and what is called the *fair market value* (shown in Figure 2.14) was conducted for the Washington, D.C., area marketplace by Hanscomb, Inc. The chart indicates what an assessment of reasonable labor and material costs and markups would produce. The late 1980s were an economic boom period, during which demand outstripped supply to

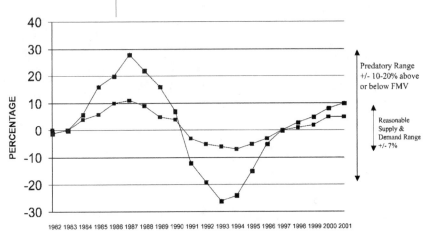

Figure 2.14 Washington, D.C., area market conditions: Comparing bid results and fair market value. Source: Hanscomb, Inc.

the point where bid prices rose 10 to 15 percent above fair market value. In contrast, in the early 1990s, there was an abrupt drop in the economy, followed by an abrupt drop in construction demand. In a very short period of time, construction prices dropped by 10 to 15 percent below fair market value. It took a number of years for the industry to compensate, and it wasn't until the late 1990s that bid prices again started to exceed fair market value.

The lesson to the cost manager is twofold: be aware that market factors are volatile; and take great care when projecting inflation using historical cost information (based on bids) and adjusting prices based exclusively on inflationary indices. Consider what happened when several government agencies used bid prices from the early '90s to establish budgets for projects scheduled for the end of the decade, and adjusted the cost only by an inflationary index. These budgets proved to be inadequate by 10 to 15 percent because market conditions were not comparable. We continue the discussion on this complicated subject in Chapter 4.

Conclusions

Developing an understanding of building economics is an important component in applying cost management. Construction projects are complicated and involve many entities in order to reach a satisfying conclusion. This chapter has concentrated on identifying the factors that directly and indirectly affect cost, as well as the major components that make up construction cost.

The next chapter will discuss cost-estimating methods to predict costs and to work with those costs within the context of design and construction. Responsive estimating is essential to effective cost management.

Cost-Estimating Methodology

3

An essential element of successful cost management is the ability to accurately and quickly estimate costs. Numerous publications, workbooks, and textbooks have been published on the broad subject of cost estimating. The express purpose of this chapter, however, is to approach cost estimating from a cost management perspective. To that end, this chapter focuses on the essential elements and aspects of cost estimating that are critical in the cost management process. These critical elements include:

- ➤ Standard formats
- ➤ Identification of cost drivers
- ➤ Consistent principles of estimate preparation
- ➤ Cost-estimating methods
- ➤ Escalation and contingencies
- ➤ Risk management and range estimating
- ➤ Special estimating challenges
- ➤ Life-cycle costing
- ➤ Value management

This chapter discusses these issues and makes recommendations as to how to utilize and apply these issues in the context of cost management.

Establishing Standard Formats

An essential component of any cost-estimating approach is to establish a standard framework from which to classify and manage information. The framework should accommodate the needs of the system throughout its life cycle and be able to respond to the viewpoint and requirements of the various users. If the framework is not standardized, inconsistencies will occur between projects and between stages of each project. Confusion and, ultimately, loss of control will result.

A standard framework for construction information will serve the following basic purposes:

- ➤ Ensure consistency of work products over time and from project to project.
- ➤ Provide a frame of reference for collecting and managing information and, eventually, for delivering feedback based on experience.
- ➤ Provide a checklist to aid in both management and technical decision making.
- ➤ Facilitate clear communication among all disciplines.
- ➤ Establish a basis for ongoing training of personnel.
- ➤ Lay an efficient base for automation.

The Facility Cycle and Standardization

The facility cycle by which buildings are procured and operated—that is, *planning, design, construction and operation*—requires a method to collect data on a progressively increasing level of detail. The facility cycle process usually starts with a program of needs and an initial budget. The design process starts with a conceptual solution and results in a set of construction documents, specifications, and a cost estimate. This leads to a procurement process (construction) and, eventually, to the managing of an owned asset (facility management). Providing feedback from the process to the initial planning and design stages is essential for effective management. This relationship is shown in Figure 3.1.

Practitioners in the major disciplines in the construction process—design architects and engineers, specifiers, estimators, construction managers, general contractors, trade contractors and suppliers, design-builders, and facilities managers—all have different perspectives on the facility cycle and the use of construction information. These individual perspectives often determine the required format for presenting and organizing data.

Buildings and facilities also possess attributes as to their individual components. Attributes describe how a component is designed and constructed and what function it performs. Attributes can take the following forms:

- *Functional.* What purpose is the component serving?
- *Material.* What material or materials make up the component?

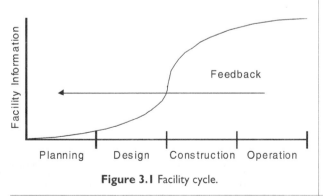

Figure 3.1 Facility cycle.

- *Installation.* What methods are used to install or construct the component?

- *Locational.* Where in the building is the component located?

- *Dimensional.* What are the physical dimensions of the component?

- *Quantitative.* How many of the components exist within the building, and how much of the materials making up the components is used?

- *Qualitative.* What are the qualitative and performance properties of the component, including physical form, appearance, capacity, and so on?

An effective data format for cost estimating and cost management should respond to the classification of the components of a building using these attributes; moreover, this format should enable the data relating to each attribute to be separately identified, tracked, and retrieved.

Figure 3.2 shows how the various disciplines view and use building component attributes. Each discipline has different priorities and, hence, uses the same information in different ways. For example, a designer is concerned with functional and qualitative attributes as part of the design of the structure (e.g., properly size a column for a given load). In contrast, a trade contractor whose job it is to physically construct a column is concerned with the specific method to be used to erect the column. Both, however, are directly concerned with the "dimensional attributes" of the column, in that it be properly sized and constructed.

Likewise, the point of view of an estimator and that of a specifier can be different. The estimator uses the dimensions of the column and the number

Discipline	Functional	Material	Installation	Locational	Dimensional	Quantitative	Qualitative
Design Architect/Engineer	■	■	□	■	■	□	■
Specifier	◪	■	■	□	□	□	■
Cost Estimator	□	■	■	◪	■	■	■
Value Engineer	■	◪	◪	□	◪	◪	■
General Contractor/Construction Manager	□	◪	◪	■	◪	◪	■
Trade Contractor/Supplier	□	■	■	■	■	■	■
Design-Builder	■	■	■	■	■	■	■
Facilities Manager	■	■	□	■	■	■	■

Attribute

Legend: □ Low Utilization   ◪ Moderate Utilization   ■ High Utilization

Figure 3.2 Utilization of building information.

of occurrences to calculate quantities of materials and labor in order to prepare a cost estimate. The specifier defines the materials and methods that are to be used to construct the column, but usually is not directly concerned with column dimensions or the number of columns.

A construction manager (or general contractor) is responsible for scheduling the work and for establishing how the various suppliers and trade contractors will interface over time; therefore, the construction manager is very concerned with the timing of construction events. On the other hand, the designer's concern with phasing of the actual construction is limited; seldom is phasing indicated on the documents (except in reconstruction work). And though many of the actual construction steps—excavating, forming, and so on—are not shown on the documents at all, they should be accounted for by the construction manager, trade contractor, and estimator. Means and methods are generally the responsibility of the installing contractor. The expanding use of design-build and design-build-operate methodologies increases the importance of utilizing and sharing common data by focusing all the activity through a single entity.

There are a number of ways to view cost data format issues, just as there are a number of different points of view and ways to utilize and classify information. For example, a trade or installing contractor will be interested in information that is organized by trades, crafts, and materials, whereas a designer will want material organized around design-driven issues that relate to building components such as structure and enclosure. A construction manager or general contractor will seek to group information by contract

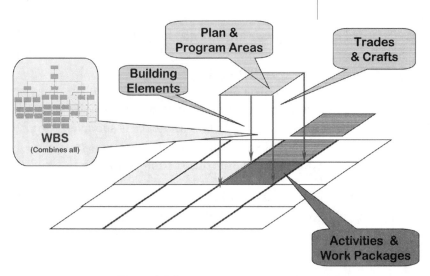

Figure 3.3 Data organization approaches.

packages or major construction activities. Often, the owner will require an extensive definition and breakdown of the work (referred to as the Work Breakdown Structure, or WBS). The facility manager will be interested in plan or program areas of the facility, in terms of where components are located and perhaps by cost associated with building-out space. This relationship is shown in Figure 3.3, which presents multiple ways that data can be organized.

Estimating Formats

The most common data standard in use in the construction industry today is the 16-division Master-Format. The format was originally conceived during the 1960s as a joint effort of the Construction Specification Institute (CSI) in association with other trade, professional, construction, and product organizations. After joining with Canadian groups, a joint publication, titled *Uniform Construction Index* (UCI), was made available in 1972. Eventually redefined as MasterFormat in 1978, the first revised edition was published in 1983; it was revised again in 1988 and in 1995.

MasterFormat is a system of numbers and titles for organizing construction information into a standard sequence. This sequence is subdivided into 16 divisions organized by major products and trades associated with construction, as follows:

DIVISION
1	General Requirements
2	Sitework
3	Concrete
4	Masonry
5	Metals
6	Wood and Plastics
7	Thermal and Moisture Protection
8	Doors and Windows
9	Finishes
10	Specialties
11	Equipment
12	Furnishings
13	Special Construction
14	Conveying Systems
15	Mechanical
16	Electrical

MasterFormat is organized into four levels of detail. Level 1 comprises major groupings such as "Bidding requirements," "Contracting requirements," and the 16 division trades. Levels 2, 3, and 4 provide progressively more detailed subgroupings within divisions. An example of these levels is shown in Figure 3.4.

MasterFormat is used extensively throughout the industry as a format for project manuals, specifica-

Level 1	Level 2	Level 3	Level 4
07 Thermal and Moisture Protection	07400 Roofing and Siding Panels	07410 Metal Roof and Wall Panels	- Metal roof panels - Metal wall panels
		07420 Plastic Roof and Wall Panels	- Plastic roof panels - Plastic wall panels
		07430 Composite Panels	- Composite surface roof panels - Composite surface wall panels
		07440 Facia Panels	- Aggregate coated panels - Porcelain enameled-faced panels - Tile-faced panels
		07450 Fiber-Reinforced Cementitious Panels	- Glass-Fiber-Reinforced cementitious panels - Mineral-Fiber-Reinforced cementitious panels
		07460 Siding	- Aluminum siding - Composition siding - Hardboard siding - Mineral fiber cement siding - Plastic siding - Plywood siding - Steel siding - Wood siding
		07470 Wood Roof and Wall Panels	- Wood roof panels - Wood wall panels
		07480 Exterior Wall Assemblies	- Assemblies including framing, insulation, substrate, and wall panels

Figure 3.4 Example of MasterFormat level of details.

tions, and project data, and is now the accepted standard for various reference sources, such as R. S. Means Co., for unit cost publications, and Sweets, for product literature. And because the format resembles the basic form by which projects are procured (subtrades and contract packages), it is often used as a cost control, scheduling, and estimating framework.

Though MasterFormat provides an effective system for defining material and installation attributes, it does not provide an effective format for defining functional or locational attributes because it does not generally address a complete system or building element. For example, an exterior wall system standard detail could consist of masonry block backup, insulation, and precast concrete panel and would reference the following specification sections:

03450–Plant-Precast Architectural Concrete
04230–Concrete Masonry Units
07210–Building Insulation

Three sections from three separate divisions are required to define the wall system. This relates well to the means of specifying and constructing the wall, but the needs of the designer are somewhat different. The designer views the wall as a complete functional entity or system and relates to a data format that uses a "system" or "elemental" approach to defining building components. Thus, during the early 1970s, many design and construction professionals recognized the need to develop a format that would relate better to the language of design. In particular, it was important that the format relate to conceptual design issues when material decisions had not been finalized, and when cost, budget, and performance aspects (U-value [heat transfer coefficient of a wall], STC [sound transfer coefficient], etc.) of building components were major considerations.

Relating to the previous example, using Master-Format to determine the cost of the wall system could require searching under three headings. Furthermore, each of the three sections might contain costs for the same materials used in other components. Therefore, the question "What is the cost of the exterior wall?" might be difficult and time-consuming to answer.

The industry response was to begin to structure estimates into components, or elements, of design more meaningful to architects and engineers. This allowed estimates of the building components to be gathered under one heading, regardless of the type of material being specified.

British and Canadian design and quantity surveying professionals had begun to develop "elemental" classification systems in the mid-1950s; the first U.S. initiative, called the MASTERCOST framework, wasn't developed until 1973, by Hanscomb, Inc., for the American Institute of Architects (AIA) in 1973. This work involved coordinating an AIA committee effort with initiatives being taken by the General Services Administration (GSA), which eventually produced a commonly agreed framework, christened UNIFORMAT. GSA also provided additional funding to take the hierarchically based UNIFORMAT classification and expand it until it reached a level of compatibility with the MasterFormat.

Continuing efforts have resulted in the development of UNIFORMAT II, which refined certain aspects of the original UNIFORMAT. These refinements are relatively cosmetic, and this second version retains the hierarchical structure and elemental makeup of the original UNIFORMAT. Now an American Society for Testing and Materials (ASTM) Standard (E1557-96), CSI has accepted an oversight role over both UNIFORMAT II and MasterFormat.

Each element within UNIFORMAT II is a discrete functional part of the building. In practice, this facilitates cost and performance comparisons regardless of the actual materials chosen. Furthermore, UNIFORMAT II is hierarchical, which allows information (in particular, cost information) to be developed at different levels appropriate to the degree of information available. UNIFORMAT II lends itself well to use during the concept stage of projects, where preliminary estimates and specifications can be formatted in this manner. For example, a wall system can be budgeted on a cost-per-wall-area basis, complete with targeted U-values and other performance characteristics well in advance to the selection of a particular wall.

UNIFORMAT II is subdivided into these 22 major building elements:

A10	Foundations
A20	Basement Construction
B10	Superstructure
B20	Exterior Closure
B30	Roofing
C10	Interior Construction
C20	Staircases
C30	Interior Finishes
D10	Conveying Systems
D20	Plumbing
D30	HVAC
D40	Fire Protection
D50	Electrical
E10	Equipment
E20	Furnishings
F10	Special Construction
F20	Selective Building
G10	Site Preparation
G20	Site Improvements
G30	Site Mechanical Utilities
G40	Site Electrical Utilities
G50	Other Site Construction

Figures 3.5 (a) and (b) serve a threefold purpose: They provide a comparison between UNIFORMAT II and UNIFORMAT; a listing of UNIFORMAT II

UNIFORMAT II Categories

MASTERFORMAT Categories:
01 General conditions
02 Site work
03 Concrete
04 Masonry
05 Metals
06 Wood-plastic
07 Thermal & moisture protection
08 Doors & windows
09 Finishes
10 Specialties
11 Equipment
12 Furnishings
13 Special construction
14 Conveying systems
15 Mechanical
16 Electrical

Level 1	Level 2	Level 3
A SUBSTRUCTURE	A 10 Foundations	A 1010 Standard Foundations
		A 1020 Other Foundations
		A 1030 Slab on Grade
	A 20 Basement Construction	A 2010 Basement Excavation
		A 2020 Basement Walls
B SHELL	B 10 Superstructure	B 1010 Floor Construction
		B 1020 Roof Construction
	B 20 Exterior Enclosure	B 2010 Exterior Walls
		B 2020 Exterior Windows
		B 2030 Exterior Doors
	B 30 Roofing	B 3010 Roof Coverings
		B 3020 Roof Openings
C INTERIORS	C 10 Interior Construction	C 1010 Partitions
		C 1020 Interior Doors
		C 1030 Specialties
	C 20 Stairs	
	C 30 Interior Finishes	C 3010 Wall Finishes
		C 3020 Floor Finishes
		C 3030 Ceiling Finishes
D SERVICES	D 10 Conveying Systems	
	D 20 Plumbing	
	D 30 HVAC	
	D 40 Fire Protection	
	D 50 Electrical	D 5010 Electrical Service & Distribution
		D 5020 Lighting & Branch Wiring
		D 5030 Communications & Security
		D 5040 Other Electrical Systems
E EQUIPMENT & FURNISHINGS	E 10 Equipment	
	E 20 Furnishings	
F SPECIAL CONSTR & DEMO	F 10 Special Construction	
	F 20 Selective Building Demolition	
G BUILDING SITEWORK	G 10 Site Preparation	
	G 20 Site Improvements	
	G 30 Site Mechanical Utilities	
	G 40 Site Electrical Utilities	
	G 50 Other Site Construction	

General Conditions, Overhead & Profit may be spread throughout or added after sub-totaling

Figure 3.5(a) Relationship between UNIFORMAT II and MasterFormat.

Level 1		Level 2		Level 3
A	SUBSTRUCTURE	A 10	Foundations	A 1010 Standard Foundations
				A 1020 Other Foundations
				A 1030 Slab on Grade
		A 20	Basement Construction	A 2010 Basement Excavation
				A 2020 Basement Walls
B	SHELL	B 10	Superstructure	B 1010 Floor Construction
				B 1020 Roof Construction
		B 20	Exterior Enclosure	B 2010 Exterior Walls
				B 2020 Exterior Windows
				B 2030 Exterior Doors
		B 30	Roofing	B 3010 Roof Coverings
				B 3020 Roof Openings
C	INTERIORS	C 10	Interior Construction	C 1010 Partitions
				C 1020 Interior Doors
				C 1030 Specialties
		C 20	Stairs	C 2010 Stair Construction
				C 2020 Stair Finishes
		C 30	Interior Finishes	C 3010 Wall Finishes
				C 3020 Floor Finishes
				C 3030 Ceiling Finishes
D	SERVICES	D 10	Conveying Systems	D 1010 Elevators & Lifts
				D 1020 Escalators & Moving Walks
				D 1030 Materials Handling
				D 1040 Other Conveying Systems
		D 20	Plumbing	D 2010 Plumbing Fixtures
				D 2020 Domestic Water Distribution
				D 2030 Sanitary Waste
				D 2040 Rain Water Drainage
				D 2050 Other Plumbing Systems
		D 30	HVAC	D 3010 Energy Supply
				D 3020 Heat Generation
				D 3030 Refrigeration
				D 3040 HVAC Distribution
				D 3050 Terminal & Package Units
				D 3060 Controls and Instrumentation
				D 3070 Other HVAC Systems
				D 3080 Testing, Adjusting & Balancing
		D 40	Fire Protection	D 4010 Fire Protection Sprinkler Systems
				D 4020 Standpipe and Hose Systems
				D 4030 Fire Protection Specialties
				D 4040 Other Fire Protection Systems
		D 50	Electrical	D 5010 Electrical Service & Distribution
				D 5020 Lighting & Branch Wiring
				D 5030 Communications & Security
				D 5040 Other Electrical Systems
E	EQUIPMENT & FURNISHINGS	E 10	Equipment	E 1010 Commercial Equipment
				E 1020 Institutional Equipment
				E 1030 Vehicular Equipment
				E 1040 Other Equipment
		E 20	Furnishings	E 2010 Fixed Furnishings
				E 2020 Moveable Furnishings
F	SPECIAL CONSTR.& DEMO	F 10	Special Construction	F 1010 Special Structures
				F 1020 Integrated Construction
				F 1030 Special Construction Systems
				F 1040 Special Facilities
				F 1050 Special Controls & Instrumentation
		F 20	Selective Building Demolition	F 2010 Building Elements Demolition
				F 2020 Hazardous Components Abatement
G	BUILDING SITEWORK	G 10	Site Preparation	G 1010 Site Clearing
				G 1020 Site Demolition & Relocations
				G 1030 Site Earthwork
				G 1040 Hazard Waste Remediation
		G 20	Site Improvements	G 2010 Roadways
				G 2020 Parking Lots
				G 2030 Pedestrian Paving

UNIFORMAT

	Level 2		Level 3
01	Foundations	011	Standard Foundations
		012	Special Foundations
02	Substructure	021	Slab On Grade
		022	Basement Excavation
		023	Basement Walls
03	Superstructure	031	Floor Construction
		032	Roof Construction
		033	Stair Construction
04	Exterior Closure	041	Exterior Walls
		042	Exterior Doors & Windows
05	Roofing		
06	Interior Construction	061	Partitions
		062	Interior Finishes
		063	Specialties
07	Conveying Systems		
08	Mechanical		
		081	Plumbing
		082	HVAC
		083	Fire Protection
		084	Special Mechanical Systems
09	Electrical	091	Service & Distribution
		092	Lighting & Power
		093	Special Electrical Systems
10	**General Conditions, OH&P**		
11	Equipment	111	Fixed & Moveable Equipment
		112	Furnishings
		113	Special Construction
12	Sitework	121	Site Preparation
		122	Site Improvements

Figure 3.5(b) Comparison of UNIFORMAT II and UNIFORMAT.

at levels 1, 2, and 3; indicate the hierarchical nature of the format; and show the relationship between UNIFORMAT II and MasterFormat.

Using the previous example again, the first construction element is B-Shell, which subdivides into:

B20–Exterior Enclosure
B2010–Exterior Walls
B2020–Exterior Windows
B2030–Exterior Doors

Referencing Figure 3.5(a) indicates that MasterFormat Divisions 03-07, 09, and 10 could potentially be used for exterior walls. Figure 3.6 offers an example of how the wall system used in the previous examples would break down into the UNIFORMAT II hierarchy.

UNIFORMAT II also provides an efficient means of comparing historical cost information for complete buildings. Buildings and systems can be compared on a functional basis regardless of the particular materials used (e.g., cost of superstructure for concrete versus steel framed buildings). However, collecting useful historical data can be difficult

UNIFORMAT II LEVEL					DESCRIPTION	MASTERFORMAT REFERENCE
1	2	3	4	5		
B					Shell	
	B20				Exterior Enclosure	
		B2010			Exterior Walls	
			(a)		Exterior Wall Construction	
				(1)	Precast Conc. Ext. Panels	(03450)
				(2)	Rigid Insulation	(07210)
				(3)	Concrete Block	(04220)

Figure 3.6 Wall system example using UNIFORMAT.

because most buildings are actually "bought out" by trades that tend to follow MasterFormat and because actual "hard cost" information is not usually organized in an elemental fashion. The subject of developing and maintaining cost data files is presented in more detail in Chapter 4.

Suggested Uses for UNIFORMAT II and MasterFormat

There is no absolute right or wrong way to utilize data formats. Each basic approach has advantages and disadvantages and circumstances in which one, rather than another format, will save a great deal of time and facilitate communication; but experience has shown that in most situations, it is necessary to use *both* systems and refer back and forth between them as the project develops.

That said, it is possible to distinguish specific advantages and disadvantages of each system. We begin by describing the advantages of MasterFormat:

> ▶ *It has been accepted by contractors.* Contractors have accepted and used MasterFormat for some time now; hence, they are comfortable and familiar with its application for specifications, schedules of values, pay requests, and technical documentation. And when it comes to pay requests and other financial issues, typically, contractors are not interested in trying new systems. They also have a great deal of experience collecting and processing bid and sub-bid information. Construction documents are usually subdivided and distributed to subcontractors by specification section (hence, MasterFormat) so that their bid information can be gathered and processed by the prime contractor.

TIP

There is no absolute right or wrong way to utilize data formats, but experience has shown that in most situations, it is necessary to use both systems and refer back and forth between them as the project develops.

➤ *It is trade/material-oriented.* MasterFormat is a very useful system for both defining and implementing quality control of trades and materials.

➤ *It is excellent for writing detailed/prescriptive specifications.* Because the industry has extensive experience with MasterFormat, practitioners are comfortable using this application to write and organize their specifications.

➤ *It is good for making detailed estimates.* Details on how MasterFormat is used for the quantity survey estimate are described later in this chapter.

➤ *It is excellent to implement construction-phase cost controls.* Because trade contractors are comfortable working with MasterFormat, financial and cost-tracking systems tend to be organized around its trade type categories. Seldom are major substitutions made to completely replace entire systems; rather, most changes are made on one-to-one substitutions that will more often than not remain within a single trade.

The disadvantages of MasterFormat are the following:

➤ *It has limited use for budgeting and conceptual estimating.* While MasterFormat is effective for establishing detailed estimates, it tends to be of limited use for budget and conceptual estimates because these estimates are based on conceptual designs that are seldom advanced to the point at which all materials and methods are defined. Nevertheless, reasonable budgets and cost allocations for the systems may be an absolute necessity, and they can be realistically defined using modeling techniques or by conducting a historical cost analysis. A simple example is choosing between a steel frame and a concrete frame for a structural system. In MasterFormat, a steel frame choice would be largely allocated to Division 5, whereas a concrete-based estimate would be almost exclusively allocated to Division 3. If this decision has not been made, it is awkward and potentially confusing to place cost in either of the two divisions, in particular when a steel frame is considered because it still involves substantial costs in Division 3 concrete work.

> *It is difficult to use for design-phase cost control purposes.* Design-phase cost control requires that system alternates can be considered and that changes in system choices can be easily tracked and accounted for. If, for example, the conceptual design was based on a steel frame, then during development a change was made to use a concrete frame, there would be a significant cost shift from Division 5 to Division 3. Would the reduction in Division 5 be considered savings or simply be reallocation of costs? As another example, consider the wall previously discussed, where three divisions were represented. If, instead of the precast wall panels, it was determined to use a composite type wall panel, there would be a significant drop in Division 3, and Division 7 would be significantly increased. The point is, it would be difficult to track and fully understand the ramifications of these types of changes.

> *It is difficult to use to compare competing designs.* From a cost manager's perspective, perhaps the single most difficult aspect of working with MasterFormat is that it makes it very difficult to

compare competing designs. This is particularly evident in design competitions, especially when design-build participants are involved and where the competing designs may be drastically different in terms of use of materials and methods and system choices. The previous example of choosing between a steel frame and a concrete frame building exemplifies the difficulties facing the owner who may be comparing the relative merits and cost performance of each of the systems. In this circumstance, the steel-based design would be very cost-effective in Division 3, while the concrete-based design would be very cost-effective in Division 5. Determining their relative cost performance for the structure would be very difficult, time-consuming, and have greater potential for risk for the owner.

UNIFORMAT tends to be strong where Master-Format is weak and weak where MasterFormat is strong. Thus, the systems may be said to be complementary. UNIFORMAT's advantages are as follows:

> *It has gained acceptance by designers.* UNIFORMAT and other similar element-based systems are well understood by designers; hence, they are, in general, comfortable with their use and application. Over the years, designers have developed systems to collect details and standardized designs that tend to group comfortably around UNIFORMAT. Furthermore, the way a design develops tends to follow the UNIFORMAT major elements.

> *It is function/element-oriented.* Simply, UNIFORMAT is organized around the functional and elemen-

tal components of a building. For this reason, designers can relate comfortably to the language of UNIFORMAT.

▶ *It is excellent for to use for performance specifications.* It is difficult if not impossible to develop usable and traceable performance specifications around any system that is not based on building elements or components. For example, a critical performance aspect of a wall system is its U-value or R-value, which establishes a wall's thermal performance. This thermal performance is entirely a function of the composite wall system; it is not necessarily an individual attribute of any single wall material. Therefore, the performance requirements as defined in a performance specification would be for the entire wall assembly. This works well with UNIFORMAT, but would be very difficult to implement through MasterFormat.

▶ *It is good for making conceptual estimates.* The characteristics of building elements make UNIFORMAT a very effective and comfortable system and format to use for conceptual estimates. UNIFORMAT makes it possible to establish building system budgets without necessarily having to define exactly the means and methods being designed. Even when specific systems have been determined, their budgets are expressed in terms of the systems or elements rather than the materials and methods.

▶ *It can be used for detailed estimating.* Although UNIFORMAT relates more directly to conceptual estimates, it can also be used as a system or format for establishing detailed estimates. As a result, trades will cross several UNIFORMAT categories. This is demonstrated in Figure 3.5.

➤ *It is excellent for design-phase cost control purposes.* Since UNIFORMAT is useful as a budgeting and conceptual estimating format, it is likewise valuable and useful for design-phase cost control. The basic process of budgeting and cost control, which is described in more detail in Chapter 5, consists of establishing budgets for each design discipline and subdiscipline for the building work that is defined by their respective discipline. As the design develops and, invariably, changes are made, UNIFORMAT provides an effective system for assessing cost impact of design changes as they occur. Referring again to the wall example, specifically the tracking that would be associated with a change from a precast wall cladding to the composite panel: The cost of the wall would remain in the same UNIFORMAT categories even though the materials were changing. This would allow for comparisons and analysis to be conducted. In addition, life-cycle costing, sustainability, and other assessments are facilitated because entire building components can be assessed at the same time.

➤ *It is effective for comparing competing designs.* Unlike MasterFormat, which has very limited viability as a format for comparing competing designs, UNIFORMAT is ideally suited for this purpose, especially at a conceptual level when basic system approaches may vary considerably between designs or may not fully be defined. UNIFORMAT allows for a one-to-one comparison for each building element among many potentially competing designs. Using the previous example, a steel-framed building could be compared to a concrete-framed building in a fair and equitable way, as could multiple wall-system alternates, both for initial cost as well as life-cycle considerations. Performing these types of analyses using MasterFormat would be difficult if not impossible.

► *It is valuable for use in assembling and maintaining historical project information.* Historical project costs can be formatted using UNIFORMAT as a basis for categorization by building type, as well as, potentially, by building system or element. Though most historical costs on buildings are extracted from schedules of values that typically are organized according to Master-Format divisions, storing and extracting information for multiple projects with dissimilar materials and methods in this system can be a challenging process for all of the reasons previously stated. In contrast, storing projects using UNIFORMAT makes extracting and comparing historical costs more effective. Doing so may even facilitate extracting building element costs from dissimilar buildings, for example, comparing wall system costs from an office building and institutional building. Other systems, such as HVAC, might vary dramatically between the two building types, but the wall system might be useful as a comparison because of design approach, use of materials, and environmental drivers. The problem of collecting information using MasterFormat (schedules of values) and converting this information to UNIFORMAT is addressed in more detail in Chapter 4. In short, however, effective use of

Cost-Estimating Methodology

historical information requires the use of an elemental approach such as UNIFORMAT.

The disadvantages of UNIFORMAT are the following:

> *It makes it more difficult for contractors to assemble subcontractor quotes.* The characteristic of trades spanning several UNIFORMAT elements and categories is precisely what makes it very difficult for contractors to use UNIFORMAT to collect and process subcontractor quotes and bids. In fact, requiring a contractor to submit a bid or price offer in a UNIFORMAT structure would be considered a significant imposition. Even if the prime contractor is familiar with UNIFORMAT, it is unlikely that the trade subcontractors would be, raising the risk of missing and overlapping bids. When a contract requires the submission of bids in the UNIFORMAT structure, it is necessary to allow additional time for the contractor to collect bids in traditional MasterFormat categories and then convert them to UNIFORMAT form. It is important to recognize that a contractor may be receiving bids and quotes until the very last moment the bid is open. This is difficult and challenging enough without the additional task of reformatting and reallocating those bids. Therefore, if UNIFORMAT is the system being used, the preferred approach is to require the contractor to submit a total bid at the bid due date but then be given a reasonable amount of time to substantiate and back up that bid in whatever format is necessary. Though the bid in total is fixed, the contractor has time

to properly categorize and group subcontractor bids. Chapter 5 delves further into this subject.

▶ *It finds limited use for construction-phase cost control.* While UNIFORMAT has obvious benefits during the design phase, as described above, it is of limited value during the construction phase, when focus tends to shift toward individual trades and crafts rather than on building components.

Identifying and Managing Cost Drivers

The Pareto principal states that 20 percent of the components of the building will represent 80 percent of the costs. Expanding on the principle, it can be interpreted that 20 percent of the decisions made in the course of design will govern 80 percent of the costs. It therefore becomes essential to identify, estimate, and ultimately control those decisions that will drive the majority of the cost of the facility. These cost drivers can be identified early in the process and focused on throughout the entire design process.

How can these drivers be identified? Simply, they comprise the same key issues that were identified as part of the entire alignment process described in Chapter 1, and fall into predictable categories of scope and expectations. For reference, the material presented as Figure 1.2 is presented again as Figure 3.7.

Specifically, the cost drivers entail: program, design, phasing and scheduling, site and environment, market, and risk. Each is discussed in turn in the following subsections.

RULE OF THUMB

Twenty percent of the decisions made in the course of design will govern 80 percent of the costs.

SCOPE	EXPECTATIONS	BUDGET
• **Program** - Functional Space Program - Blocking & Stacking - Public Space - Efficiency • **Geometric Drivers** - Wall Area Ratio - Degree of Articulation • **Volume Drivers** - Clear Ceiling Height - Plenum Height - Interstitial Needs - Atria - Light Shelves • **Facility Parameters** - HVAC SF/Ton - Watts/SF - Plumbing Fixtures - Ductwork Poundage - Steel Pounds/SF - Etc.	• **Aesthetics** - Form & Massing - Image - Community Requirements - Design Issues • **Quality** - Systems - Materials - Workmanship • **Project Delivery** - Phasing & Scheduling - Continued Occupancy - Delivery System • **Systems Performance** - Functional Space Elements - Building Management - Maintainability - Energy Consumption - Sustainability • **Facility Performance** - Live Loads - Expandability - Flexibility - Security & Safety - Access & Egress - Adjacencies - Natural Light • **External Requirements** - Codes - Standards & Criteria	• **Initial Costs** - Site Acquisition - Fees - Construction - Inflation and Market Conditions - Contingencies - Other Costs • **Future One-Time Costs** - Replacements - Alterations - Salvage - Other One-Time Costs • **Facility Annual Costs** - Operations - Maintenance - Financing - Taxes - Insurance - Security - Other Annual Costs • **Functional Use Costs** - Staffing - Materials - Denial of Use - Other Functional Use Costs

Figure 3.7 Hierarchy of scope, expectations, and budget.

Program

Cost drivers related to program typically include space efficiency, security requirements, circulation requirements, Americans with Disabilities Act (ADA) requirements, blocking and stacking, and adjacency requirements; but by far the most significant program driver is the *mix* of space types contained within the building. For example, laboratory space can easily cost in excess of $400 per square foot, whereas standard administrative or office space can be built for $100 to $150 per square foot. An exact 50/50 program mix would yield a building cost of $200 to $220 per square foot. If, instead, that same building had 70 percent laboratories and 30 percent office space, the building cost would exceed $300 per square foot. It is interesting to note that, in practice, as building designs develop, expensive spaces tend to increase while inexpensive spaces tend to decrease as a compensation. So, while the overall gross area may remain constant, the program mix changes toward the expensive spaces, and consequently, the cost per square foot increases. This phenomenon repeats over and over again.

The next most significant issue is space efficiency. Again, experience has shown that the actual delivered space efficiency in buildings, especially complicated buildings, such as laboratories, is usually lower than originally planned in the program. Simply put, it is very difficult to deliver a net program within the geometric limitations of a design, and the effects of this tend to be underestimated in the programming and design processes. From a cost manager's perspective, tracking delivered program in terms of both program mix and space efficiency can be the single most important cost management activity undertaken for the project.

Design

Design factors represent both the physical measures as defined in the scope and the performance and quality measures defined by expectations. Some of the more common drivers relative to design include wall area ratio and degree of articulation of the footprint itself. Since the exterior enclosure can represent a substantial portion of the cost of the building, the relationship between the amount of wall built and the enclosed space can have a dramatic impact on the cost of the building. The amount of wall is affected by the basic aspect ratio of the footprint. For example, a square footprint 200 feet on a side represents an area of 40,000 square feet; and assuming the wall height is 15 feet, the exterior wall area will be 12,000 square feet (200 × 4 × 15) for a wall or ratio of 0.3. A footprint 400 feet long by 100 feet wide represents the same 40,000 square feet but has an exterior wall area 15,000 square feet (400 × 2 × 15 + 100 × 2 × 15). All other things being equal, if the exterior wall cost is $40 per wall square foot, then the building cost will increase by $120,000, or $3 per gross square foot. The degree of articulation of the wall affects the costs of the wall system because an articulated wall will increase the wall area ratio; in addition, as explained earlier, the number of corners increases the delivered wall cost per wall square foot. Therefore, highly articulated walls will cost more than a more plainly articulated wall—again, all other things being equal.

Other design-related drivers affect the volume of the facility in a number of ways. Obviously, clear ceiling height and plenum height will drive the volume directly. However, such elements as atria and the inclusion of light shelves can have a substantial impact on the overall volume of the building, depending on where they are placed and how they are structurally included in the overall building.

Numerous other measures are presented in Figure 3.7 that relate to the effectiveness of building systems. Experienced estimators can focus on critical aspects of the design, such as steel pounds per square foot. And, to repeat, the quality of systems, materials, and workmanship has a substantial impact on cost.

Also, owner requirements relative to facility performance are obviously major cost drivers. These include live loads, security requirements, the desire for natural light, energy performance, and sustainability. And owner needs for such factors as expandability and flexibility are more complicated to measure but nonetheless can be expected to affect project cost. A simple example of expandability will make the point. If, say, the owner wants to expand the building in a particular direction, the building must be sited to accommodate future expansion. In addition, the materials chosen for the exterior wall in the design of the structural system supporting the wall and frame will be affected. Furthermore, utilities serving the potential expansion will either have to be sized accordingly or be included in such a way that future changes can be facilitated. All these issues affect cost. The cost manager should recognize early in the process which decisions are going to affect cost most and track those decisions carefully throughout the design process.

Phasing and Scheduling

Phasing and scheduling of a project will affect the price of the project in terms of both the direct costs as well as the indirect costs, such as general conditions. A majority of projects are launched under scheduling assumptions that are either unrealistic or impractical for the time of year; and, too often, insufficient time and effort is invested in determining the adequacy of schedule issues, or the owner's assumptions or requirements will be carried forward into the schedule without sufficient scrutiny. Specifically, unreasonably long schedules will raise the cost of the project in the general conditions and financing categories, while unreasonably short schedules will incur added costs because there is inadequate time to do the work, thus requiring multiple shifts, overtime, and additional supervision. In these situations, something as simple as curing of concrete can be overlooked.

The logistics associated with movement of people and equipment either in and out of a new building or inside a building being renovated may often drive the schedule. In the case of a renovation, if the work is being conducted while the building continues to be occupied, this will dramatically add to and/or alter the schedule, and in some cases will affect the actual design choices to accommodate work that must be done in increments.

A primary scheduling determinant is the delivery method chosen for the project, whether design-bid-build, CM at risk, or design-build. Cost will be both directly and indirectly affected. Delivery methods are covered in more detail in Chapter 5. The cost manager should accurately define, track, and monitor scheduling and phasing issues.

Site and Environment

Good sites—meaning easy to develop and inexpensive to build on—are becoming rare. Today, more sites than ever before have environmental problems, such as ground contamination, presence of hazardous materials, or use limitations, because of the presence of wetlands, stormwater retention requirements, or treatment requirements for groundwater. In many cases, large-scale sites have very limited areas that can be developed.

In addition to environmental issues, slopes and soil conditions should be factored into the cost of developing and building on the site. Historically, not having adequate site and geotechnical information has caused cost difficulties. In defining, budgeting, and eventually managing costs, the cost manager should keep a careful eye on assumptions concerning site and environment.

Market

We discussed the economic effects of market conditions Chapter 2. From an estimating perspective, we must now answer how market conditions can be tracked relative to project cost over time. If a market change takes place, how can the project estimator document and account for it?

One of the simplest, but most important, activities for a project estimator is to evaluate the impact of other projects going on at the same time, because knowing this can be critical from the overall supply and demand aspects of the construction industry in the area. Also it's important for estimators to recognize that certain types of construction tend to draw from limited fields for labor and construction trades. General contractors, construction managers, and trade contractors tend to specialize in certain areas—say, for example, in building schools for grades K-12. Since construction of these schools is booming in many metropolitan and suburban areas, competition for the same resources has increased. Even when the overall economy is relatively flat, if school construction is high, the prices for this work will likewise be high, perhaps even prohibitive. In 2000, one of the major counties in the Maryland suburbs of Washington, D.C. stopped all school construction because of extremely poor bids.

Another market-related issue is caused by short supply of specific materials and trades. Over the years, shortages have occurred in structural steel,

REMINDER!
A project estimator should be aware of other construction projects in the same area since construction industry supply and demand will affect costs.

portland cement, precast concrete, gypsum wall board, and glass and glazing. The cost manager should stay abreast of potential material and labor shortages.

Risk

Risk drivers on a project can involve many areas and come from many sources. As discussed in Chapter 1, risk—and specifically the impacts of risk on cost—need to be carefully managed. It may be beneficial for the cost manager to prepare risk-based estimates that focus on major cost components where risk is a significant issue. Formalized risk-estimating methods are available that may be appropriate for certain circumstances. These are discussed later in this chapter.

The key in risk assessment is, first, to identify those elements of an estimate at highest risk and, second, to evaluate the implications of variances in these elements. In extreme circumstances, it may be appropriate to alter the design to minimize the risk of a particular decision. For example, a major public authority undertaking the design and development of a bridge spanning a river was forced to confront the potential that contaminated soils were located where the major structural components were to be placed. The problem was complicated by the fact that, until work began, the nature and degree of contamination could not be clearly known. The potential for added cost was upward of $60 to $70 million, in terms of disposal and time. In this case, the authority chose a revised design approach that increased the span of the bridge, to avoid the high-risk area, thereby adding approximately $30 million to the cost of the bridge but avoiding the contaminated soil and potentially saving $30 to $40 million overall. The point is, proper risk management may require making alternate design choices and eventually design changes.

Estimate Preparation Principles

If estimating is to be an effective component of the overall cost management process, the cost manager should clearly understand certain principles and be able to clearly and correctly interpret the results of an estimate. Also, it is essential that those *using* an estimate, as well as those *producing* an estimate, understand clearly the intentions behind the estimate, the basis of the estimate, and the reasons why the estimate is being produced.

Estimating versus Bidding

A first, and critical, step in the estimating process is to recognize the differences between estimating and bidding. Briefly, bidding is a *procurement* process, whereas estimating is a *predictive* process. General contractors will prepare an estimate as part of the bidding process, but will rely primarily on quotes from subcontractors and suppliers. Usually, only the direct work conducted by the general contractor will be estimated as part of the bid.

Estimating

The estimating process for an installing contractor is somewhat different from the estimating process at either the general contractor or consulting estimator level. An installing contractor's estimate represents a quote for completing the work and is regarded as an agreement. The general contractor expects that the work will be conducted per the quote and that changes will occur only if conditions vary from those

EXPLANATION

Bidding is a procurement process. Estimating is a predictive process.

outlined in the contract. To minimize risk to the installing contractor, the estimating approach may be very detailed and be based on the procurement actions and assemblage of labor and supporting equipment necessary to conduct the work. Figures 3.8 and 3.9 contain examples of installing contractor's estimates.

The challenge to the contractor is to calculate the quantity of materials necessary (in the case of the

---

Problem: Estimate the cost of laying 6" x 6" x ½" quarry tile flooring and 6" cove base to the room illustrated below.

Estimating Data:

6" x 6" x ½" quarry tile	$70.00 per carton of 100
6" x 6" Quarry tile base (straight)	$ 1.50 each
6" x 6" Quarry tile base (angles/corners)	$ 5.00 each
Cement setting mix (3 bags required per 100 SF)	$ 3.50 per bag
Tax on all materials	5%
Allow for "waste" on tile	5%
Allow for "waste" on base	2%
Tile setter (setting 120 SF or 100 linear ft. of base per 8-hour day)	$26.00 per hour
Helper (one required for each setter)	$21.00 per hour
Burden/Fringe benefits	35% on labor cost
Job Overhead	5% on labor and materials
Head Office Overhead	2% labor, materials & job overhead
Profit	10% on labor, materials & job overhead

Figure 3.8 Sample estimating task for installing contractor.

Cost-Estimating Methodology

examples, tile), including the probable waste, then order/purchase the materials. Next, the contractor has to calculate the amount of labor and time that will be necessary to install the tile on-site. This is done by assessing labor availability and productivity relative to the amount of work that must be done.

Estimate:

a) Materials:

6" x 6" x 1/2 quarry tile	18	at	$70.00	$1,260
6" x 6" base - straight	172	at	$ 1.50	$ 258
6" x 6" base - angles /corners	6	at	$ 5.00	$ 30
Cement setting mix	12 bags		$ 3.50	$ 42

		$1,590
Tax	5%	80	$1,670

b) Labor:

Tile setting	34 hrs	at	$26.00	$ 884
Helper	34 hrs	at	$21.00	$ 714
				$1,598
Burden		35%		$ 559	$2,157

Labor & Materials:		$3,827

c) Job Overhead:	5%	$ 191
		$4,018

d) Head Office Overhead:	2%	
Profit	10%	
	12%	$ 482

Total Estimated Cost	$4,500

Area of room	409 SF
Cost per SF	$11.00

Figure 3.9 Sample estimate for installing contractor.

The last two steps in the process are to determine how to distribute overheads (the inherent cost of doing business) and how to calculate profit on the project. These last two steps are judgmental and will vary significantly depending on the circumstances of the contractor and the supply and demand characteristics of the marketplace.

Figure 3.9 presents the results of the estimate shown in Figure 3.8. Calculating the material cost involves, first, figuring the amount of quarry tile, bases, corners, and cement setting necessary to complete the job, then adding the sales tax that must be paid. Estimating labor is a somewhat more complicated process. The first step is to assess the labor or crew time that it will take to install the tile and accessories. In the example case, the tile setter working with a helper can produce 120 square feet of tile per day, or 100 lineal feet of base per day, calculated on an eight-hour day. In total amount of time, this comes to 34 hours. Applying the direct wage rates and including the 35 percent wage burden results in the calculation of total labor cost. The job overheads and profits are then added, to arrive at a total estimate of $4,400.

Though this process is laborious and time-consuming, it is essential to do because contractors are risking their own costs on predicting this outcome. In the example, it is interesting to note that calculating the cost per square foot over the room area comes to $11 per square foot. For similar size and quality of tile, $11 a square foot would therefore be a reliable figure. But keep in mind that it is important to ensure that two situations are in fact comparable.

As stated in the first paragraph of this chapter, numerous publications, workbooks, and textbooks are available on the subject of estimating, and depending on the interests of the individual, these sources can be very useful to anyone interested in preparing estimates or in becoming an estimator. The purpose of this book is not to define nor detail the estimating process, but to explain how to use estimates as part of an overall process. The point here is that a variety of estimating methods exist for use by installing contractors, general contractors, or consulting estimators.

Clearly, not all estimates can be prepared exclusively at the level of detail of an installing contractor, or there would not be sufficient time for everyone to do their job. Moreover, such a fine level of detail is inappropriate to conceptual or schematic work. Estimating done by professional consultants or by general contractors is usually done on a unit price basis, using either historical records or published sources. The $11-per-square-foot rate in Figure 3.9 is an example of what might be extracted from published sources or that might be a preliminary quote from an installing contractor who would use similar projects as a basis. Needless to say, this requires selecting a unit price that matches the actual work anticipated.

Bidding

The next significant consideration in the estimating sequence is the process by which a bid is assembled and prepared. Assuming that each of the installing subcontractors is preparing an estimate similar to the one described in Figures 3.8 and 3.9, the general contractor would assemble the quotes and prepare a bid. This process will take anywhere from two weeks to several months. And, invariably, the final day, even the final hours or minutes, may be an action-filled series of events.

The "bid room" in a contractor's office is a fascinating and complex environment. Phones may be ringing off the hook and e-mails may be flying through cyberspace until the bid is finalized, which may not be until the last moment. This is one reason that general contractors object so strenuously to complicated bid forms. It is virtually impossible to complete one of these forms and insert the results of final quotes coming so late in the process. Chapter 5 offers suggestions for dealing with bid forms and schedules of values.

Understanding the Difference

The cost manager has to understand the differences between estimating and bidding, as well as the implications of those differences. For example, when several trades are involved in an element of work, resolving a particular question may require those trades and, therefore, subcontractors, to be involved in any negotiation or clarification. This can become complicated when a relatively simple change impacts several trades and, hence, several estimates. Change-order negotiating is difficult and challenging for these reasons, among others.

Defining the Contents of Estimate

Before preparing an estimate, or calling for an estimate to be prepared, a critical activity is to carefully define the contents or anticipated contents of the estimate. This is essentially a six-step procedure, as follows:

1. *Define and agree to the scope of the estimate.* This step should represent both inclusions and exclusions to the estimate. The nature of the business is such that estimate exclusions tend to be more signifi-

CHECKLIST

Defining the Contents of an Estimate

▶ Define and agree to the scope of the estimate.

▶ Clearly document the basis of all costs and the timeframe of the estimate.

▶ Define precisely what unit pricing represents in the estimate.

▶ Factor in contingencies and escalation as important components of estimates.

▶ Cross-check and validate estimates.

▶ Reconcile two or more estimates that have been prepared for a project in an orderly and comprehensive manner.

Cost-Estimating Methodology

cant than inclusions; specifically, if an item is not stated to be excluded from an estimate, it will be assumed to be in the estimate. This is the exact opposite in a bid situation, where scope is defined by what is included rather than by what is excluded; that is, if an item of work isn't specifically defined as being included in a bid, it will be excluded. Figure 3.10 presents examples of what is typically included and excluded in an estimate.

2. *Clearly document the basis of all costs and the timeframe of the estimate.* This should include expected construction start time, any construction phasing, and the expected construction completion time. There are few standards in the United States regarding basis of measurement for the estimate and estimate components. Consequently, it is the cause of many disagreements. In the United Kingdom, in contrast, the quantity surveying profession has been accepted for many, many years and the method of measurement has been meticulously defined for building components and subcomponents. Most standards in this country apply to major building measurements, such as gross and net area; and even in these, significant discrepancies exist between standards. It is therefore extremely important that the cost manager ensure that the method of measurement for critical items has been agreed on by all concerned. A simple example would be for sitework sheet piling: it is equally valid to measure the sheet piling by the actual area or by only that area exposed above grade. The unit price for the sheet piling, however, would vary dramatically on the basis of how it is measured, assuming that the total cost is the same in either case. The first step, in this case, is to agree on the method of measurement. The issue of standards clearly needs attention in this country. A variety of initiatives from

Items usually excluded from construction contracts	Items sometimes excluded from construction contracts
• Loose & movable furniture	• Lockers
• Furnishings (drapes, rugs, etc.)	• Chalk & tack boards
• Movable equipment	• Built-in seating
• Tenant work (partitions, finishes, etc.)	• Venetian blinds & curtain track
• Telecommunications installation (except conduit)	• Carpeting
	• Signs & graphics
• Demolition	• Built-in equipment (e.g. food service, window washing, etc.)
	• Vaults (doors)
	• Conveyors & hoists
	• Heat & chilled water generation (decentralized)
	• Special electrical systems (e.g. stage lighting, CCTV, etc.)
	• Transformers & switchgear (when by utility)
	• Site work elements (e.g. site furniture, landscaping, signs, etc.)
	• Insurance, bonds & permits
	• CM fees

Figure 3.10 Example of typical inclusions and exclusions in an estimate.

governing bodies such as ASTM and NIST are intended to help clarify this process, but until standards are put in place, cost managers should ensure proper communication on a project-by-project basis.

Cost-Estimating Methodology

3. *Define precisely what unit pricing represents in the estimate.* For example, do prices quoted within the body of the estimate represent costs to the general contractor or costs to the installing contractor; or are they the raw costs of the installing contractor? In each case, the cost will be substantially different and subject to a series of various markups. There are no absolute rights or wrongs in this step, but in most cases the cost manager will want to know what the cost will be to the general contractor exclusive of general contractor markups. Regardless, consistency is of paramount importance here. Consider which forms or formats will be used in the estimate. If costs are going to be summarized in a number of different ways, it is important that those costs include all of the markups associated with their work in place so that once costs are moved, the markups move with them.

4. *Factor in contingencies and escalation as important components of estimates.* This step is especially important when preparing preliminary estimates on the basis of limited documentation. Generally, quotes from subcontractors submitted as part of a bid or in the general contractor's preliminary estimate will usually include any expected cost growth and are representative of an in-place cost at the time that the work needs to be done. Otherwise, a quote would represent the work in place at the time of the quote. If the work is to be conducted at a later time, the quote would have a "sunset provision," which is a time at which the quote is no longer valid, or would be subject to an inflation or escalation increase. Thus, escalation in the context of estimating moves prices forward (or backward) in time. It is also important to distinguish whether escalation is being applied to an estimate or to a sub-bid. An estimate represents a

collection of costs all on the same baseline of time, usually the point at which the estimate is being prepared. A bid represents a quote of work to be conducted over a given timeframe and includes all costs. A bid and an estimate for the same scope of work are equivalent only if their respective timeframes are equivalent. A bid can be moved through time by escalating between bid dates, whereas an estimate will usually be moved through time by escalating to midpoint of that construction period. Ostensibly, a bid includes any escalation that would occur during the conduct of the work. Figure 3.11 presents a comparison of a bid versus an estimate, and Figure 3.12 presents how bids and estimates are escalated through time.

Contingency, on the other hand, is a function of confidence in the estimate and completeness of the documentation on which the estimates are based. Generally, bids prepared entirely on the basis of construction documents will have no contingencies expressly defined. Pricing on the basis of incomplete documentation will always include some degree of contingency. The cost manager should assure that any contingency is expressly defined in the estimate. This is not always easy to do because estimators consider risk as an inherent part of their process and do not always wish to identify contingency separately. Nevertheless, it is important that the allocation of contingency be documented. The topics of contingencies and escalation are covered in more depth later in this chapter.

5. *Cross-check and validate estimates.* This important step is sometimes overlooked. A cost manager can review and cross-check an estimate in a number of ways. Critical components can be verified by independent estimates or by cross-checking in-

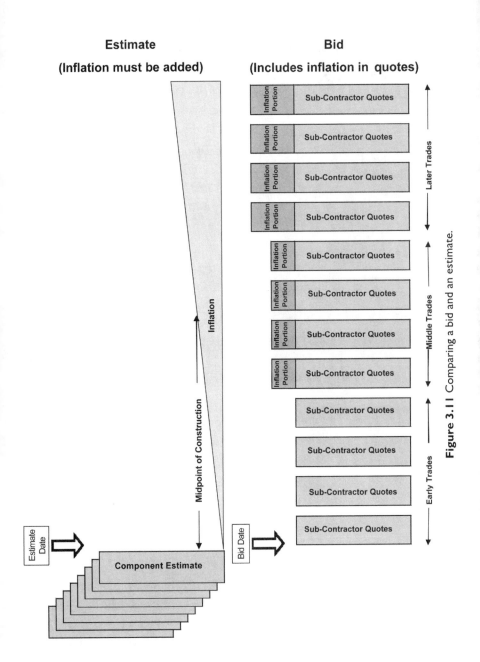

Figure 3.11 Comparing a bid and an estimate.

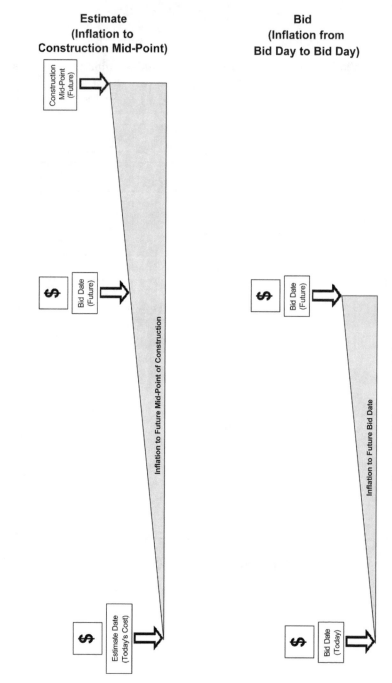

Estimate
(Inflation to
Construction Mid-Point)

Bid
(Inflation from
Bid Day to Bid Day)

Construction Mid-Point (Future)

$

Bid Date (Future)

Inflation to Future Mid-Point of Construction

Estimate Date (Today's Cost)

$

Bid Date (Future)

Inflation to Future Bid Date

$

Bid Date (Today)

Figure 3.12 Escalating a bid versus escalating an estimate.

place costs on the unit basis. The tile example presented previously demonstrated how work could be cross-checked using a previous project. Critical measures of an estimate can be cross-checked simply by, for example, adding up all the floor finishes in an estimate and comparing them to the total gross area to ascertain overlapping versus underlapping finishes. If the total area of finishes exceeds the floor area, obviously there is an error; if the total is less than the overall gross area, then a quick check of unfinished spaces and construction area contained inside walls or voids can provide validation. Another way to cross-check an estimate is to rely on some of the standard measures defined previously in the scope chart in Figure 3.7. Calculating, say, the total tons of air conditioning, and assessing the total in-place cost per ton, can give a quick check. If the cost per ton varied off accepted standards, then either an error has occurred or the basis of the estimate was different from the accepted standard. Similarly, calculating the total pounds of steel per square foot of a building is useful for cross-checking a steel frame building based on reasonable standards from past projects.

6. *Reconcile two or more estimates that have been prepared for a project in an orderly and comprehensive manner.* This step is important to take in order to avoid wasting time and energy to no real purpose. The following offer suggestions for a reconciliation process:

   ▶ *Define the format for the estimates before they're prepared.* If possible, have parties involved in the preparation of the estimate discuss and, ultimately, agree on the exact format to be used, whether UNIFORMAT or MasterFormat, as discussed previously in this chapter.

- *Define and agree to method of pricing in advance.* This may require one or more of the parties to alter either the method of pricing or the way by which they present their estimate. This is not to suggest that any of the parties use a method with which they are unfamiliar. The point is, everyone should understand how to summarize the estimate. Any markups included in the pricing or in the body of the estimate should be clearly identified. And, if possible, the method of measurement associated with critical components should be agreed on as well, to avoid spending unnecessary time and energy determining how something is being measured.

- *Clearly document the schedule and timeframe for the project.* In some cases a schedule detailing individual activities or phases may be attached to the estimate.

- *Clearly identify and define, if necessary, any escalation in contingency.* Clarify bid date escalation or midpoint escalation, if used.

- *Follow both a "top-down" and "bottom-up" strategy for the actual reconciliation process.* Generally, it is not feasible for the reconciliation of two estimates to follow a line-item-by-line basis. The top-down strategy calls for an examination of the overall cost of an estimate, followed by the comparison of major components of the estimate. Focus attention initially on disagreements over significant components of the estimate. A wise approach is to separately identify major quantities of critical items and to clearly document any calculations associated with them. Also, assess significant risks driving or affecting the project, and take the time to understand how these risks have been factored in (or not) each of the estimates. Carefully scrutinize these "drivers," because differences of any consequence in the estimate should result from differences in interpretation of the drivers. Simply put, it is neither feasible nor beneficial to spend a great deal of time and effort on details of the estimate when significant disagreements may exist over the drivers. The top-down approach forces discussion and reconciliation over the major drivers. The bottom-up approach, in contrast, is useful for examining scope inclusions and exclusions and overall consistency. That said, a line-item-by-line-item examination of individual pricing usually will not prove valuable because it requires a great deal of definition over what each line item includes. A review of line items is beneficial when examining overall trends and patterns of pricing in particular areas. Experience has shown that two or more estimates, even when all are extremely competently prepared, may still vary dramatically from component to component and certainly from item to item. Any estimate represents a prediction, so the first conclusions over any reconciliation should be at the highest levels first. Initially, this reconciliation should include scope, inclusions, and exclusions, along with major pricing assumptions concerning markups, profit, and overheads, as well as any significant restrictions over the work. Subsequently, attention should be focused on a review of the major drivers as they are identified. The line-item-by-line-item bottom-up reconciliation should be used only as a means of adjusting any individual estimate when the top-down review indicates significant differences. Again, it is important to understand that two or more estimates will seldom, if ever, be made to match at any lower level.

Cost-Estimating Methods

Cost estimates can be prepared using a variety of methods appropriate to the level of information available and the time available to prepare the estimate. The methods fall into four major categories:

- Single-unit rate (SUR) methods
- Parametric/cost modeling
- System/elemental cost analysis
- Quantity survey

Figure 3.13 illustrates how these estimating methods can be applied to the overall delivery of a project. Single-unit rate methods are usually more appropriate for the preplanning and programming phases of the project. Parametric and cost model estimates are generally utilized during schematic design and early design development. Systems and elemental estimates are best implemented during design development or for early construction documents. Quantity survey-based estimates are generally prepared during construction documents and into bid-

Predesign	Schematic	Design Development	Construction Documents	Bidding	Construction
SUR					
	Parametric/Cost Modeling				
		Systems/Elemental			
			Quantity Survey		

Figure 3.13 Application of estimating methods during project delivery.

ding and construction. However, at any point in time, the techniques may be utilized as a cross-check of overall costs or, in the case of a quantity survey estimate, as a check of an individual model assumption or particular critical driving detail.

Single-Unit Rate Estimating Methods

Single-unit rate estimating methods also can be subdivided into four major categories:

- ► Accommodation Method
- ► Cubic Foot Method
- ► Square Foot Method
- ► Functional Area Method

Accommodation Method

The accommodation method is based on an overall calculation of the cost to deliver the facility, based on a *major measure* of the facility. For example, parking garages could be measured per parking stall. Apartment buildings might be measured on cost per apartment. Performing arts facilities and auditoriums could be measured on cost per seat. Hospitals may be measured on cost per bed. The accommodation method is often used to provide very preliminary estimates or a quick check and assessment of a current project. The key to utilizing accommodation estimates is, as might be expected, the basis of the accommodation unit in the first place. Take the example of the parking garage. A simple above-grade parking garage would generally be budgeted at $10,000 per space. The question is, what is the basis of that figure? It would probably be based on the following: approximately 300 to 350 square feet per stall; spans optimized accordingly; reasonable soil conditions; a flat site with all above-grade construc-

MAXIM

The easier the measurement, the more difficult the pricing; the more detailed the measurement, the easier the pricing.

tion; very limited exterior cladding; and open space with minimal mechanical ventilation. In contrast, a below-grade construction in poor soils could push the number above $30,000 per space, and extensive exterior cladding could add significantly to the number. Furthermore, extensive van-pool parking might increase the average area per space to 400 to 450 square feet, thereby increasing the cost by 25 or 30 percent. The cost manager, therefore, must exercise great care to ensure that comparisons are truly comparable. And, when comparing measures from past projects, the cost manager must carefully consider geographical, time, and market adjustments as well.

Cubic Foot Method

The cubic foot method of analysis is not generally used in the United States, except for volume-dependent facilities such as warehouses. By nature of the measure, the cubic foot method will be sensitive to the volume of facility and to variances affecting the volume of facility. Interestingly, European countries, especially Germany, routinely use cubic measures as a means of budgeting facilities. The method can certainly be effective, but it tends to be awkward for use in general facilities.

Square Foot Method

The square foot method is the most commonly used initial budgeting mechanism in the United States. The method is routinely applied in both government and private industry and for buildings and process industries as well. Though effective, the square foot method is extremely dependent on the basis on which the square footage is compared and on the measurement method used to produce

TIP

The square foot method is the most commonly used initial budgeting mechanism in the United States.

the square foot comparison in the first place. For example, comparing the cost per square foot of an office building using net measures versus gross measures could vary the resulting number by 30 or 40 percent. There are a number of published sources for square foot costs; one of the most commonly referenced is the R. S. Means Company. Figure 3.14 shows an excerpt from R. S. Means's building construction cost data book that contains a summary of various building types, how the unit costs per square foot vary over a large number of projects, and how unit costs can be adjusted for facility size. This method is useful because it indicates expected variances both for the total cost of the project and for major building components, such as plumbing, HVAC, and electrical.

Functional Area Method

The functional area method of estimating is based on functional space types. A functional space type is defined as an area within the building that has a distinct purpose; for example, in a school, functional spaces are classrooms, cafeterias, gymnasiums, and so on. The advantage of the functional area method over the square foot method is that variations in space types and, therefore, program can be accommodated in the basic estimate. Using the school example, a classroom might cost $100 per square foot to build in place, whereas the gymnasium component might cost as much as $200 per square foot to build in place. The overall proportions in a typical program will yield an overall cost per gross square foot. If the programs of different facilities are similar, it is likely that the cost per square foot will be similar; conversely, if the programs are significantly different, the resulting cost per

		17100| S.F. & C.F. Costs		UNIT	UNIT COSTS			% OF TOTAL			
					1/4	MEDIAN	3/4	1/4	MEDIAN	3/4	
700	1800	Equipment	R17100	S.F.	5.40	14.40	22	6.10%	13.40%	15.60%	700
	2720	Plumbing	-100		7.15	8.70	12.40	6.10%	8.30%	9.10%	
	2770	Heating, ventilating, air conditioning			9.45	12.60	16.45	9.40%	12.20%	13%	
	2900	Electrical			9.60	11.85	15.40	8.50%	10.60%	11.60%	
	3100	Total: Mechanical & Electrical		↓	30	31.50	39.50	21.10%	24%	29.50%	
	5000										
	9000	Per seat unit, total cost		Seat	3,300	4,400	5,600				
	9500	Total: Mechanical & Electrical		"	700	995	1,300				
720	0010	**RETAIL STORES**	R17100	S.F.	42	56.50	74.50				720
	0020	Total project costs	-100	C.F.	2.86	4.08	5.65				
	2720	Plumbing		S.F.	1.54	2.56	4.38	3.20%	4.60%	6.80%	
	2770	Heating, ventilating, air conditioning			3.32	4.54	6.85	6.70%	8.70%	10.10%	
	2900	Electrical			3.79	5.15	7.45	7.30%	9.90%	11.60%	
	3100	Total: Mechanical & Electrical		↓	10.15	13	16.85	17.10%	21.40%	23.80%	
740	0010	**SCHOOLS** Elementary	R17100	S.F.	67	82.50	99.50				740
	0020	Total project costs	-100	C.F.	4.53	5.80	7.50				
	0500	Masonry		S.F.	6.20	9.75	13.65	7.10%	10.50%	15.20%	
	1800	Equipment			2.11	3.56	6.30	2.50%	4.20%	7.60%	
	2720	Plumbing			3.87	5.60	7.50	5.70%	7.10%	9.40%	
	2730	Heating, ventilating, air conditioning			5.95	9.50	13.25	8.10%	10.80%	15.20%	
	2900	Electrical			6.25	7.95	10.15	8.40%	10%	11.60%	
	3100	Total: Mechanical & Electrical		↓	21.50	24	33.50	22.20%	28%	30.40%	
	9000	Per pupil, total cost		Ea.	6,700	11,000	36,000				
	9500	Total: Mechanical & Electrical		"	2,250	2,825	11,300				
760	0010	**SCHOOLS** Junior High & Middle	R17100	S.F.	68	84	98.50				760
	0020	Total project costs	-100	C.F.	4.47	5.85	6.55				
	0500	Masonry		S.F.	7.65	10.20	12.60	8.80%	11.10%	14%	
	1800	Equipment			2.28	3.67	5.65	2.60%	4.30%	5.90%	
	2720	Plumbing			4.52	5	6.65	5.60%	6.90%	8.10%	
	2770	Heating, ventilating, air conditioning			5.20	10.05	14	8.70%	12.70%	17.40%	
	2900	Electrical			6.55	8.25	9.95	7.80%	9.40%	10.60%	
	3100	Total: Mechanical & Electrical		↓	18.95	24	31.50	23.30%	25.70%	27.30%	
	9000	Per pupil, total cost		Ea.	8,500	9,800	12,200				
780	0010	**SCHOOLS** Senior High	R17100	S.F.	73.50	84	118				780
	0020	Total project costs	-100	C.F.	4.70	6.10	8.60				
	1800	Equipment		S.F.	1.95	4.59	6.80	2.30%	3.70%	5.40%	
	2720	Plumbing			3.79	6.85	11.40	5%	6.90%	12%	
	2770	Heating, ventilating, air conditioning			8.50	9.65	18.55	8.90%	11%	15%	
	2900	Electrical			7.20	9.50	15.80	8.30%	10.10%	12.60%	
	3100	Total: Mechanical & Electrical		↓	19.70	26	48.50	19.80%	23.10%	27.80%	
	9000	Per pupil, total cost		Ea.	7,000	11,900	17,800				
800	0010	**SCHOOLS** Vocational	R17100	S.F.	60	83.50	106				800
	0020	Total project costs	-100	C.F.	3.67	5.30	7.40				
	0500	Masonry		S.F.	3.52	8.70	13.30	4%	10.90%	19.90%	
	1800	Equipment		"	1.88	2.54	6.45	2.90%	3.40%	4.70%	
	2720	Plumbing		S.F.	3.84	5.85	8.40	5.40%	7%	8.50%	
	2770	Heating, ventilating, air conditioning			5.35	10	16.70	8.80%	11.90%	14.60%	
	2900	Electrical			6.15	8.55	12.05	8.40%	11.20%	13.80%	
	3100	Total: Mechanical & Electrical		↓	16.25	21.50	41.50	21.70%	27.30%	33.10%	
	9000	Per pupil, total cost		Ea.	8,400	22,400	33,400				
830	0010	**SPORTS ARENAS**	R17100	S.F.	51	70	103				830
	0020	Total project costs	-100	C.F.	2.85	5.05	6.60				
	2720	Plumbing		S.F.	2.71	4.51	8.50	4.50%	6.30%	9.40%	
	2770	Heating, ventilating, air conditioning			5.55	7.75	10.10	5.80%	10.20%	13.50%	
	2900	Electrical			4.51	7.10	8.90	7.70%	9.80%	12.30%	
	3100	Total: Mechanical & Electrical		↓	13.25	23.50	30.50	13.40%	22.50%	30.80%	

Figure 3.14 Example of R. S. Means historical square foot costs.

R17100-100   Square Foot Project Size Modifier

One factor that affects the S.F. cost of a particular building is the size. In general, for buildings built to the same specifications in the same locality, the larger building will have the lower S.F. cost. This is due mainly to the decreasing contribution of the exterior walls plus the economy of scale usually achievable in larger buildings. The Area Conversion Scale shown below will give a factor to convert costs for the typical size building to an adjusted cost for the particular project.

The Square Foot Base Size lists the median costs, most typical project size in our accumulated data and the range in size of the projects.

The Size Factor for your project is determined by dividing your project area in S.F. by the typical project size for the particular Building Type. With this factor, enter the Area Conversion Scale at the appropriate Size Factor and determine the appropriate cost multiplier for your building size.

Example: Determine the cost per S.F. for a 100,000 S.F.
Mid-rise apartment building.

$$\frac{\text{Proposed building area} = 100,000 \text{ S.F.}}{\text{Typical size from below} = 50,000 \text{ S.F.}} = 2.00$$

Enter Area Conversion scale at 2.0, intersect curve, read horizontally the appropriate cost multiplier of .94. Size adjusted cost becomes .94 x $72.00 = $67.70 based on national average costs.

Note: For Size Factors less than .50, the Cost Multiplier is 1.1
For Size Factors greater than 3.5, the Cost Multiplier is .90

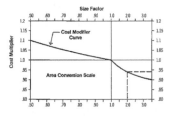

Square Foot Base Size							
Building Type	Median Cost per S.F.	Typical Size Gross S.F.	Typical Range Gross S.F.	Building Type	Median Cost per S.F.	Typical Size Gross S.F.	Typical Range Gross S.F.
Apartments, Low Rise	$ 57.00	21,000	9,700 - 37,200	Jails	$174.00	40,000	5,500 - 145,000
Apartments, Mid Rise	72.00	50,000	32,000 - 100,000	Libraries	103.00	12,000	7,000 - 31,000
Apartments, High Rise	82.55	145,000	95,000 - 600,000	Medical Clinics	98.20	7,200	4,200 - 15,700
Auditoriums	95.30	25,000	7,600 - 39,000	Medical Offices	92.25	6,000	4,000 - 15,000
Auto Sales	58.95	20,000	10,800 - 28,600	Motels	70.65	40,000	15,800 - 120,000
Banks	128.00	4,200	2,500 - 7,500	Nursing Homes	92.10	23,000	15,000 - 37,000
Churches	86.05	17,000	2,000 - 42,000	Offices, Low Rise	76.95	20,000	5,000 - 80,000
Clubs, Country	85.80	6,500	4,500 - 15,000	Offices, Mid Rise	80.80	120,000	20,000 - 300,000
Clubs, Social	83.45	10,000	6,000 - 13,500	Offices, High Rise	103.00	260,000	120,000 - 800,000
Clubs, YMCA	83.70	28,300	12,800 - 39,400	Police Stations	129.00	10,500	4,000 - 19,000
Colleges (Class)	112.00	50,000	15,000 - 150,000	Post Offices	95.30	12,400	6,800 - 30,000
Colleges (Science Lab)	164.00	45,600	16,600 - 80,000	Power Plants	716.00	7,500	1,000 - 20,000
College (Student Union)	125.00	33,400	16,000 - 85,000	Religious Education	78.95	9,000	6,000 - 12,000
Community Center	89.70	9,400	5,300 - 16,700	Research	134.00	19,000	6,300 - 45,000
Court Houses	122.00	32,400	17,800 - 106,000	Restaurants	116.00	4,400	2,800 - 6,000
Dept. Stores	53.25	90,000	44,000 - 122,000	Retail Stores	56.60	7,200	4,000 - 17,600
Dormitories, Low Rise	91.95	25,000	10,000 - 95,000	Schools, Elementary	82.45	41,000	24,500 - 55,000
Dormitories, Mid Rise	120.00	85,000	20,000 - 200,000	Schools, Jr. High	84.00	92,000	52,000 - 119,000
Factories	51.60	26,400	12,900 - 50,000	Schools, Sr. High	83.95	101,000	50,500 - 175,000
Fire Stations	90.15	5,800	4,000 - 8,700	Schools, Vocational	83.65	37,000	20,500 - 82,000
Fraternity Houses	88.65	12,500	8,200 - 14,800	Sports Arenas	70.10	15,000	5,000 - 40,000
Funeral Homes	99.10	10,000	4,000 - 20,000	Supermarkets	56.80	44,000	12,000 - 60,000
Garages, Commercial	62.95	9,300	5,000 - 13,600	Swimming Pools	131.00	20,000	10,000 - 32,000
Garages, Municipal	80.55	8,300	4,500 - 12,600	Telephone Exchange	153.00	4,500	1,200 - 10,600
Garages, Parking	33.00	163,000	76,400 - 225,300	Theaters	84.05	10,500	8,800 - 17,500
Gymnasiums	83.30	19,200	11,600 - 41,000	Town Halls	92.45	10,800	4,800 - 23,400
Hospitals	157.00	55,000	27,200 - 125,000	Warehouses	38.10	25,000	8,000 - 72,000
House (Elderly)	77.95	37,000	21,000 - 66,000	Warehouse & Office	44.00	25,000	8,000 - 72,000
Housing (Public)	72.15	36,000	14,400 - 74,400				
Ice Rinks	80.20	29,000	27,200 - 33,600				

Figure 3-14 (continued)

square foot would be different. The functional area method allows for sensitivity to program elements.

There are two options for applying the functional area method: first, by space type; second, by core and shell plus functional space type build-out. The first assumes an equal sharing of the core and shell costs among space types. The second derives the core and shell costs separately and then assesses the build-out costs of the space types. Figure 3.15 provides an example of the calculation for a school using both methods, and demonstrates that they can result in the same total cost.

By Space Type:

Area			Space Type		Unit Cost		Total Cost
25,000	SF	of	Classroom	x	$ 90.00	=	$ 2,250,000.00
6,000	SF	of	Laboratories	x	$ 175.00	=	$ 1,050,000.00
12,000	SF	of	Gymnasium	x	$ 145.00	=	$ 1,740,000.00
8,000	SF	of	Auditorium	x	$ 205.00	=	$ 1,640,000.00
Total	*51,000 SF*				*$ 130.98*		*$ 6,680,000.00*

By Core & Shell + Function:

Area			Space Type		Unit Cost		Total Cost
51,000	SF		Core & Shell	x	$ 65.00	=	$ 3,315,000.00
25,000	SF	of	Classroom	x	$ 25.00	=	$ 625,000.00
6,000	SF	of	Laboratories	x	$ 110.00	=	$ 660,000.00
12,000	SF	of	Gymnasium	x	$ 80.00	=	$ 960,000.00
8,000	SF	of	Auditorium	x	$ 140.00	=	$ 1,120,000.00
Total	*51,000 SF*				*$ 130.98*		*$ 6,680,000.00*

By Core & Shell + Function (modified):

Area			Space Type		Unit Cost		Total Cost
51,000	SF		Core & Shell	x	$ 60.00	=	$ 3,060,000.00
25,000	SF	of	Classroom	x	$ 25.00	=	$ 625,000.00
6,000	SF	of	Laboratories	x	$ 110.00	=	$ 660,000.00
12,000	SF	of	Gymnasium	x	$ 80.00	=	$ 960,000.00
8,000	SF	of	Auditorium	x	$ 140.00	=	$ 1,120,000.00
Total	*51,000 SF*				*$ 125.98*		*$ 6,425,000.00*

Figure 3.15 Example of functional area method approaches.

Both methods are effective, but the second tends to be more accurate and sensitive, in that the core and shell drivers and space type build-out drivers usually are different. Figure 3.15 shows the change in design approach from the base assumptions, such that the core and shell incorporates the high-bay functions in a different manner to reduce the impact on core and shell; therefore, the results may be different. In this case, the core and shell cost could be reduced by $5 per square foot from $65 to $60. The build-out costs would remain the same, but the overall cost could be reduced by approximately $250,000. The core and shell plus function method provides greater flexibility and sensitivity, to reflect optional design approaches. This method is particularly valuable when exterior design issues are drivers on a project.

Using functional area methods, owners have devised systems for preparing initial budgeting estimates. The federal government, too, has prepared budgeting systems using this method; in particular, the General Services Administration (GSA) has produced the "General Construction Cost Review Guide for Federal Office Buildings and Courthouses" (GCCRG) since the early 1990s. An excerpt of the GCCRG approach for space type costs is provided in Figure 3.16; a complete example of a GCCRG estimate is presented in Figure 3.17. The GSA method classifies space type by 16 standard categories and by a reasonable range from low to high. The costs shown here were derived from a model that included basic building types and basic space types. The system process takes net area, expands it into gross area, and determines a cost per total gross square foot per space type. Note that courtrooms are

Item		Space Type*	Low Cost $/Gross SF $/Gross M^2$	Typical $/Gross SF $/Gross M^2$	High Cost $/Gross SF $/Gross M^2$
1		General Office	$120.00/GSF $1290.00/GM^2$	$126.00/GSF $1350.00/GM^2$	$147.00/GSF $1590.00/GM^2$
2		Office (Enhanced Finish Buildings - Courthouses)	$136.00/GSF $1460.00/GM^2$	$143.00/GSF $1545.00/GM^2$	$168.00/GSF $1800.00/GM^2$
3	ST-1	General Storage	$74.00/GSF $800.00/GM^2$	$104.00/GSF $1120.00/GM^2$	$136.00/GSF $1460.00/GM^2$
4	ST-2	Inside Parking	$57.00/GSF $610.00/GM^2$	$68.00/GSF $731.00/GM^2$	$74.00/GSF $800.00/GM^2$
5		Outside Parking (Garage Structure)	$30.00/GSF $320.00/GM^2$	$34.00/GSF $370.00/GM^2$	$39.00/GSF $420.00/GM^2$
6	ST-3	Warehouse	$75.00/GSF $810.00/GM^2$	$83.00/GSF $900.00/GM^2$	$98.00/GSF $1050.00/GM^2$
7	SP-1A	Laboratories	$170.00/GSF $1820.00/GM^2$	$171.00/GSF $1845.00/GM^2$	$229.00/GSF $2460.00/GM^2$
8	SP-1B	Private Toilets, Clinics, Health Facilities/Child Care	$163.00/GSF $1750.00/GM^2$	$168.00/GSF $1800.00/GM^2$	$171.00/GSF $1840.00/GM^2$
9	SP-2	Food Service	$150.00/GSF $1620.00/GM^2$	$164.00/GSF $1761.00/GM^2$	$186.00/GSF $2010.00/GM^2$
10	SP-3A	Structurally Changed Areas	$163.00/GSF $1750.00/GM^2$	$183.00/GSF $1980.00/GM^2$	$201.00/GSF $2160.00/GM^2$
11	SP-3B	Courtrooms	$200.00/GSF $2150.00/GM^2$	$221.00/GSF $2380.00/GM^2$	$241.00/GSF $2600.00/GM^2$
12	SP-4	Automatic Data Processing	$166.00/GSF $1780.00/GM^2$	$180.00/GSF $1940.00/GM^2$	$216.00/GSF $2330.00/GM^2$
13	SP-5A	Conference and Classroom Training	$133.00/GSF $1430.00/GM^2$	$145.00/GSF $1570.00/GM^2$	$160.00/GSF $1720.00/GM^2$
14	SP-5B	Judicial Hearing Rooms, Small Courtrooms	$185.00/GSF $2000.00/GM^2$	$207.00/GSF $2225.00/GM^2$	$226.00/GSF $2430.00/GM^2$
15	SP-5C	Judicial Chambers	$157.00/GSF $1690.00/GM^2$	$159.00/GSF $1710.00/GM^2$	$176.00/GSF $1900.00/GM^2$
16	SP-6	Light Industrial	$106.00/GSF $1140.00/GM^2$	$114.00/GSF $1230.00/GM^2$	$124.00/GSF $1330.00/GM^2$

Figure 3.16 GSA's "General Construction Cost Review Guide" (GCCRG): space costs.

almost twice as expensive to build as a general office, including the circulation and support spaces allocated to each space type. The cost of the net square footage associated with courtrooms is much higher. Currently, the GSA is changing its system to convert

GENERAL CONSTRUCTION COST ANALYSIS

Project Name: New Federal Building Courthouse	Submission or Purpose: Planning Cost Analysis - New Construction Alternative			GCCRG Issue Date: 10/01/96
City, State: Raleigh, North Carolina	Applied GCCRG Location: North Carolina	Annual Const. Esc. Rate: 3.00%	GCCRG Cost Index: 0.83	Cover Sheet Analysis Date: 12/15/96
Estimator: John Doe	Organization Symbol: XPCP	Telephone Number: (202) 501-0000	Seismic Zone Factor: 1.00	Estimate Date For Specials: 12/25/96
Portfolio Management Coordinator: Steve Smith	Organization Symbol: XPLX	Telephone Number: (202) 501-1321	Other Space Factor: 1.00	Desired Reference Date: 01/01/00

Space Types (Directly Involved or Impacted)	Area Occupiable	Area Efficiency	Area Gross	Unit Cost From GCCRG Table	Space Cost For Location & Factors On GCCRG Date	Space Cost Escalated To Reference Date
General Office (Equal Mix Plan)	150,000	72%	208,333	$126.00	$21,788,000	$23,986,000
Office (Within Enhanced Finish Building)	0	0%	0	$0.00	$0	$0
ST-1 General Storage	2,450	81%	3,025	$104.00	$261,000	$287,000
ST-2 Inside Parking	35,900	86%	41,744	$68.00	$2,356,000	$2,594,000
Outside Parking (Garage Structure)	0	0%	0	$0.00	$0	$0
ST-3 Warehouse	0	0%	0	$0.00	$0	$0
SP-1A Laboratories	0	0%	0	$0.00	$0	$0
SP-1B Priv.Toilets/Clinics/Health/Child Care	4,100	61%	6,721	$168.00	$937,000	$1,032,000
SP-2 Food Service	5,800	68%	8,529	$164.00	$1,161,000	$1,278,000
SP-3A Structurally Changed Areas	3,000	74%	4,054	$183.00	$616,000	$678,000
SP-3B Courtrooms	24,000	65%	36,923	$221.00	$6,773,000	$7,456,000
SP-4 Automated Data Processing	10,580	65%	16,277	$180.00	$2,432,000	$2,677,000
SP-5A Conference and Classroom Training	6,500	65%	10,000	$145.00	$1,204,000	$1,325,000
SP-5B Judicial Hearing Rms./Sm. Courtrooms	12,000	65%	18,462	$207.00	$3,172,000	$3,492,000
SP-5C Judicial Chambers	18,000	65%	27,692	$159.00	$3,655,000	$4,024,000
SP-6 Light Industrial	0	0%	0	$0.00	$0	$0
Other	0	0%	0	$0.00	$0	$0
Other	0	0%	0	$0.00	$0	$0
Space Totals	272,300 OSF		381,800 GSF		$44,355,000	$48,829,000

Note: Unit Costs and Efficiency Factors Provide for Building Support Space. Site Development Costs Are Also Proportioned Within Space Unit Costs. Space Unit Costs Reflect: Contingencies (Design & Construction), General Conditions/Profit, Art-In-Architecture And Other Reservations.

Overall Building Space Efficiency = 70% Without Parking, = 71% With All Indicated Parking

Figure 3.17 GSA's "General Construction Cost Review Guide" (GCCRG): example estimate.

to a core and shell plus functional area approach for the same reasons mentioned previously, to gain a greater degree of accuracy and sensitivity for budgeting purposes. It is anticipated that this material will become publicly available by mid-2002.

Privately developed systems also can be utilized to prepare space-based estimates. An example is the product called PACES, produced by Talisman Partners. PACES can be viewed on the firm's Web site at www.talpart.com.

Parametric and Cost-Modeling Methods

Parametric and cost-modeling methods seek to utilize predetermined models and statistical analyses to predict facility costs. These approaches are generally applied to repetitive facilities or to replicate theoretical analyses and expectations over building programs. In the process, facilities statistics can be utilized as a means of predicting and assessing costs, especially for complicated systems involving piping and process components. These approaches have less application in building construction.

An example of a statistically based cost-modeling approach is presented in Figure 3.18, where an analysis has been made to determine the statistical variation in costs for different-size facilities. The chart was constructed based on a regression analysis, which is a statistical process to project a curve fit to point-specific data. Interestingly, the R. S. Means Company also uses a statistically derived curve to adjust building costs for size (refer to Figure 3.14). It is possible to use statistical analysis in conjunction with more traditional measures and methods.

Cost models can also be prepared based on computer models that project form, shape, and composi-

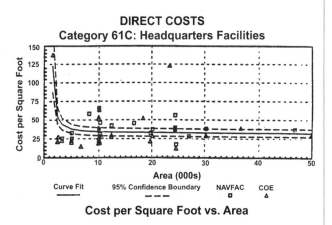

DIRECT COSTS
Category 61C: Headquarters Facilities

Cost per Square Foot vs. Area

Figure 3.18 Example of statistical cost-modeling system.

tion of building types. In the last several years, several computer-based systems have been developed for modeling purposes; they have been intended primarily to help designers visualize form and shape and determine magnitude. These systems can also be used as front-end devices to a cost-modeling process. Experience has shown, however, that it is surprisingly difficult to connect such systems to pricing systems in a practical way. One such system, by REVIT Technology Corporation, can be viewed at the company Web site, www.revit.com.

Systems/Elemental Cost Analysis

The systems/elemental cost analysis approach bridges the conceptual estimating methods described previously and the detailed quantity survey-based estimating that is described next. The basic concept behind this approach is to subdivide the facility into its elemental components, generally using UNIFORMAT as a basis. The actual level of detail is generally a function of the amount of design detail that is available.

When very limited design information is available, it becomes necessary for the estimator, working in conjunction with the designers, to make a set of assumptions on which to base an estimate. It is possible to use historical information from similar facilities or from building components and elements as a basis for these estimates, or it may be necessary to develop what are generally referred to as "assemblies."

Relying on historical cost is appropriate when facility types and programmatic components are very similar. Adjustments to the historical cost basis could then be made on the basis of deviations from that historical basis—essentially a plus–minus adjustment of a statistically significant baseline. An example of programmatically similar facilities that would lend themselves to an elemental analysis is elementary schools. Figure 3.19 presents a systems/elemental summary of an elementary school recently built in the Washington, D.C., area. The project has a gross area of 77,200 gross square feet and a building cost of $6.6 million at an average cost of $85 per square foot. Some of the key statistics of the school are also included in the figure. This model could be used subsequently as the basis of an analysis of a new school being designed, assuming that the programs and the construction and design approaches are similar.

It is also possible to adjust this model on a plus-minus basis. For example, the school in Figure 3.19 has a brick exterior wall; alternate wall materials could be considered that might be more or less expensive per square foot than brick. Once the overall wall area is known, the cost projection can be adjusted based on the choice of different materials.

Published sources of information are also available that can be used to prepare estimates and to

Project Description:	**Elementary School, Virginia - Example 1**				Bid Date:		11/96	
Project Type:	**School**				Construction time(Months):		14	
Gross Building Area:(GSF)	77,200				Market Conditions:		good	

SYSTEM / ELEMENT DESCRIPTION	UNIFORMAT REFERENCE	TOTAL COST	COST PER GSF	% OF BUILDING	ELEMENTAL ANALYSIS MEASURE	UNIT	VALUE	COST/UNIT
BUILDING:		*b*	*b / GSF*	*b / 27*				*b / c*
1 Foundations	(A10)	506,192	6.56	9.3%	Ground Floor Area	SF	77,200	6.56
2 Standard Foundations	(A1010)	302,142	3.91	5.6%	Ground Floor Area	SF	77,200	3.91
3 Other Foundations	(A1020)	-	-	0.0%	Ground Floor Area	SF	77,200	-
4 Slab on Grade	(A1030)	204,050	2.64	3.8%	Ground Floor Area	SF	77,200	2.64
5 Basement Construction	(A20)	-	-	0.0%	Ground Floor Area	SF	77,200	-
6 Substructure - Sub-Total (A)		506,192	6.56	9.3%	Ground Floor Area	SF	77,200	6.56
7 Superstructure	(B10)	400,900	5.19	7.4%	Gross Bldg. Area	SF	77,200	5.19
8 Exterior Enclosure	(B20)	537,917	6.97	9.9%	Gross Enclosure Area	SF	31,000	17.35
9 Roofing	(B30)	273,275	3.54	5.0%	Roof Surface Area	SF	80,000	3.42
10 Shell - Sub-Total (B)		1,212,092	15.70	22.3%	Gross Bldg. Area	SF	77,200	15.70
11 Interior Construction	(C10)	560,523	7.26	10.3%	Gross Bldg. Area	SF	77,200	7.26
12 Stairs	(C20)	-	-	0.0%	Gross Bldg. Area	SF	77,200	-
13 Interior Finishes	(C30)	394,833	5.11	7.3%	Gross Bldg. Area	SF	77,200	5.11
14 Interiors - Sub-Total (C)		955,356	12.38	17.6%	Gross Bldg. Area	SF	77,200	12.38
15 Conveying Systems	(D10)	7,288	0.09	0.1%	Total No. of Stops	EA	1	7,288
16 Plumbing	(D20)	447,800	5.80	8.2%	No. of Fixtures	EA	150	2,985
17 HVAC	(D30)	1,049,400	13.59	19.3%	Tons (or MBH)	EA	200	5,247
18 Fire Protection	(D40)	151,800	1.97	2.8%	Protected Area	SF	77,200	1.97
19 Electrical	(D50)	859,866	11.14	15.8%	Gross Bldg. Area	SF	77,200	11.14
20 Electrical Service & Distribution	(D5010)	182,120	2.36	3.4%	Connected KW	KW	650	280
21 Lighting & Branch Wiring	(D5020)	286,132	3.71	5.3%	Gross Bldg. Area	SF	77,200	3.71
22 Communications & Security	(D5030)	205,778	2.67	3.8%	Gross Bldg. Area	SF	77,200	2.67
23 Other Electrical Systems	(D5040)	185,836	2.41	3.4%	Gross Bldg. Area	SF	77,200	2.41
24 Services - Sub-Total (D)		2,516,154	32.59	46.3%	Gross Bldg. Area	SF	77,200	32.59
25 Equip. & Furnishings - Sub-Total (E)		211,210	2.74	3.9%	Gross Bldg. Area	SF	77,200	2.74
26 Spec. Construct. & Demo - Sub-Total (F)		28,500	0.37	0.5%	Gross Bldg. Area	SF	77,200	0.37
27 **TOTAL BUILDING**		$ 5,429,504	$ 70.33	100.0%	Accommodation Units	EA	750	$ 7,239
28 **SITEWORK & UTILITIES:**		-						
29 Site Preparation	(G10)	467,598	6.06	8.6%	Gross Site Area	SF	600,000	0.78
30 Site Improvements	(G20)	85,122	1.10	1.6%	Gross Site Area	SF	600,000	0.14
31 Site Mechanical Utilities	(G30)	301,500	3.91	5.6%	Gross Site Area	SF	600,000	0.50
32 Site Electrical Utilities	(G40)	-	-	0.0%	Gross Site Area	SF	600,000	-
33 Other Site Construction	(G50)	-	-	0.0%	Gross Site Area	SF	600,000	-
34 **TOTAL SITEWORK & UTILITIES:** (G)		854,220	11.07	15.7%	Gross Site Area	SF	600,000	1.42
35 General Conditions, Overhead, & Profit @ 5.1%		322,647	4.18	5.9%				
36 **TOTAL FACILITY COST - CURRENT**		$ 6,606,371	$ 85.57	121.7%	Accommodation Units	EA	750	$ 8,808
37 Contingency @		-	-	0.0%				
38 Escalation @		-	-	0.0%				
39								
40 **TOTAL FACILITY COST - PROJECTED**		$ 6,606,371	$ 85.57	121.7%	Accommodation Units	EA	750	$ 8,808

Parameters:		Measure	Value	Area Analysis:	Area (SF)
1	Gross Bldg. Area	SF	77,200		
2	Ground Floor Area	SF	77,200	Basement	-
3	Gross Enclosure Area	SF	31,000	Ground Floor	77,200
4	Percent Fenestration	%	12%	Upper Floors	
5	Roof Surface Area	SF	80,000	Penthouses	
6	Total No.of Conveying Stops	STOPS	1	Other Areas	-
7	Tons Cooling (or MBH Htg)	TONS	200		
8	No. of Plumbing Fixtures	EA	150	Gross Floor Area	77,200
9	Fire Protected Area	SF	77,200		
10	Connected KW	KW	650		
11	Accommodation Units	EA	750		
12	Floor to Floor Height (Avg.)	LF	12		
13	Gross Site Area	SF	600,000		
14	Gross Bldg. Area/Accommod Unit	SF/EA	103		
			-		

Figure 3.19 Example of a systems/elemental estimate.

Model costs calculated for a 2 story building with 12' story height and 110,000 square feet of floor area

			Unit	Unit Cost	Cost Per S.F.	% Of Sub-Total
A. SUBSTRUCTURE						
1010	Standard Foundations	Poured concrete: strip and spread footings	S.F. Ground	1.66	.83	
1030	Slab on Grade	4" reinforced concrete with vapor barrier and granular base	S.F. Slab	3.42	1.71	5.4%
2010	Basement Excavation	Site preparation for slab and trench for foundation wall and footing	S.F. Ground	1.09	.55	
2020	Basement Walls	4' foundation wall	L.F. Wall	52	.91	
B. SHELL						
	B10 Superstructure					
1010	Floor Construction	Open web steel joists, slab form, concrete, columns	S.F. Floor	16.30	8.15	15.2%
1020	Roof Construction	Metal deck, open web steel joists, columns	S.F. Floor	6.34	3.17	
	B20 Exterior Enclosure					
2010	Exterior Walls	Face brick with concrete block backup 75% of wall	S.F. Wall	21	6.53	
2020	Exterior Windows	Window wall 25% of wall	Each	34	3.53	14.0%
2030	Exterior Doors	Double aluminum & glass	Each	1405	.37	
	B30 Roofing					
3010	Roof Coverings	Built-up tar and gravel with flashing; perlite/EPS composite insulation	S.F. Roof	3.96	1.98	2.7%
3020	Roof Openings	Roof hatches	S.F. Roof	.04	.02	
C. INTERIORS						
1010	Partitions	Concrete block 20 S.F. Floor/L.F. Partition	S.F. Partition	6.04	3.02	
1020	Interior Doors	Single leaf kalamein fire doors 750 S.F. Floor/Door	Each	537	.72	
1030	Fittings	Toilet partitions, chalkboards	S.F. Floor	1.17	1.17	
2010	Stair Construction	Concrete filled metal pan	Flight	5075	.28	25.2%
3010	Wall Finishes	50% paint, 40% glazed coatings, 10% ceramic tile	S.F. Surface	5.96	2.98	
3020	Floor Finishes	50% vinyl composition tile, 30% carpet, 20% terrazzo	S.F. Floor	6.88	6.88	
3030	Ceiling Finishes	Mineral fiberboard on concealed zee bars	S.F. Ceiling	3.71	3.71	
D. SERVICES						
	D10 Conveying					
1010	Elevators & Lifts	One hydraulic passenger elevator	Each	51,700	.47	0.6%
1020	Escalators & Moving Walks	N/A	-	-	-	
	D20 Plumbing					
2010	Plumbing Fixtures	Kitchen, toilet and service fixtures, supply and drainage 1 Fixture/1170 S.F. Floor	Each	2480	2.12	
2020	Domestic Water Distribution	Gas fired water heater...	S.F. Floor	.22	.22	3.5%
2040	Rain Water Drainage	Roof drains	S.F. Roof	.46	.23	
	D30 HVAC					
3010	Energy Supply	N/A	-	-	-	
3020	Heat Generating Systems	Included in D3030	-	-	-	
3030	Cooling Generating Systems	Multizone unit, gas heating, electric cooling	S.F. Floor	13.85	13.85	18.6%
3050	Terminal & Package Units	N/A	-	-	-	
3090	Other HVAC Sys. & Equipment	N/A	-	-	-	
	D40 Fire Protection					
4010	Sprinklers	Sprinklers, light hazard 10% of area	S.F. Floor	.27	.27	0.4%
4020	Standpipes	N/A	-	-	-	
	D50 Electrical					
5010	Electrical Service/Distribution	1600 ampere service, panel board and feeders	S.F. Floor	.84	.84	
5020	Lighting & Branch Wiring	Fluorescent fixtures, receptacles, switches, A.C. and misc. power	S.F. Floor	7.08	7.08	14.3%
5030	Communications & Security	Alarm systems, communications systems and emergency lighting	S.F. Floor	2.46	2.46	
5090	Other Electrical Systems	Emergency generator, 100 kW	S.F. Floor	.32	.32	
E. EQUIPMENT & FURNISHINGS						
1010	Commercial Equipment	N/A	-	-	-	
1020	Institutional Equipment	Laboratory counters	S.F. Floor	.08	.08	0.1%
1030	Vehicular Equipment	N/A	-	-	-	
1090	Other Equipment	N/A	-	-	-	
F. SPECIAL CONSTRUCTION & DEMOLITION						
1020	Integrated Construction	N/A	-	-	-	0.0%
1040	Special Facilities	N/A	-	-	-	
G. BUILDING SITEWORK	**N/A**					
			Sub-Total		74.45	100%
	CONTRACTOR FEES (General Requirements: 10%, Overhead: 5%, Profit: 10%)			25%	18.61	
	ARCHITECT FEES			7%	6.49	
			Total Building Cost		**99.55**	

Figure 3.20 Excerpt of R. S. Means's building square foot costs for a junior high school.

cross-check estimates that have been prepared using other methods. The R. S. Means Company produces a publication, called *Square Foot Costs,* that contains cost models of various building types, along with descriptions of the assumptions (for example, choice of walls, finishes, mechanical systems, etc.) that drove the model. An excerpt of this publication is presented in Figure 3.20 for a school building. Here, too, it is possible to adjust the information presented in this model on a plus–minus basis and apply it to other project conditions. An advantage of this method is that it allows the total cost to be adjusted upward or downward based on unknown conditions, all with a reasonably high degree of confidence; hence, it can be useful for early-stage decision making.

The next step using this approach is to prepare an estimate in an elemental format to represent specific conditions of the developing design. This may require combining pricing mechanisms, for example, historical costs, systems or assemblies, or a detailed cost analysis for selected items. Based on standard designs or design details of a project, systems or assemblies can be prepared early, when they are used on a repetitive basis; or they can be extracted from published cost information; or "mini-estimates" can be prepared for individual components. Figure 3.21 gives an example of an assembly for a built-up roofing system. In this instance, using a cost of $4.00 per square foot for the roof would be justified if the design anticipated were similar.

Essentially, the process consists of the following steps:

1. Measure and interpret key elemental quantities, based on a design or assumptions.

```
┌─────────────────────────────────────────────────────────────────────┐
│ Roofing System – 4-Ply Built-Up Roof                                │
│                                                                       │
│ – 4-ply built-up roofing including 2"    7,840 SF @ $3.45   ...  $27,048 │
│   insulation and vapor barrier                                        │
│                                                                       │
│ – Aluminum flashing and cants to         438 linear ft. @   ...    3,197 │
│   parapet and upstands                    $7.30                       │
│                                                                       │
│ – Double-skin plastic skylights,         27 SF @ $45.00     ...    1,215 │
│   including curbs, etc.                                               │
│                                                                      ─────── │
│                                                              ...   $31,460 │
│                                                                   ═══════ │
│ Elemental cost = $31,460 ÷ 7,840 SF                          ...  $4.02 SF │
└─────────────────────────────────────────────────────────────────────┘
```

Figure 3.21 Example of an assembly.

2. Select unit prices to reflect quality and performance required using mini-estimates or published information.

3. Assess major elemental costs on the basis of judgment and historical information; adjust as appropriate.

4. Aggregate to total estimate.

Assemblies are also available from published sources, such as R. S. Means's *Assemblies Cost Data*. An example is presented in Figure 3.22(a) and (b).

Quantity Survey Method

The quantity survey method is usually utilized when detailed design information is available and the estimator is in a position to measure and price the entire project or at least its major components. The actual pricing approach may include only total unit prices or may include labor, materials, and equipment. Regardless, the level of detail is on an individual unit of work basis, to reflect how the work will be carried out.

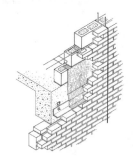

Exterior brick face composite walls are defined in the following terms: type of face brick and backup masonry, thickness of backup masonry and insulation. A special section is included on triple wythe construction at the back. Seven types of face brick are shown with various thicknesses of seven types of backup. All systems include a brick shelf, ties to the backup and necessary dampproofing, flashing, and control joints every 20'.

System Components			COST PER S.F.		
	QUANTITY	UNIT	MAT.	INST.	TOTAL
SYSTEM B2010 130 1120					
COMPOSITE WALL, STANDARD BRICK FACE, 6" C.M.U. BACKUP, PERLITE FILL					
Face brick veneer, standard, running bond	1.000	S.F.	2.92	7.75	10.67
Wash brick	1.000	S.F.	.02	.67	.69
Concrete block backup, 6" thick	1.000	S.F.	1.46	4.25	5.71
Wall ties	.300	Ea.	.04	.11	.15
Perlite insulation, poured	1.000	S.F.	.32	.22	.54
Flashing, aluminum	.100	S.F.	.09	.25	.34
Shelf angle	1.000	Lb.	.52	.68	1.20
Control joint	.050	L.F.	.06	.05	.11
Backer rod	.100	L.F.		.08	.08
Sealant	.100	L.F.	.02	.20	.22
Collar joint	1.000	S.F.	.31	.44	.75
TOTAL			5.76	14.70	20.46

B2010 130		**Brick Face Composite Wall - Double Wythe**						
	FACE BRICK	BACKUP MASONRY	BACKUP THICKNESS (IN.)	BACKUP CORE FILL		COST PER S.F.		
						MAT.	INST.	TOTAL
1000	Standard	common brick	4	none		6.25	17.65	23.90
1040		SCR brick	6	none		8.40	15.75	24.15
1080		conc. block	4	none		4.97	14.20	19.17
1120			6	perlite		5.75	14.70	20.45
1160				styrofoam		6.35	14.50	20.85
1200			8	perlite		6.05	15.05	21.10
1240				styrofoam		6.45	14.75	21.20
1280		L.W. block	4	none		5.15	14.10	19.25
1320			6	perlite		5.90	14.60	20.50
1360				styrofoam		6.50	14.40	20.90
1400			8	perlite		6.40	14.95	21.35
1440				styrofoam		6.85	14.65	21.50
1520		glazed block	4	none		10.95	15.15	26.10
1560			6	perlite		11.65	15.60	27.25
1600				styrofoam		12.25	15.40	27.65
1640			8	perlite		12.15	16	28.15
1680				styrofoam		12.60	15.75	28.35

Figure 3.22(a) Example of an assembly from R. S. Means.

B2010 Exterior Walls

B2010 130		Brick Face Composite Wall - Double Wythe						
	FACE BRICK	BACKUP MASONRY	BACKUP THICKNESS (IN.)	BACKUP CORE FILL		COST PER S.F.		
						MAT.	INST.	TOTAL
1720	Standard	clay tile	4	none		8.10	13.65	21.75
1760			6	none		8.15	14	22.15
1800			8	none		9.50	14.50	24
1840		glazed tile	4	none		11.45	18	29.45
1880								
2000	Glazed	common brick	4	none		10.80	18	28.80
2040		SCR brick	6	none		13	16.10	29.10
2080		conc. block	4	none		9.55	14.55	24.10
2120			6	perlite		10.35	15.05	25.40
2160				styrofoam		10.90	14.85	25.75
2200			8	perlite		10.60	15.40	26
2240				styrofoam		11.05	15.10	26.15
2280		L.W. block	4	none		9.75	14.45	24.20
2320			6	perlite		10.50	14.95	25.45
2360				styrofoam		11.05	14.75	25.80
2400			8	perlite		11	15.30	26.30
2440				styrofoam		11.45	15	26.45
2520		glazed block	4	none		15.50	15.50	31
2560			6	perlite		16.25	15.95	32.20
2600				styrofoam		16.80	15.75	32.55
2640			8	perlite		16.75	16.35	33.10
2680				styrofoam		17.15	16.10	33.25
2720		clay tile	4	none		12.70	14	26.70
2760			6	none		12.75	14.35	27.10
2800			8	none		14.05	14.85	28.90
2840		glazed tile	4	none		16	18.35	34.35
2880								
3000	Engineer	common brick	4	none		6.45	16.45	22.90
3040		SCR brick	6	none		8.65	14.55	23.20
3080		conc. block	4	none		5.20	13	18.20
3120			6	perlite		6	13.50	19.50
3160				styrofoam		6.55	13.30	19.85
3200			8	perlite		6.25	13.85	20.10
3240				styrofoam		6.70	13.55	20.25
3280		L.W. block	4	none		4.26	9.20	13.46
3320			6	perlite		6.10	13.40	19.50
3360				styrofoam		6.70	13.20	19.90
3400			8	perlite		6.65	13.75	20.40
3440				styrofoam		7.05	13.45	20.50
3520		glazed block	4	none		11.15	13.95	25.10
3560			6	perlite		11.85	14.40	26.25
3600				styrofoam		12.45	14.20	26.65
3640			8	perlite		12.35	14.80	27.15
3680				styrofoam		12.80	14.55	27.35
3720		clay tile	4	none		8.35	12.45	20.80
3760			6	none		8.40	12.80	21.20
3800			8	none		9.70	13.30	23
3840		glazed tile	4	none		11.65	16.80	28.45
4000	Roman	common brick	4	none		8	16.70	24.70
4040		SCR brick	6	none		10.20	14.80	25

Figure 3.22(b) Example of an assembly from R. S. Means.

Figure 3.23(a) contains an excerpt from a detailed quantity survey-based estimate. In this example, the format used, as a Work Breakdown Structure (WBS), is UNIFORMAT (the original version). There are numerous sources for published unit cost data. Probably the most recognized is R. S. Means's *Building Construction Cost Data* (BCCD), an excerpt of which is presented in Figure 3.23(b).

Dealing with Escalation and Contingencies

Escalation and contingencies are real costs that, simply put, have not been specifically identified at the time of estimate preparation. All estimates, by their nature, will potentially include escalation and contingencies.

Escalation can be defined as the inflationary cost growth anticipated between the time the estimate is prepared and the project is bid or finally costed. Pricing can only represent known costs at the time the estimate is prepared, so that future escalation will be added to move the cost forward in time. Escalation can be divided into two subcomponents:

► Escalation that may occur during the duration of construction on the project. For simplicity, assume 50 percent of the work will take place before the midpoint of construction and 50 percent will take place after. Therefore, the estimate is escalated to the *midpoint of construction* to reflect what a potential bid would represent at the time of estimate preparation. This could be called a *bid estimate.*

► Escalation that may occur from the time of the estimate to a projected bid date. In order for an

WBS	Description	Quantity	Unit	Rate	Subtotal
01	**SUBSTRUCTURE**				
0101	Standard Foundations				
010101	Wall Foundations				
01010101	Excavate for foundation wall footings	457	M³	15.70	7,175
01010102	Over excavate for foundation wall footing	229	M³	15.70	3,595
01010103	Form sides of foundation wall footings	144	M²	37.70	5,429
01010104	Form foundation wall	340	M²	37.70	12,818
01010105	Form brick ledge in foundation wall at sides of dock	18	M	8.50	153
01010106	Reinforce foundation wall	2	Te	1,500.00	3,000
01010107	Reinforce foundation wall footings (allow 3 x #5 per footing width)	2	Te	1,500.00	3,000
01010108	Perimeter drain at foundation wall (no detail)	252	M	26.25	6,615
01010109	Concrete foundation wall	56	M³	165.00	9,240
01010110	Concrete foundation wall footing	44	M³	135.00	5,940
01010111	2" Rigid insulation on foundation wall	216	M²	10.76	2,324
01010112	Backfill to foundation wall strip footing foundation	548	M³	7.80	4,274
010102	Column Foundations and Pile Caps				
01010201	Excavate for spread footing	361	M³	15.70	5,668
01010202	Over excavate for spread footing	181	M³	15.70	2,842
01010203	Form sides of spread footing	115	M²	37.70	4,336
01010204	Reinforcing steel to spread footings	2	Te	1,500.00	3,000
01010205	Concrete spread footing	54	M³	165.00	8,910
01010206	Backfill to spread footing foundation	497	M³	7.80	3,877
01010207	Haul surplus excavated material off site	183	M³	11.00	2,013
010204	Dewatering				
01020401	Dewatering, allowance	1	LS	10,000.00	10,000
0103	Slab on Grade				
010301	Standard Slab on Grade				
01030101	150mm Crushed stone base course under slab on grade	377	M³	20.00	7,540
01030102	Fine grade area under slab on grade	2,516	M²	5.30	13,335
01030103	127mm Concrete slab on grade, including curing, mesh reinforcement	2,483	M²	32.30	80,201
01030104	6 Mil Polyethylene vapor barrier under slab on grade	2,483	M²	2.20	5,463
01030105	Concrete loading dock slab, complete with fill, subbase and base course	33	M²	54.00	1,782
01030106	Concrete steps on grade	4	M²	161.50	646
01030107	Edge form slab on grade	280	M	5.00	1,400
01030108	Form slab depression	34	M²	50.00	1,700
010305	Pits and Bases				
01030501	Elevator pit, 2.1m x 2.5m x 1.2m deep, complete	1	EA	3,500.00	3,500
	Total 01 Substructure Carried to Summary				**$ 219,774**

Figure 3.23(a) Example of quantity survey estimate.

	04090	Masonry Accessories	CREW	DAILY OUTPUT	LABOR-HOURS	UNIT	2002 BARE COSTS MAT.	LABOR	EQUIP.	TOTAL	TOTAL INCL O&P	
420	0500	8" x 8" units, 8" thick				S.F.	.66			.66	.73	420
	0550	12" thick				↓	.82			.82	.90	
650	0010	PARGETING Regular Portland cement, 1/2" thick	D-1	2.50	6.400	C.S.F.	13.20	173		186.20	280	650
	5100	Waterproof Portland cement	"	2.50	6.400	"	14.55	173		187.55	281	
700	0010	SCAFFOLDING & SWING STAGING See division 01540 [R01540-100]										700
850	0010	VENT BOX See division 04090-860										850
860	0010	VENT BOX Extruded aluminum, 4" deep, 2-3/8" x 8-1/8"	1 Bric	30	.267	Ea.	30.50	8.15		38.65	46	860
	0050	5" x 8-1/8"		25	.320		42.50	9.75		52.25	61.50	
	0100	2-1/4" x 25"		25	.320		85	9.75		94.75	109	
	0150	5" x 16-1/2"		22	.364		44	11.10		55.10	65.50	
	0200	6" x 16-1/2"		22	.364		85	11.10		96.10	111	
	0250	7-3/4" x 16-1/2"	▼	20	.400		80	12.20		92.20	107	
	0400	For baked enamel finish, add					35%					
	0500	For cast aluminum, painted, add					60%					
	1000	Stainless steel ventilators, 6" x 6"	1 Bric	25	.320		91	9.75		100.75	115	
	1050	8" x 8"		24	.333		96	10.15		106.15	122	
	1100	12" x 12"		23	.348		112	10.60		122.60	139	
	1150	12" x 6"		24	.333		96	10.15		106.15	122	
	1200	Foundation block vent, galv., 1-1/4" thk, 8" high, 16" long, no damper	▼	30	.267	▼	18	8.15		26.15	32.50	
	1250	For damper, add					6			6	6.60	
900	0010	WALL PLUGS For nailing to brickwork, 26 ga., galvanized, plain	1 Bric	10.50	.762	C	25	23		48	63	900
	0050	Wood filled	"	10.50	.762	"	84	23		107	128	

	04210	Clay Masonry Units	CREW	DAILY OUTPUT	LABOR-HOURS	UNIT	2002 BARE COSTS MAT.	LABOR	EQUIP.	TOTAL	TOTAL INCL O&P	
100	0010	COMMON BUILDING BRICK C62, TL lots, material only [R04210-120]										100
	0020	Standard, minimum				M	270			270	297	
	0050	Average (select)	▼			"	315			315	345	
120	0010	BRICK VENEER Scaffolding not included, truck load lots [R04210-120]										120
	0015	Material costs incl. 3% brick and 25% mortar waste										
	0020	Standard, select common, 4" x 2-2/3" x 8" (6.75/S.F.) [R04210-180]	D-8	1.50	26.667	M	360	740		1,100	1,525	
	0050	Red, 4" x 2-2/3" x 8", running bond		1.50	26.667		400	740		1,140	1,575	
	0100	Full header every 6th course (7.88/S.F.) [R04210-500]		1.45	27.586		400	765		1,165	1,625	
	0150	English, full header every 2nd course (10.13/S.F.)		1.40	28.571		395	790		1,185	1,650	
	0200	Flemish, alternate header every course (9.00/S.F.)		1.40	28.571		395	790		1,185	1,650	
	0250	Flemish, alt. header every 6th course (7.13/S.F.)		1.45	27.586		400	765		1,165	1,625	
	0300	Full headers throughout (13.50/S.F.)		1.40	28.571		395	790		1,185	1,650	
	0350	Rowlock course (13.50/S.F.)		1.35	29.630		395	820		1,215	1,675	
	0400	Rowlock stretcher (4.50/S.F.)		1.40	28.571		400	790		1,190	1,675	
	0450	Soldier course (6.75/S.F.)		1.40	28.571		400	790		1,190	1,675	
	0500	Sailor course (4.50/S.F.)		1.30	30.769		400	850		1,250	1,750	
	0601	Buff or gray face, running bond, (6.75/S.F.)		1.50	26.667		400	740		1,140	1,575	
	0700	Glazed face, 4" x 2-2/3" x 8", running bond		1.40	28.571		1,500	790		2,290	2,875	
	0750	Full header every 6th course (7.88/S.F.)		1.35	29.630		1,475	820		2,295	2,850	
	1000	Jumbo, 6" x 4" x 12",(3.00/S.F.)		1.30	30.769		1,250	850		2,100	2,675	
	1051	Norman, 4" x 2-2/3" x 12" (4.50/S.F.)	▼ ▼	1.45	27.586	▼	735	765		1,500	1,975	

Figure 3.23(b) Example of R. S. Means's BCCD cost file.

estimate to reflect a future bid date, the bid estimate would be escalated for the amount of time between the date of the bid estimate and the bid date.

Note that if a subcontractor submits a firm quote for the work, cost growth, if any, will be included in the quote. Refer back to Figures 3.11 and 3.12 for a graphical representation of escalation.

Contingency is an allowance for work that is not fully defined at the time of the estimate but that is anticipated to be part of the project scope. Contingency tends to be added in as a single factor, but it can be made up of several components:

▶ *Design contingency* reflects the degree of completeness of the design and the level of confidence.

▶ *Estimating contingency* represents the estimator's confidence in the estimate; it may also reflect the development of the design as well as other factors affecting cost, such as availability, access/egress, and conditions of the work. The design and estimating contingencies are usually included together and will generally approach zero as the documents are completed.

▶ *Construction contingency* is intended to reflect the amount of cost increase that will occur after award of the construction contract. This will include unknown site conditions, weather, and uncontrollable delays, as well as a portion for change orders due to inconsistencies/incompleteness of the construction documents.

▶ *Owner's contingency* is intended to potentially include the construction contingency as well as an allowance for scope increases and owner-elected changes.

☑ **CHECKLIST**

FOR CONTINGENCY

▶ Design contingency
▶ Estimating contingency
▶ Construction contingency
▶ Owner's contingency

Standard Contingency Guidelines Used by a Major Architect/Engineering Firm	
– Program Estimates	10%–15%
– Schematic Cost Estimates	7.5%–12.5%
– Design Development Estimates	5%–10%
– Construction Documents Estimates	2%–5%
– Pre-bid Estimates	0%

Figure 3.24 Contingency allowances used by a major architect/engineering firm.

What are reasonable allowances for contingencies? There are no absolutely accepted standards, but a major architect/engineering firm advocates those presented in Figure 3.24, and experience has shown these figures to be sensible.

Risk Management and Range Estimating

Risk management is an organized method of identifying and measuring risk, then developing, selecting, implementing, and managing options for addressing that risk. There are several types of risk that an owner should consider as part of risk management methodology. These include:

> ► Schedule risk

> ► Cost risk

> ► Technical feasibility

> ► Risk of technical obsolescence

> ► Dependencies between a new project and other projects

> ► Physical events beyond direct control

Risk management seeks to identify and, ultimately, control possible future events, and should be proactive rather than reactive. To be effective, risk management should rely on tools and techniques that help predict the likelihood of future events, the effects of these future events, and methods for dealing with these future events. Risk management is the responsibility of everyone involved in a project.

Risk management consists of four basic steps:

1. *Risk assessment.* The first step is to identify and assess all potential risk areas. A risk area is any part of a project or any outside effect on the project that raises uncertainty regarding future events. This is particularly critical if these events could have a negative effect on meeting a project, program, or owner goal. Risk assessment should start early and be continuous throughout the life of a project because as the project progresses, new risks will be identified.

2. *Risk analysis.* Once risks have been identified, each should be assessed as to the likelihood of its occurrence and the severity of potential consequences. Risk analysis should assess the list of potential areas of risk and identify the likely conditions or characteristics of the risk event as it starts to happen. Risk analysis is also a continuous activity over the life of the project.

3. *Risk mitigation.* After a risk has been assessed and analyzed, the owner should consider what can be done to mitigate the risk. There are several alternate approaches:

   a. *Transfer.* The owner can transfer risk to a third party—a contractor or other entity. It may be appropriate to transfer the risk to the contractor who may be in a better position to exercise effective control and manage the risk within economically reasonable bounds. Schedule risks associated with sep-

Cost-Estimating Methodology

arate contracts are a good example of an opportunity to transfer the contracts to a single entity. At other times, it may be more appropriate to transfer the risk to a third party, such as a bonding company or insurance company.

b. *Avoidance.* Risk conditions that are so significant and whose impact would be so detrimental to the project should be removed from further consideration, and alternative approaches should be found. A common example of this type of risk situation occurs with site soil conditions, where it's wise to bypass the risk of unknown soil by developing a design that avoids the condition. Mat type foundations are often used for this purpose.

c. *Reduction.* Similarly, it may be advantageous to consider measures that minimize the likelihood that a risk event will occur and thereby minimize any negative effects to the project or project goals. Typically, owners will consider contingency plans that can be devised ahead of time to address the risk should it occur.

d. *Assumption.* The owner may choose to assume a particular risk if the owner is in the best position to exercise effective control. It may be that the cost to a contractor to manage the risk could be extreme, while the owner may have a clear method of dealing with the risk, or the risk itself may be very minimal to the owner in the first place. The decision should depend exclusively on whether the reduced cost to the contractor is sufficient to compensate the owner for assuming the risk. A good example is the owner who takes responsibility for the purchase and installation of equipment that may be difficult for the contractor to purchase or install.

e. *Sharing.* When the risk cannot be appropriately transferred, the owner and contractor may share the risk. Examples are allowances added to contracts to cover the likelihood of an event that limits the contractor's risk or sets some bounds on the magnitude of event. In some cases, unit prices are predefined as a means to minimize the owner's risk. In other cases, cost-sharing arrangements may be appropriate. Regardless, shared risks require monitoring and continuous attention.

4. *Feedback.* After encountering problems on a project, the owner and the owner's consultants should document the conditions that led to the problems and determine if, in fact, there were any warning signs that were overlooked. It is also important to document the approach taken to address the risk, the effects on cost in schedule, and the outcome, whether satisfactory or not. Effective feedback will not only help future projects, but could help identify recurring problems within the existing project.

Range Estimating

Paying attention to detail and implementing appropriate cost and schedule control systems are obviously important activities inherent to risk analysis and management. Another tool, however, deserves closer scrutiny: *range estimating*. Range estimating can be done in a rather simple fashion by selecting the 20 percent of the line items in an estimate that represent 80 percent of the cost, then developing a range for each of those items and adding the low and high ranges. A sensitivity analysis can also be prepared to vary the key risk parameters and calculate the results. A more advanced approach is to take the same 20-percent items, establish the range, then use any one of several available software packages to perform a Monte Carlo (probabilistic) simulation and produce a risk profile. This approach would give a more accurate projection of the logical highs and lows involved with the 20-percent drivers.

Finally, it is possible to use a complete risk analysis package that includes range estimating and prepares a risk profile that estimates confidence ranges and contingency amounts. Organizations such as the New York/New Jersey Port Authority have used this type of approach to establish contingencies not only for individual projects but for entire programs.

Special Estimating Challenges

Preparing an estimate is always a challenge, even under the most benign of circumstances. In addition, there are several special project considerations that exacerbate the challenge and require additional attention. Two areas are worthy of discussion: estimating renovations and alterations and estimating international projects.

Estimating Renovations and Alterations

Estimating renovations and alterations is a complicated process that is always difficult to predict in advance of doing the actual work. That said, several basic potential problems can be accounted for and documented. These include:

- *Existing drawings.* Are they accurate and dependable?

- *Codes.* Have codes that will affect the work changed over time?

- *Continued occupancy.* Will the facility remain occupied during construction? Are there special cleaning requirements or environmental limitations?

- *Hidden work.* What is the likelihood of hidden work revealing itself, and what might the ramifications be?

- *Changes in function.* Is the new use of the building different from the original use? Have potential code issues been identified? Are environmental issues likely to arise?

- *Structural changes.* Structural changes are often associated with changes in function, but might they result from changes in codes or building deterioration?

- *Adjoining buildings.* Might adjoining buildings be impacted in such a way as to require underpinning or environmental work? What are these buildings used for? Must any vibration or environmental conditions be met?

- *Salvage.* Salvage can occasionally be a significant factor. Who will own the salvage rights?

- *Access to space and staging areas.* This factor often is not adequately considered in an estimate. Is there sufficient access to the site, including turning radii and bearing capacity? Is there sufficient space on-site to stage materials and avoid double handling?

Estimating International Projects

When estimating international projects, there are several factors to consider:

- ► Design issues pertinent to the country that are different from those in the United States
- ► Construction issues and approaches that vary from U.S. standards
- ► Codes, regulations, and procedures
- ► Project location and specific local issues
- ► Financial and currency issues, including taxes, currency fluctuations, and differential inflation
- ► Approaches to estimating
- ► Cost in U.S. dollars (In many cases, it is beneficial to price the estimate on a U.S. basis, then factor to a location.)
- ► Market survey and price in U.S. dollars (A local market survey can better assess productivity and availability.)

It's a good idea to retain a local consultant to assist in any international estimating effort.

Value Management

Value management (VM) refers to the collection of value-based processes and techniques. Value engineering (VE) is a problem-solving process that has been applied in numerous ways for over 30 years in the construction industry. The terms VM and VE are often used synonymously and will be so used in this book. VE has both staunch supporters and vehement detractors, for when it is applied correctly, results are excellent, but when it is applied incorrectly, the process may simply create more problems.

The application of VE is not difficult, but it does require patience, concentration, and a certain amount of discipline. And for it to work, everyone involved should agree on objectives and be willing to work toward common goals. When implemented properly as part of the overall design process—what has been termed *value-enhanced design*—VE can be an extremely useful tool to the designer and cost manager for general problem solving, cost optimization, and value enhancement.

Principles of Value Engineering

The intended purpose of value engineering is to *improve the value obtained by an owner from a constructed project*. Value is the relationship between the *functional benefits* and the *cost* to obtain those benefits. Improved value results from optimizing this relationship, as follows:

$$\text{Value} = \frac{\text{Functional benefits}}{\text{Cost}}$$

To improve value:

> ► Improve functional benefits, maintain cost.
> ► Maintain functional benefits, reduce cost.
> ► Improve functional benefits, reduce cost.
> ► Reduce functional benefits, reduce cost (if benefits remain within needs and cost within limitations).
> ► Increase functional benefits, increase cost (if benefits remain within needs and cost within limitations).

Cost is relatively easy to measure, but benefits can be very difficult and obtuse to interpret. Benefits represent many possibilities, as shown in Figure 3.25. (Figure 1.5 graphically displayed the cost–qual-

• Esteem	• Aesthetics
• Use	• Safety
• Reliability	• Durability
• Cost	• Convenience
• Maintainability	• Accessibility
• Security	• Flexibility
• Expandability	• Adaptability
• Sustainability	• Perception

Figure 3.25 Functional benefits: How are they measured?

ity relationship, which is one measure of functional benefits.)

The owner is responsible for defining quality expectations, while the designer is responsible for delivering a design that meets those expectations. Realistically, most owner criteria, standards, and program requirements tend to define only the lower limits. Well-intentioned designers often exceed these minimums, believing that better quality always equates to better value. This is not, however, necessarily true since value is cost-dependent and cost and quality do not usually have a linear relationship. An incremental improvement in quality may come at a two- to three-increment increase in cost. When too many elements of a facility approach this "vertical cost curve," budgets are exceeded and problems occur.

The value engineering process focuses attention on the quality-cost relationship by seeking solutions that provide required quality at a minimal cost. Adding quality that can be obtained at a low-increment added cost (i.e., a "flat" cost curve) is usually a good idea. However, when higher quality incurs a large incremental cost (i.e., a "steep" cost curve), careful attention should be paid. Balancing quality and cost will usually result in a design that responds to best life-cycle cost.

A further VE objective is to attain balance in the overall design, where all aspects of a facility are achieving reasonably equal value targets. Figure 3.26 graphs the relationship between an overall facility value target and value delivered from the individual building elements. VE seeks to balance the elements in a fair and reasonable way to achieve the best *overall* value.

It is important to note that simply reducing cost at the expense of quality, outside of acceptable limits, is

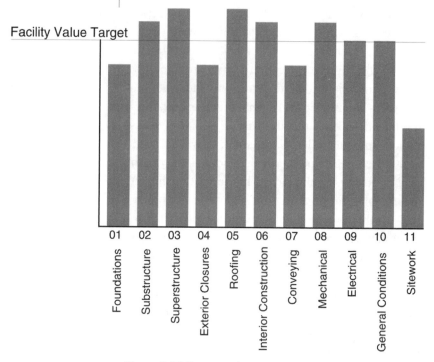

Figure 3.26 Systems value assessment.

not value engineering. This is simple cost-cutting, which often leads to problems and fractured relationships on all too many projects. If, however, cost reduction is necessary because of limited funds, VE can be an excellent tool. But any value engineering effort should be first based on a reassessment of value objectives and quality targets that can lead to sensible cost reduction. One way or another, the key to success when using value engineering is a more precise and appropriate definition of value.

Basic Approaches to Value Engineering

Historically, most formal value engineering has been conducted by an independent, outside team of planners, architects, engineers, and construction specialists facilitated by a VE specialist. Informal VE has been conducted by design teams, construction managers, and owners, but usually without a formal plan and process. While there is no necessarily right or wrong way to implement value engineering, experience has shown that informal VE tends to veer in the direction of either a unidiscipline design review or a cost-cutting exercise, with value often sacrificed in the process. Again, for VE to be successful, there should be a consolidated team effort, where everyone focuses on the major cost drivers and clearly understands interdiscipline issues. This relationship is graphically displayed in Figure 3.27.

Three basic approaches to conducting a VE study have been shown to be successful:

1. The "traditional" approach that employs a VE specialist to facilitate the study team made up of an outside, independent "cold team."
2. A VE specialist facilitates a study using a team made up of personnel from the design firm,

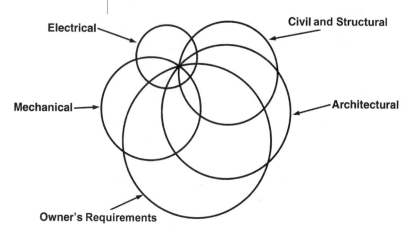

Figure 3.27 VE focus on interdisciplinary areas.

consultants, and owner personnel, all of whom were not associated directly with the project.

3. A VE specialist facilitates the study using the existing design team and consultants and owner personnel associated with the project.

All three approaches can provide meaningful results, but if option 3 is employed, it is critical that the study be conducted early in the process, preferably no later than the conceptual/schematic design phase. Otherwise, it is unrealistic to expect objectivity and open-mindedness from the design team. And the early-stage study can be followed by a second study that focuses more on details and constructibility issues. This second study is also used to verify the implementation from the first study.

Establishing Value Objectives and Study Constraints

The objectives of any VE study should be consistent with the overall philosophy and objectives of the owner, while considering the individual require-

Cost-Estimating Methodology

ments of the project. For a project whose construction cost is within budget, the emphasis should be on maintaining or improving value in terms of operations, flexibility, expandability, and so on within the budget. If improved value can be delivered at reduced cost, then cost reduction becomes a secondary goal with the possibility of reducing the budget.

When a project is determined to be above budget, the emphasis of the VE study will tend to be on reducing construction cost to within budget without compromising the program of requirements or eroding the value of the finished project. The VE study should not be used as a device for producing reductions by cost-cutting with an accompanying reduction in the scope of the project or in realized value over the life cycle of the completed facility. If substantial cost reduction is required (in excess of 10 percent), the VE study should focus on reconsidering owner objectives.

As a general rule, no constraints are placed on the VE study in terms of the areas under scrutiny. Likewise, governing criteria, except as required by codes or law, can be considered open for challenge by the VE team—providing that the value and cost benefits are worthwhile and that no compromises are made to important project functions. Typically, even program requirements can be open to challenge by the VE team, to the extent that inefficiencies can be eliminated without sacrificing the basic project objectives and intended functionality of the completed facility.

All that said, it is important to recognize that, often, the owner may seek to constrain the VE team to work within certain limits and to keep certain issues "off the table." When that is the case, these

REMINDER!
Typically, even program requirements can be open to challenge by the VE team, to the extent that inefficiencies can be eliminated without sacrificing the basic project objectives and intended functionality of the completed facility.

limitations should be clearly communicated and understood prior to the launch of any efforts.

As to the VE team, its members are expected to use common sense in challenging design decisions or criteria that are deep-seated and important to the owner or designer. Common sense will also preclude the team expending valuable time on far-fetched or frivolous ideas that have little or no chance of acceptance.

Value Engineering Study Techniques

An effective VE study will generally follow the basic VE workplan and procedures acknowledged by the SAVE, The Value Society (formerly The Society of American Value Engineers) and VE practitioners. More information is available on the SAVE Web site (www.value-eng.org). This technique comprises three distinct phases:

➤ Phase A: Preworkshop

➤ Phase B: Workshop

➤ Phase C: Presentation of results, decision-making meeting, and report presentation

The approach is structured and directed toward obtaining the maximum effect from the expended efforts. This involves:

Phase A: Preworkshop

A comprehensive preworkshop will effectively prepare the owner, design team, consultants, and construction management team. It may include assembling a workbook, conducting a briefing on project status, selecting appropriate VE team personnel, and doing all the logistical organization necessary to ensure that the workshop session will be productive and proceed smoothly. Materials required for an efficient workshop typically include:

- ▶ Project program and budget development documents
- ▶ Drawings for the level of design under study
- ▶ Outline or definitive specifications of major construction elements
- ▶ Program areas/spaces analysis with respect to program
- ▶ Line-item cost estimates for the level of design under study
- ▶ Definition of major systems and subsystems, including architectural, structural, mechanical, electrical, sitework, and utilities
- ▶ Plot plan, topography, and site planning; photographs are useful when available
- ▶ Verification of power, sewer, gas, and other service availability for selected site
- ▶ Soils report, with response for foundation design concepts indicated on drawings
- ▶ Special systems or requirements
- ▶ Economic data, budget constraints, discount rate, useful life of facility
- ▶ Staffing costs and other appropriate financial information

A timely and careful preparation carried out prior to the VE workshop will enhance the results of the study. It will also ensure that, subsequently, each VE team member will be well informed and well prepared for the project briefing given at the commencement of each workshop. Of course, if design team personnel are used for the study, the degree of initial preparation can be reduced.

Cost-Estimating Methodology

The following material is usually completed prior to a workshop session to help focus the workshop effort:

- Cost model(s), using the project cost estimate
- Function analysis for total project and pertinent high-cost systems as appropriate
- Identification of key issues and value objectives

Phase B: Workshop

The VE workshop is the major component of a VE study. The systematic methodology used by the VE team to accomplish the workshop is typically called the VE *job plan* or *workplan,* although various other terms are used throughout the professions to describe this methodology. Regardless what it is called, however, all workplans represent the same basic methodology, which assists the VE team in a number of ways:

- It is an organized approach that allows the VE team to analyze a project quickly by identifying high cost to worth areas and selecting alternatives that minimize costs while maximizing quality.
- It encourages the VE team to think in a creative manner, that is, to look beyond the use of common or standard approaches.
- It emphasizes total ownership costs (life-cycle costs) for a facility, rather than just initial capital costs.
- It leads the VE team to develop a concise understanding of the purposes and functions of the facility.

The recommended VE workplan consists of the following five distinct phases:

1. Information gathering
2. Speculation/creation
3. Evaluation/analysis
4. Development/recommendation
5. Reporting

Briefly, each phase is marked by a series of activities, as follows:

▶ *Information gathering.* During this phase, the VE team reviews the material gathered prior to the workshop to gain as good an understanding as possible about the project design, background, constraints, and projected costs. The team performs a function analysis and relative cost ranking of systems and subsystems to identify potential high-cost areas.

▶ *Speculation/creation.* The VE team uses a creative group interaction process to identify alternative ideas for accomplishing the function of a system or subsystem.

▶ *Evaluation/analysis.* The ideas generated during the speculation/creation phase are screened and evaluated by the team. Those showing the greatest potential for cost savings and project improvement are selected for further study.

▶ *Development/recommendation.* The VE team researches the selected ideas and prepares descriptions, sketches, and life-cycle cost estimates to support the recommendations as formal VE proposals. The results of a VE workshop are presented through the development of proposals. These proposals communicate information and better enable informed decision making. The proposal consists of a description of the recommended change, the cost of implementing the proposal, supplemented by sketches, advantages, and disadvantages. The cost data should be sufficient to indicate the probable order of magnitude of the cost savings (or added cost) that may reasonably be expected from the implementation of the VE alternate design proposal.

> *Reporting.* The VE team, in concert with the designer and owner representative, produces a preliminary written VE report that is intended to represent the results of the VE workshop activities and meet the VE program objectives. Emphasis is placed upon innovative recommendations that avoid simple cost-cutting ideas and that are tailored to fit the particular project, its objectives, the overall budget status, and, especially, the key value objectives.

Phase C: Presentation of Results, Decision-making Meeting, and Report Presentation

If implementation of the VE study methodology must be time-compressed, it's a good idea to present an informal briefing of the workshop results to the owner, designer, construction manager, and other consultants at the conclusion of the workshop session. It's also a good idea to present preliminary copies of the proposals to allow an initial review to start.

The VE specialist responsible for facilitating the study may also meet with the owner, design team, or consultants for an implementation meeting after the VE workshop. Doing so will allow the designers to prepare their responses and comments on the results of the VE workshop; it also gives the facilitator the opportunity to clarify any misunderstandings that might arise from the recommendations.

Level-of-Effort Guidelines

The overall effort required to conduct a VE study is a function of three primary variables: the magnitude and complexity of the project, the degree of repetition within a project, and the owner's willingness to commit time and money. In addition, budget, schedule, and constructibility issues may also have impact. The graph presented in Figure 3.28 expresses in hours the potential level of effort for VE studies for two workshops, with a full technical team of from 5 to 10 people, including a cost estimator/manager. The three curves are interpreted as follows.

- ➤ *Average,* for projects of average complexity and repetition, such as an office building

- ➤ *High,* for projects of high complexity, such as courthouses, laboratories, or hospitals with complex space requirements

- ➤ *Low,* for less-complex projects, such as warehouses, or for projects with a very high degree of repetition

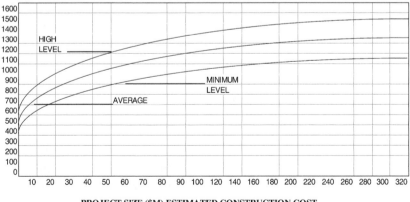

Figure 3.28 Recommended VE level of effort.

Implementation Strategies

A VE study, no matter how well conducted, can only *suggest* changes in the design or program of requirements. The ultimate responsibility for the design rests with the designer and owner; therefore, the designer should either accept and implement, or reject, changes for valid reasons. The risk involved in doing so is a factor for consideration when suggesting new ideas.

Though the VE team should assist in the implementation process and provide technical backup as needed, it is the owner, in consultation with the designer and other consultants, who is responsible for administering the implementation process. A recommended strategy to improve implementation will follow these eight guidelines:

1. Assure that the designer fully understands the nature and benefits of each VE proposal under consideration. If necessary, the VE team should provide additional backup information to better clarify the proposal.

2. Verify that reasons given by the designer for rejection are valid and based on technical considerations, and are not just a critique of the validity of the VE proposal. Rejections should be accompanied by distinct technical analysis. Where choices represent opinions, this should be so stated.

3. When a proposal is rejected because the designer claims that the issue had been studied previously, confirm that the conditions are in fact the same, not just similar. The failure of one idea is not necessarily justification for the rejection of a similar idea, especially if the circumstances are different.

4. Investigate new and comparatively untried ideas carefully before acceptance. And keep in mind that newness by itself is not a valid reason for rejection.

5. Do not regard a disagreement with the VE team's cost estimate for a proposal as the sole reason for rejection. Where the designer disclaims that a savings actually exists, the proposal should be evaluated on other merits. In other words, cost saving should not be the sole reason for acceptance, nor should the lack of cost saving be the sole reason for rejection.

6. Do not treat redesign cost and/or time alone as a reason for rejection, rather as one consideration among others. If substantial redesign effort is required, the designer will be eligible for additional compensation if the effort proves to have been beyond normal design evolution and not reasonably identifiable by the designer. A major benefit of conducting VE early in the design process is to identify and make any broad-based changes in design direction before detailed design begins.

7. Consider for implementation proposals that provide improved value, regardless of added or reduced cost. If added cost is required, other proposals that reduce cost can offset it. In other words, any cost-saving goals are *collective* to the project.

8. Do not summarily reject proposals that offer substantial reductions in life-cycle cost because of increased first-cost, even on a project with actual or potential budget overrun problems. Life-cycle cost-savings opportunities should not be passed over simply because a project is over-budget or was not properly budgeted at the outset.

Reporting and Follow-up Procedures

The report that results from a VE study should be a concise yet self-contained document, comprising enough technical project description so that someone not knowledgeable about the project can understand the major issues. In addition, the individual VE proposals should clearly document the original concept, the proposed concept, advantages and disadvantages, and economic consequences. Summaries should allow for a quick overview and provide the designer with a simple means of review and inclusion into the design.

Recent Developments in Value Engineering

Currently, the VE profession appears to be moving in two somewhat contradictory directions, one to continue to rely on mandated requirements from government and corporate entities; the other to emphasize VE, as a "value-added" service that becomes part of the overall design and construction process. Techniques, such as *zero-based design*, have evolved in the industrial sector as a means to apply VE techniques to cost optimization in plant design and construction.

Many in the profession believe that VE can be much better integrated into the design process. Development of value-enhanced design is one such approach.

The increasing use of design-build as a project delivery method also creates new opportunities to apply VE during design and construction. In the design-build environment, VE can be applied for the owner's benefit, for the design-builder's benefit, and for both. Chapter 5 has a more in-depth discussion of delivery methods.

TIP

The increasing use of design-build as a project delivery method also creates new opportunities to apply VE during design and construction.

Also, refer to *Value Engineering, Practical Applications*, by Alphonse J. Dell'Isola (R. S. Means Company, Inc., 1997) for a more detailed presentation of value engineering.

Life-Cycle Costing

Life-cycle costing (LCC) is an economic assessment of an item, system, or facility achieved by considering all significant costs of ownership over an economic life, expressed in terms of equivalent costs. In order to ensure that costs are compared on an equivalent basis, the baselines used for initial cost should be the same as those used for all other costs associated with each option, including maintenance, operating cost, and replacement.

Life-cycle costing is used to compare various options by identifying and assessing economic impacts over the whole life of each alternative. Future costs in terms of operations, maintenance, and replacement will typically match or exceed the initial cost of procurement in facilities. If staffing and other use costs are factored into the analysis, the initial procurement may be less than 20 percent of the total cost of ownership. Owners are recognizing these relationships and considering methods to reduce or minimize initial capital expenses without adding an undue burden to total life-cycle cost.

This section discusses methods for defining, estimating, and managing life-cycle costs, as well as approaches that can be utilized to sensitize procurement to life-cycle issues and optimize overall facility costs.

Economic Analysis Principles

In making cost decisions, both present and future costs need to be taken into account and related to one another. Today's dollar is not equal to tomorrow's dollar. Money invested in any form earns, or has the capacity to earn, interest. For example, $100 invested at 10 percent annual interest, compounded annually, will grow to $673 in 20 years. In other words, it can be said that $100 today is equivalent to $673 in 20 years time, provided that the money is invested at the rate of 10 percent per year. A current dollar is worth more than the prospect of a dollar at some future time. The exact amount depends on the investment rate (cost of money) and the length of time.

> **Note**
>
> The terms *interest rate* and discount rate are generally used synonymously to refer to the annual growth rate for the time value of money.

Figure 3.29 illustrates the time value of money for various discount rates. Note that for a 5 percent discount rate, a dollar will grow in value by a factor of approximately 3.5 over the 25-year period, while at a 15 percent discount rate, the factor is nearly 35. Even though the discount rates are a factor of 3, the resulting relationship is nearly 10. Obviously, therefore, the selection of a discount rate is important to an LCC analysis.

The discount rate means either the minimum acceptable rate of return for the client for investment purposes or the current prime or borrowing rate of interest. In establishing this rate, several factors may be considered, including the source of finance (borrowed money or capital assets), the client (government agency or private industry), and the rate of return for the industry (before or after income taxes).

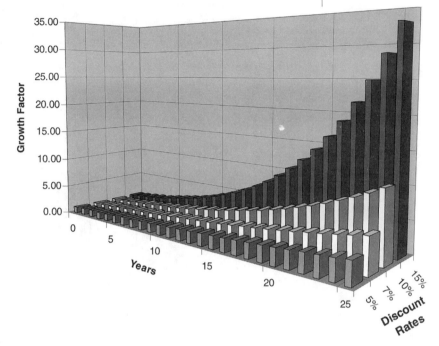

Figure 3.29 Investment return on $1.

At times, the owner may establish the minimum attractive rate of return based only on the cost of borrowed money. Although the approach is particularly common in government projects and in personal economic studies, the same approach may not be applicable to a project in competitive industry.

Inflation also can affect an economic analysis in that, over time, inflation reduces the purchasing power of currency. This effect, more correctly termed *deflation,* means that more currency in the future will be required to purchase the same goods. Figure 3.30 graphs this effect over time and, as with discounting, demonstrates the nonlinear relationship between the rate and the end result.

Cost-Estimating Methodology

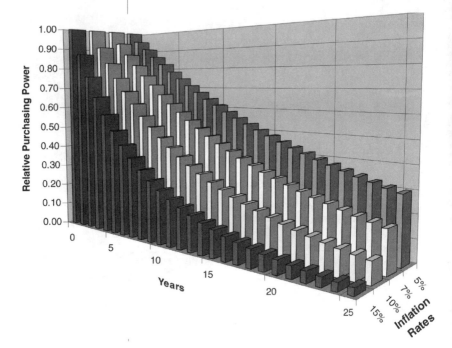

Figure 3.30 Price deflation for various inflation rates.

Inflation does not directly affect the actual time value of money since under all circumstances, money must have a time value. Inflation does, however, affect how the time value is calculated and so should be added to the calculation. In other words, if the real time value of money is 7 percent to a particular owner, and inflation is predicted to be 3 percent, then any discounting analysis would need to use 10 percent as an interest rate and inflate all future costs by 3 percent. This is called a *current dollars analysis*.

As a simplification, especially in comparative analyses not used for cash flow calculations, *constant dollars* may be used. In this case, a 7 percent discount rate would be used and all future costs would be held at the base-date relative cost and not inflated. The one exception would be for any future costs expected to not follow inflation. For example, energy costs have tended to increase at 1 to 2 percent above inflation over the last 10 years. In this case, future energy costs would be inflated differentially (above the general inflation rate) by 1 to 2 percent. This effect is referred to in economic analyses as *escalation*.

Published charts and tables are available, and spreadsheet programs provide discounting formulae. Figures 3.31 and 3.32 provide examples of factors used to calculate the present value of single costs and annual costs at a rate of 10 percent and for various inflation rates.

Economic Analysis Period

The economic or study period used in comparing alternatives is an important consideration. Generally, 25 to 40 years is long enough to predict future costs for economic purpose to capture the most significant costs. Figure 3.33 illustrates and plots accumulated annual costs for 100 years, discounted to present worth at a 10 percent interest rate. Note that 90 percent of the total equivalent cost is consumed in the first 25 years. This result is due to the effect of discounting: early-year dollars are worth much more than later-year dollars. Therefore, periods longer than 40 years will generally have no significant benefit to the analysis.

A timeframe should also be used for each system under analysis. The useful life of each system, component, or item under study may be the physical, technological, or economic life. The useful life of any item depends on such things as the frequency with which it is used, its age when acquired, the pol-

Present Worth of a Single Escalating Amount, Discount Rate = 10%													
	Escalation Rate												
Year	0%	1%	2%	3%	4%	5%	6%	7%	8%	9%	10%	11%	12%
1	0.909	0.918	0.927	0.936	0.945	0.955	0.964	0.973	0.982	0.991	1.000	1.009	1.018
2	0.826	0.843	0.860	0.877	0.894	0.911	0.929	0.946	0.964	0.982	1.000	1.018	1.037
3	0.751	0.774	0.797	0.821	0.845	0.870	0.895	0.920	0.946	0.973	1.000	1.028	1.056
4	0.683	0.711	0.739	0.769	0.799	0.830	0.862	0.895	0.929	0.964	1.000	1.037	1.075
5	0.621	0.653	0.686	0.720	0.755	0.792	0.831	0.871	0.912	0.955	1.000	1.046	1.094
6	0.564	0.599	0.636	0.674	0.714	0.756	0.801	0.847	0.896	0.947	1.000	1.056	1.114
7	0.513	0.550	0.589	0.631	0.675	0.722	0.772	0.824	0.879	0.938	1.000	1.065	1.134
8	0.467	0.505	0.547	0.591	0.638	0.689	0.744	0.802	0.863	0.930	1.000	1.075	1.155
9	0.424	0.464	0.507	0.553	0.604	0.658	0.717	0.780	0.848	0.921	1.000	1.085	1.176
10	0.386	0.426	0.470	0.518	0.571	0.628	0.690	0.758	0.832	0.913	1.000	1.095	1.197
11	0.350	0.391	0.436	0.485	0.540	0.599	0.665	0.738	0.817	0.904	1.000	1.105	1.219
12	0.319	0.359	0.404	0.454	0.510	0.572	0.641	0.718	0.802	0.896	1.000	1.115	1.241
13	0.290	0.330	0.375	0.425	0.482	0.546	0.618	0.698	0.788	0.888	1.000	1.125	1.264
14	0.263	0.303	0.347	0.398	0.456	0.521	0.595	0.679	0.773	0.880	1.000	1.135	1.287
15	0.239	0.278	0.322	0.373	0.431	0.498	0.574	0.660	0.759	0.872	1.000	1.145	1.310
16	0.218	0.255	0.299	0.349	0.408	0.475	0.553	0.642	0.746	0.864	1.000	1.156	1.334
17	0.198	0.234	0.277	0.327	0.385	0.453	0.533	0.625	0.732	0.856	1.000	1.166	1.358
18	0.180	0.215	0.257	0.306	0.364	0.433	0.513	0.608	0.719	0.848	1.000	1.177	1.383
19	0.164	0.198	0.238	0.287	0.344	0.413	0.495	0.591	0.706	0.841	1.000	1.188	1.408
20	0.149	0.181	0.221	0.268	0.326	0.394	0.477	0.575	0.693	0.833	1.000	1.198	1.434
21	0.135	0.167	0.205	0.251	0.308	0.376	0.459	0.560	0.680	0.825	1.000	1.209	1.460
22	0.123	0.153	0.190	0.235	0.291	0.359	0.443	0.544	0.668	0.818	1.000	1.220	1.486
23	0.112	0.140	0.176	0.220	0.275	0.343	0.427	0.529	0.656	0.811	1.000	1.231	1.514
24	0.102	0.129	0.163	0.206	0.260	0.327	0.411	0.515	0.644	0.803	1.000	1.243	1.541
25	0.092	0.118	0.151	0.193	0.246	0.313	0.396	0.501	0.632	0.796	1.000	1.254	1.569
26	0.084	0.109	0.140	0.181	0.233	0.298	0.382	0.487	0.621	0.789	1.000	1.265	1.598
27	0.076	0.100	0.130	0.169	0.220	0.285	0.368	0.474	0.609	0.781	1.000	1.277	1.627
28	0.069	0.092	0.121	0.159	0.208	0.272	0.354	0.461	0.598	0.774	1.000	1.288	1.656
29	0.063	0.084	0.112	0.149	0.197	0.259	0.342	0.448	0.587	0.767	1.000	1.300	1.686
30	0.057	0.077	0.104	0.139	0.186	0.248	0.329	0.436	0.577	0.760	1.000	1.312	1.717
31	0.052	0.071	0.096	0.130	0.176	0.236	0.317	0.424	0.566	0.753	1.000	1.324	1.748
32	0.047	0.065	0.089	0.122	0.166	0.226	0.306	0.413	0.556	0.747	1.000	1.336	1.780
33	0.043	0.060	0.083	0.114	0.157	0.215	0.295	0.402	0.546	0.740	1.000	1.348	1.812
34	0.039	0.055	0.077	0.107	0.149	0.206	0.284	0.391	0.536	0.733	1.000	1.360	1.845
35	0.036	0.050	0.071	0.100	0.140	0.196	0.274	0.380	0.526	0.726	1.000	1.373	1.879
36	0.032	0.046	0.066	0.094	0.133	0.187	0.264	0.370	0.517	0.720	1.000	1.385	1.913
37	0.029	0.042	0.061	0.088	0.126	0.179	0.254	0.359	0.507	0.713	1.000	1.398	1.948
38	0.027	0.039	0.057	0.082	0.119	0.171	0.245	0.350	0.498	0.707	1.000	1.410	1.983
39	0.024	0.036	0.053	0.077	0.112	0.163	0.236	0.340	0.489	0.700	1.000	1.423	2.019
40	0.022	0.033	0.049	0.072	0.106	0.156	0.227	0.331	0.480	0.694	1.000	1.436	2.056

Figure 3.31 Present worth of a single escalating amount at a discount rate of 10 percent.

Present Worth of an Annual Escalating Amount, Discount Rate = 10%												
Escalation Rate												
Year	0%	1%	2%	3%	4%	5%	6%	7%	8%	9%	10%	11%	12%
1	0.909	0.918	0.927	0.936	0.945	0.955	0.964	0.973	0.982	0.991	1.000	1.009	1.018
2	1.736	1.761	1.787	1.813	1.839	1.866	1.892	1.919	1.946	1.973	2.000	2.027	2.055
3	2.487	2.535	2.584	2.634	2.684	2.735	2.787	2.839	2.892	2.946	3.000	3.055	3.110
4	3.170	3.246	3.324	3.403	3.483	3.566	3.649	3.735	3.821	3.910	4.000	4.092	4.185
5	3.791	3.899	4.009	4.123	4.239	4.358	4.480	4.605	4.734	4.865	5.000	5.138	5.279
6	4.355	4.498	4.645	4.797	4.953	5.115	5.281	5.453	5.630	5.812	6.000	6.194	6.394
7	4.868	5.048	5.234	5.428	5.628	5.837	6.053	6.277	6.509	6.750	7.000	7.259	7.528
8	5.335	5.553	5.781	6.019	6.267	6.526	6.796	7.078	7.372	7.680	8.000	8.334	8.683
9	5.759	6.017	6.288	6.572	6.871	7.184	7.513	7.858	8.220	8.601	9.000	9.419	9.859
10	6.145	6.443	6.758	7.090	7.441	7.812	8.203	8.616	9.053	9.513	10.000	10.514	11.057
11	6.495	6.834	7.194	7.575	7.981	8.411	8.868	9.354	9.870	10.418	11.000	11.619	12.276
12	6.814	7.193	7.598	8.030	8.491	8.983	9.510	10.072	10.672	11.314	12.000	12.733	13.517
13	7.103	7.523	7.972	8.455	8.973	9.530	10.127	10.770	11.460	12.202	13.000	13.858	14.781
14	7.367	7.825	8.320	8.853	9.429	10.051	10.723	11.449	12.233	13.082	14.000	14.993	16.068
15	7.606	8.103	8.642	9.226	9.860	10.549	11.297	12.109	12.993	13.954	15.000	16.139	17.378
16	7.824	8.358	8.941	9.576	10.268	11.024	11.849	12.752	13.738	14.818	16.000	17.294	18.713
17	8.022	8.593	9.218	9.903	10.653	11.477	12.382	13.377	14.470	15.674	17.000	18.461	20.071
18	8.201	8.808	9.475	10.209	11.018	11.910	12.895	13.985	15.189	16.523	18.000	19.638	21.454
19	8.365	9.005	9.713	10.496	11.362	12.323	13.390	14.576	15.895	17.363	19.000	20.825	22.862
20	8.514	9.187	9.934	10.764	11.688	12.718	13.867	15.151	16.588	18.196	20.000	22.024	24.296
21	8.649	9.353	10.139	11.015	11.996	13.094	14.326	15.711	17.268	19.022	21.000	23.233	25.756
22	8.772	9.506	10.329	11.251	12.287	13.454	14.769	16.255	17.936	19.840	22.000	24.453	27.243
23	8.883	9.647	10.505	11.471	12.562	13.797	15.196	16.784	18.591	20.650	23.000	25.685	28.756
24	8.985	9.776	10.668	11.678	12.822	14.124	15.607	17.299	19.235	21.454	24.000	26.927	30.297
25	9.077	9.894	10.819	11.871	13.069	14.437	16.003	17.800	19.867	22.250	25.000	28.181	31.866
26	9.161	10.003	10.960	12.052	13.301	14.735	16.384	18.287	20.488	23.038	26.000	29.446	33.464
27	9.237	10.102	11.090	12.221	13.521	15.020	16.752	18.761	21.097	23.820	27.000	30.723	35.090
28	9.307	10.194	11.211	12.380	13.729	15.291	17.107	19.222	21.695	24.594	28.000	32.012	36.746
29	9.370	10.278	11.323	12.528	13.926	15.551	17.448	19.671	22.283	25.361	29.000	33.312	38.433
30	9.427	10.355	11.426	12.667	14.112	15.799	17.777	20.107	22.859	26.122	30.000	34.624	40.150
31	9.479	10.426	11.523	12.798	14.287	16.035	18.095	20.532	23.426	26.875	31.000	35.947	41.898
32	9.526	10.491	11.612	12.920	14.453	16.261	18.400	20.944	23.982	27.622	32.000	37.283	43.678
33	9.569	10.551	11.695	13.034	14.610	16.476	18.695	21.346	24.527	28.362	33.000	38.631	45.490
34	9.609	10.606	11.771	13.141	14.759	16.682	18.979	21.736	25.063	29.095	34.000	39.992	47.335
35	9.644	10.657	11.843	13.241	14.899	16.878	19.252	22.116	25.589	29.821	35.000	41.364	49.214
36	9.677	10.703	11.909	13.335	15.032	17.065	19.516	22.486	26.106	30.541	36.000	42.749	51.127
37	9.706	10.745	11.970	13.423	15.158	17.244	19.770	22.845	26.613	31.254	37.000	44.147	53.075
38	9.733	10.784	12.027	13.505	15.276	17.415	20.014	23.195	27.111	31.961	38.000	45.558	55.058
39	9.757	10.820	12.079	13.582	15.389	17.578	20.250	23.535	27.600	32.661	39.000	46.981	57.077
40	9.779	10.853	12.128	13.654	15.495	17.733	20.478	23.866	28.080	33.355	40.000	48.417	59.133

Figure 3.32 Present worth of an annual escalating amount at a discount rate of 10 percent.

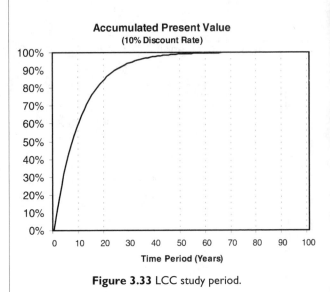

Accumulated Present Value
(10% Discount Rate)

Time Period (Years)

Figure 3.33 LCC study period.

icy for repairs and replacements, the climate in which it is used, the state of the art, economic changes, inventions, and other developments within the industry. There may be several periods for component replacement in an overall facility cycle.

Economic Equivalence

If an item costs $10,000 today and has a life expectancy of 20 years, how much would have to be put aside today to cover its replacement 20 years from now? Inflating at 3 percent per year, the actual replacement cost in year 20 will be just over $18,000. When discounted back to today, the present value is $2,680 ($10,000 × 0.268). Stated another way, $2,680 placed in the bank today at 10 percent interest rate would grow to provide $18,000 at year 20. This growth would reflect the real discount rate of 7 percent and the inflation rate of 3 percent. In terms of economics, $2,680 today (baseline year) is equivalent to $18,000 at year 20 at a 10 percent discount rate and a 3 percent inflation rate. A virtually identical analy-

Cost-Estimating Methodology

sis using constant dollars (uninflated replacement cost of $10,000 at year 20) and a 7 percent discount rate results in $2,580 ($10,000 × 0.258).

Another example of equivalence is presented in Figure 3.34; this one demonstrates that $1,000 per year for five years is equivalent to $4,123 today at a 10 percent interest rate and a 3 percent inflation rate. The chart also shows that $1,000 per year with no inflation and a 7 percent interest rate is virtually equivalent. Other examples of equivalence can be shown as follows (calculated for a high school project at a 10 percent discount rate and a 3 percent inflation for 30 years):

- ▸ Present value of one teacher = $685,000
- ▸ 5,500 square feet of average high school space = $685,000
- ▸ Present value of energy consumption–650-ton chiller = $685,000
- ▸ Installed cost of lighting systems in a 275,000-square-foot high school = $685,000

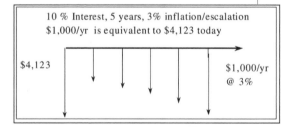

Year	Expenditure (w/o inflation)	Expenditure (with inflation) @ 3%	Discount Factor @ 10%	Present Value	Discount Factor @ 10% & 3% Infl.	Discount Factor @ 7%	Present Value
1	$1,000	$1,030	0.909	$936	0.936	0.935	$935
2	$1,000	$1,061	0.826	$877	0.877	0.873	$873
3	$1,000	$1,093	0.751	$821	0.821	0.816	$816
4	$1,000	$1,126	0.683	$769	0.769	0.763	$763
5	$1,000	$1,159	0.621	$720	0.720	0.713	$713
			3.791	$4,123	4.123	4.100	$4,100

Figure 3.34 Example of equivalence.

➤ Present value of floor maintenance in a 275,000-square-foot high school = 685,000

Cost Categories

Over the life of a facility, costs will be expended on a broad range of components and for numerous purposes. A life-cycle cost analysis is a *comparative analysis;* therefore, it is important that costs be properly identified and categorized so that common items can be eliminated from the analysis and sufficient effort can be focused on critical items. These owning costs can be subdivided as follows:

A. Initial Costs
    1. Construction
    2. Fees
    3. Other Initial Costs

B. Future Facility One-time Costs
    1. Replacements
    2. Alterations
    3. Salvage
    4. Other One-time Costs

C. Future Facility Annual Costs
    1. Operations
    2. Maintenance
    3. Financing
    4. Taxes
    5. Insurance
    6. Security
    7. Other Annual Costs

D. Functional Use Costs
    1. Staffing
    2. Materials
    3. Denial of Use
    4. Other Functional Use Costs

Initial costs include construction, fees, and others, such as land acquisition and moving. These represent "up-front" costs associated with facility development.

Future one-time costs represent major expenditures that are not annual (although they may be periodic) and include replacement, elective alterations, and salvage.

Facility annual costs include all costs to run the facility itself, exclusive of what the facility produces. These costs include operations, maintenance, and other built environment costs.

Functional use costs represent the costs associated with the production of the facility, and include staffing, materials, and any other nonfacility costs. Other items such as denial-of-use costs may be necessary during construction because of the specific option selected; these include temporary space, operations, and added security.

In parallel, it may also be necessary to consider revenue as well as costs. Eventually, there may be an income stream to offset investments and produce a viable return on those investments. While life-cycle costing tends to focus on optimizing costs, the process can also be used to optimize income as well.

Figure 3.35 presents total owning costs of a typical high school. Note that initial costs are only 25 percent of the total owning costs of the facility. Other facility types such as hospitals, research laboratories, and judicial facilities may be even more weighted toward future costs. In nearly all cases, the initial costs are 25 percent or less when compared to total owning costs.

Life-cycle Costing Procedures

Life-cycle costing focuses on comparing competing alternatives. In order to compare alternatives, both

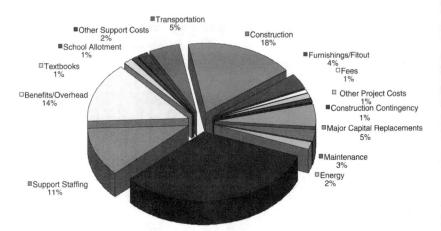

Statistics:		
Number of Years for Period	30	
Discount Rate (Interest)	8%	
Escalation Rate (Inflation)	3%	
Gross Area	sf	244,000
Students	Each	1,600
Student per Teacher		16
Staff Support per Teacher		2.3
Benefits/Overhead	%	32%

ITEM	Measure	Units	Unit Cost	Current Cost	Factor	Present Value	Percent
Capital Costs							
Construction	$/sf	244,000	$133.00	$ 32,452,000	1	$ 32,452,000	18%
Furnishings/Fitout	$/sf	244,000	$26.50	$ 6,466,000	1	$ 6,466,000	4%
Fees	$/sf	244,000	$7.00	$ 1,708,000	1	$ 1,708,000	1%
Other Project Costs	$/sf	244,000	$7.00	$ 1,708,000	1	$ 1,708,000	1%
Construction Contingency	$/sf	244,000	$6.50	$ 1,586,000	1	$ 1,586,000	1%
Sub-Total - Initial Capital Costs	$/sf	244,000	$180.00	$ 43,920,000	1	$ 43,920,000	24%
Major Capital Replacements	$/sf/yr	244,000	$ 2.50	$ 610,000	15.63	$ 9,534,894	5%
Grand Total Capital Costs						$ 53,454,894	29%
Operations & Maintenance							
Maintenance	$/sf/yr	244,000	$ 1.40	$ 341,600	15.63	$ 5,339,541	3%
Energy	$/sf/yr	244,000	$ 0.80	$ 195,200	15.63	$ 3,051,166	2%
Sub-Total				$ 536,800		$ 8,390,707	5%
Functional Operation							
Educational Staffing	Teachers	100	$ 38,000	$ 3,800,000	15.63	$ 59,397,700	32%
Support Staffing	Staff	43	$ 31,000	$ 1,333,000	15.63	$ 20,836,088	11%
Benefits/Overhead	%	32%		$ 1,642,560	15.63	$ 25,674,812	14%
Textbooks	Student	1,600	$ 90	$ 144,000	15.63	$ 2,250,860	1%
School Allotment	Student	1,600	$ 65	$ 104,000	15.63	$ 1,625,621	1%
Other Support Costs	Student	1,600	$ 135	$ 216,000	15.63	$ 3,376,290	2%
Transportation	Student	1,600	$ 360	$ 576,000	15.63	$ 9,003,441	5%
				$ 7,815,560		$ 122,164,813	66%

Grand Total			
Present Value Cost		$	184,010,413
Equivalent Annual Cost	0.0640	$	11,772,166
Equivalent Annual Cost per Student	1,600	$	7,358
Equivalent Annual Cost per Student (Excluding Capital)	1,600	$	5,220

Figure 3.35 Life-cycle costs of a typical high school.

present and future costs for each alternative should be brought to a common point of time. One of two methods can be used. Costs may be converted into today's cost by the *present worth method*, or they may be converted to an annual series of payments by the *annualized method*. Either method will properly allow comparison between alternatives.

Present Worth Method

The present worth method requires conversion of all present and future expenditures to a baseline of today's cost. Initial (present) costs are already expressed in present worth. Future costs are converted to present value by applying the factors presented previously.

A key issue in this process is for the owner to determine the rate of return or the discount rate. The federal government, through the Office of Management and Budget (OMB) publishes Circular A-94 that defines economic analysis requirements. The circular has established 10 percent as the interest rate to be used in facility studies, excluding the lease or purchase of real property. Normally, a life cycle between 25 and 40 years is considered adequate for estimating future expenses. Differential escalation (that rate of inflation above the general economy) is taken into account for recurring costs, as necessary. (See Figure 3.36.)

Annualized Method

The second method converts initial, recurring, and nonrecurring costs to an annual series of payments; it may be used to express all life-cycle costs as an annual expenditure. Home payments are an example of this procedure; that is, a buyer opts to purchase a home for $1,050 a month (360 equal monthly payments at 10 percent yearly interest) rather than pay $150,000 all at

Present Worth of an Annual Escalating Amount, Discount Rate = 10%

Year							Escalation Rate								
	0%	1%	2%	3%	4%	5%	6%	7%	8%	9%	10%	11%	12%	13%	14%
1	0.909	0.918	0.927	0.936	0.945	0.955	0.964	0.973	0.982	0.991	1.000	1.009	1.018	1.027	1.036
2	1.736	1.761	1.787	1.813	1.839	1.866	1.892	1.919	1.946	1.973	2.000	2.027	2.055	2.083	2.110
3	2.487	2.535	2.584	2.634	2.684	2.735	2.787	2.839	2.892	2.946	3.000	3.055	3.110	3.167	3.224
4	3.170	3.246	3.324	3.403	3.483	3.566	3.649	3.735	3.821	3.910	4.000	4.092	4.185	4.280	4.377
5	3.791	3.899	4.009	4.123	4.239	4.358	4.480	4.605	4.734	4.865	5.000	5.138	5.279	5.424	5.573

Present Worth of an Annual Escalating Amount, Discount Rate = 7%

Year							Escalation Rate								
	0%	1%	2%	3%	4%	5%	6%	7%	8%	9%	10%	11%	12%	13%	14%
1	0.935	0.944	0.953	0.963	0.972	0.981	0.991	1.000	1.009	1.019	1.028	1.037	1.047	1.056	1.065
2	1.808	1.835	1.862	1.889	1.917	1.944	1.972	2.000	2.028	2.056	2.085	2.114	2.142	2.171	2.201
3	2.624	2.676	2.728	2.781	2.835	2.889	2.944	3.000	3.056	3.114	3.171	3.230	3.289	3.349	3.410
4	3.387	3.470	3.554	3.640	3.727	3.817	3.907	4.000	4.094	4.190	4.288	4.388	4.490	4.593	4.698
5	4.100	4.219	4.341	4.466	4.595	4.727	4.862	5.000	5.142	5.287	5.437	5.589	5.746	5.907	6.071

Figure 3.36 Equivalence of escalated and nonescalated discount rates.

once. Recurring costs are already expressed as annual costs; therefore, no adjustment is necessary. Initial costs, however, require equivalent cost conversion, and nonrecurring costs (future expenditures) should be converted to current cost (present worth) and then to an annual expenditure (annualized cost).

Other Economic Analysis Methods

Other methods of economic analysis can be used in a life-cycle study, depending on the client's requirements and special needs. With additional rules and mechanics, it is possible to perform a sensitivity analysis; to determine the payback period; to establish a break-even point between alternatives; to determine the rate of return and extra-investment, rate-of-return alternatives; to perform a cash-flow analysis; and to review the benefits and costs.

All methods, correctly applied, will yield results pointing to the same conclusion; in other words, the alternative with superior economic performance will be selected. That said, because the construction industry is capital-cost-intensive, the present worth method is recommended. Furthermore, the present worth method tends to be easier to use and produces results that can be easily understood.

Figure 3.37 presents a sample worksheet for use in conducting present worth life-cycle costing studies. The worksheet (as a spreadsheet) allows input of initial costs, replacement costs, and annual costs, and automatic calculation of present worth. Simple and discounted payback periods are also calculated.

The Relationship between Quality and Cost

Life-cycle costing provides a methodology to compare competing alternatives over the life of the facil-

		Option 2		Option 3	
Life Cycle Costing - General Purpose Worksheet		**Original Design**		**Option 1**	
Study Title:					
Discount Rate : Date:		Estimated	Present	Estimated	Present
Life Cycle (Yrs.)		Costs	Worth	Costs	Worth

		Occurance Year -or- Cycle	Inflation/ Escal. Rate	PW Factor	Estimated Costs	Present Worth	Estimated Costs	Present Worth
INITIAL / COLLATERAL COSTS	**Initial/Collateral Costs**							
	A. _____							
	B. _____							
	C. _____							
	D. _____							
	E. _____							
	F. _____							
	G. _____							
	H. _____							
	I. _____							
	J. _____							
	Total Initial/Collateral Costs							
	Difference							
REPLACEMENT/SALVAGE COSTS	**Replacement/Salvage (Single Expenditures)**	Occurance Year -or- Cycle	Inflation/ Escal. Rate	PW Factor				
	A. _____							
	B. _____							
	C. _____							
	D. _____							
	E. _____							
	F. _____							
	G. _____							
	H. _____							
	I. _____							
	J. _____							
	Total Replacement/Salvage Costs							
ANNUAL COSTS	**Annual Costs**		Inflation/ Escal. Rate	PW Factor				
	A. _____							
	B. _____							
	C. _____							
	D. _____							
	E. _____							
	F. _____							
	G. _____							
	H. _____							
	I. _____							
	J. _____							
	Total Annual Costs							
	Sub-Total Replacement/Salvage + Annual Costs (Present Worth)							
	Difference							
LIFE CYCLE COSTS	**Total Life Cycle Costs (Present Worth)**							N/A
	Life Cycle Cost PW Difference							N/A
	Payback - Simple Discounted (Added Cost / Annualized Savings)							N/A
	Payback - Fully Discounted (Added Cost+Interest / Annualized Savings)							N/A
	Total Life Cycle Costs - Annualized				Per Year:		Per Year:	

Figure 3.37 Sample LLC worksheet.

ity. These alternatives will generally reflect differing performance of systems relative to their useful life, required maintenance, and energy consumption. The performance of systems will tend to reflect their "quality" in that higher-quality systems usually have high initial cost and low future costs. Low-quality systems tend to be the opposite, with low initial cost but high future cost.

Refer again to Chapter 1, Figure 1.5, which diagrammed the relationship between quality and cost for initial costs as well as future costs, and demonstrated that there generally exists an "optimum life-cycle cost" design choice. If the owner's quality expectations are well founded, this point will occur within the range of quality called for and result in optimum facility costs.

It is interesting to note that in traditional design process, the tendency has been for systems to "creep" up the quality curve under the premise that better quality is always desirable. In practice, however, quality that exceeds actual needs is not necessarily a good investment, especially if the added quality is obtained at a high price. Conversely, cost-cutting, which is often done to maintain capital budget requirements, may reduce quality below needs simply to achieve that budget, and in the process achieve less-than-optimum life-cycle performance. Designers can seek to optimize the quality-cost relationship by use of increased design control and thereby optimize total life-cycle costs.

REMINDER!
Higher-quality systems usually have high initial cost and low future costs. Low-quality systems tend to have low initial cost but high future cost.

Life-Cycle Costing Applications in Overall Procurement

Life-cycle costing can be critical when analyzing better design solutions, providing better-performing facilities, and producing optimum facility financial performance.

There are three basic opportunities by which life cycle costing can impact overall procurement:

1. By owners emphasizing performance in system and facility design, and potentially requiring life-cycle cost analyses for system selection. The industry initiative to move to "performance specifying" will assist this outcome in facility design. This approach can help assure the owner that investing in facilities is a sound decision overall. Regardless of the delivery method chosen, the owner can include the impact of life-cycle costing during the initial team selection. The owner may require that life-cycle costs for the entire facility be estimated or that they be estimated only when deviations from owner specifications are considered. The owner may also insist upon a performance "guarantee" tied to future incentives or penalties. Owners also include requirements for "green" building construction, sustainable design, and workspace productivity enhancement.

2. By the design team emphasizing life-cycle performance when presenting competing design solutions. This can be in response to owner requirements or elective on the part of the design team, to gain a competitive advantage and to demonstrate efficiency. A life-cycle-efficient design will likely be most cost-competitive in the long run.

3. By "optimizing" initial cost and owning costs through effective design and operation. The benefit of carefully investing initial capital to produce more effective life-cycle facilities is clear.

Example: Life-cycle Cost Assessment of a Design-Builder's HVAC System

Figure 3.38 is the summary of an owner's independent review of a design-builder's HVAC system pro-

General Purpose Worksheet				Alternative 1 Individual Rooftop Units		Alternative 2 Central Plant with 4 - Pipe Fan Coil Units	

Study Title: **HVAC System Analysis**				Estimated Costs	Present Worth	Estimated Costs	Present Worth
Discount Rate : **8.0%** Date: **12/17/97**							
Life Cycle (Yrs.) **30**							

INITIAL / COLLATERAL COSTS

Initial/Collateral Costs							
A. Equipment				1,212,354	1,212,354	2,803,000	2,803,000
B. Screening				55,501	55,501	40,000	40,000
C. Plant Space						128,000	128,000
D.							
E.							
F.							
G.							
H.							
I.							
J.							
Total Initial/Collateral Costs				$1,267,855	$1,267,855	$2,971,000	$2,971,000
Difference							($1,703,145)

REPLACEMENT/SALVAGE COSTS

Replacement/Salvage (Single Expenditures)	Year	Inflation/ Escal. Rate	PW Factor				
A. Rooftop Units (70%)	8		0.540	770,000	416,007		
B. Rooftop Units (70%)	16		0.292	770,000	224,756		
C. Rooftop Units (70%)	24		0.158	770,000	121,428		
D. Fan Coils(100%)	15		0.315			408,888	128,899
E. Central Plant Equipment	20		0.215			600,000	128,729
F.							
G.							
H.							
I.							
J.							
Total Replacement/Salvage Costs					$762,191		$257,627

ANNUAL COSTS

Annual Costs		Inflation/ Escal. Rate	PW Factor				
A. Maintenance - Rooftops		1%	12.496	75,360	941,693		
B. Maintenance - Fan Coils		1%	12.496			37,680	470,847
C. Maintenance - Central Plant & Distrib.		1%	12.496			28,800	359,883
D. Energy		3%	15.631	468,000	7,315,296	192,000	3,001,147
E.			11.258				
F.							
G.							
H.							
I.							
J.							
Total Annual Costs				$543,360	$8,256,989	$258,480	$3,831,876
Sub-Total Replacement/Salvage + Annual Costs (Present Worth)					$9,019,180		$4,089,504
Difference							$4,929,676

LIFE CYCLE COSTS

Total Life Cycle Costs (Present Worth)					$10,287,035		$7,060,504
Life Cycle Cost PW Difference							$3,226,531
Payback - Simple Discounted (Added Cost / Annualized Savings)							3.9 Yrs.
- Fully Discounted (Added Cost+Interest / Annualized Savings)							4.8 Yrs.
Total Life Cycle Costs - Annualized				Per Year:	$913,771	Per Year:	$627,166

Figure 3.38 HVAC system analysis.

posed for a school. The analysis indicates that spending $1.7 million more initially on a better-performing HVAC system would yield net savings of $3.2 million over the life of the facility and pay back within five years.

Conclusions

This chapter presented cost-estimating methods to predict costs and additional techniques to work with those costs within the context of design and construction. Some of the key topics have included the importance of working with the effective formats, the differences between estimating and bidding, principles of cost estimating, specific cost-estimating methods, and the important subjects of value management/engineering, life-cycle costing, and risk management.

These methods and techniques provide the basic building blocks of effective cost management. The subjects covered in the next chapter deal with the importance of good information being provided, how to obtain cost data, and how to work with cost information within your organization.

Cost-Estimating Tools

4

Cost estimating and cost management are both dependent on the availability of reliable, comprehensive, and current information. Chapter 3 established the importance to cost management of using effective cost-estimating methods. This chapter emphasizes how to use published sources of cost information and how to gather and utilize cost information from internal information. The topics include:

▶ Interpreting cost information

▶ Using cost indexes

▶ Referencing published cost information

▶ Developing and maintaining cost data files

▶ Doing computer-assisted estimating

This chapter identifies sources of cost information and describes methods by which to treat and manipulate that information to make it more useful.

Interpreting Cost Information

Cost information is available from a number of sources that include published data, quotes from contractors and suppliers, public access data (widely available on the World Wide Web), contract cost histories, and cost information from personal projects. This information can be used to prepare estimates, adjust estimates, or establish economic patterns/trends geographically or through time. It is extremely important to understand the source of the information and to be able to evaluate its dependability and usefulness, keeping in mind that the timing, organization, and nature of the information can vary dramatically depending on the source. For example, schedule-of-values type information can be useful, but only if it is recognized that the contractor providing the information probably has organized it to benefit the organization. Information may, for example, be grouped in a manner that is not necessarily consistent with the way that work will actually be done. Results might include front, loading, or transferring costs from one trade to another or presenting general conditions in a desirable light along with a host of other issues. Again, this is not to say that this information is not useful, but that it should be interpreted carefully.

It is also important to understand how markups and overheads have been distributed and included in the cost information. Schedule-of-value information is often utilized as the basis of progress payments, so care should be taken to assure that overheads and markups are properly and evenly distributed.

The conditions under which the project was procured or bid should also be carefully considered. Moving costs forward in time from one market condition to another market condition can lead to substantially incorrect conclusions. Many of these issues require experience and judgment and recognizing that there are no right or wrong answers.

Using Cost Indexes

A cost index is a statistical process to measure a condition over time and through geographical comparisons. The statistical process can be based on a number of approaches that can be composed of historical information or current information that has been processed through some form of analysis. A cost index can be a simple combination of items that are measured over a consistent period of time or it may be a complicated model that measures the combined effects of numerous inputs. Regardless, the index is a "barometer" of the current status of the construction industry or some aspect of the industry.

There are numerous sources of information on trends of the construction industry in the United States. Many of these sources are provided through government agencies such as the Department of Labor and the Department of Commerce. Probably the most referenced index in day-to-day use is the Consumer Price Index (CPI) as published by the Department of Commerce. The CPI measures a "market basket" of consumer-related items that are proportioned based on their consumption in the public and priced on a regular basis. The growth or shrinkage that occurs in this index is a basic measure of inflation. Refer to Chapter 2, Figure 2.11 (page 43), which indicates the relationship between the CPI and another common index published by the R. S. Means Company. These indexes track reasonably closely and indicate that though the general condition of the construction marketplace will usually follow the general condition of the overall economy in the long run, in the short run they can vary fairly significantly.

The significant difference that occurs between indexes can be traced to their source of information. An input index is driven by factors that are inputs to the condition being measured. As an example of the CPI, consider consumer market basket inputs that deal with food, clothing, manufactured goods, housing, and so on—in other words, those items that are consumed as part of the normal process of living. Other types of indexes are based on the outputs of the items being measured, outputs being the actual product of the industry or sector being reviewed. An output index would track, for example, the current selling price of a variety of automobiles at the point of consumption. Why is the point of consumption important? Because the market will dictate the actual selling price, not necessarily the price desired by the seller. Another good example is that of home sales. The price paid is a function not only of the value of the item being sold, but of the role of supply and demand for the item in the marketplace. As demand increases past supply, the price will go up; if demand falls in comparison to the supply, the price will drop.

Most indexes prepared for the construction industry tend to be input indexes; that is, they are a measure of labor rates and materials costs, and do not necessarily reflect market conditions and supply/demand/availability factors. Input cost indexes are useful indicators of general trends across the industry, and where individual city indexes are provided, they can be used to compare the rates of increase or decrease in different locations and over time. However, input cost indexes do not necessarily reflect the price being charged by the marketplace for the actual in-place work, only the direct cost of labor and materials. This is not to say that market factors do not affect the inputs, but that these changes tend to take place over long periods of time relative to supply and demand, particularly for labor portions of the index. Materials may vary over time in the short run more from the point supplier's point of view and less from the overall industry's point of view.

An output index would track subcontractor bid prices or completed building costs. These output indexes are often also called *price indexes*. An example of an index that tracks bid prices or completed building costs is the one produced by Turner Construction, which tracks bid prices with market effects represented. Figure 4.1 diagrams the two index types. Note that though there is a certain amount of overlap between the two types of indexes, and that there may be a great deal of consistency between these types of indexes, at any point in time, because of supply and demand issues, the two indexes can vary significantly.

Typically, index producers tend not to reveal how these indexes are calculated. It is known, however,

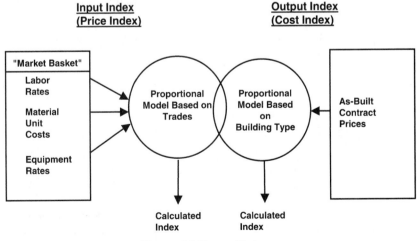

Figure 4.1 Types of indexes.

that the general method in the case of cost indexes is to survey material suppliers and track labor rates. An important step in the process is to assign the relative weights associated with each component of the index. This is usually done in proportion to the actual use of that component in the marketplace. For example, if a typical building in the analysis has 10 percent of its cost associated with concrete, then the components associated with concrete will represent 10 percent of the total cost. Once the weights are established, the pricing methodology for each component is defined. A consistent pricing methodology is necessary because the item is measured over time or from area to area, and consistency makes it possible to assume the differences to be generic, not just accidental. Figure 4.2 gives a hypothetical example of how an index can be calculated. The baseline pricing is calculated first, then the updated pricing is recalculated. The percentage relationship between the two final calculations would represent the change in the index, in this case 12.5 percent. The number of items in the index and the appropriateness of the propor-

Item	Baseline Pricing				Updated Pricing			
	Price Baseline	Unit	Weight	Initial Index Component Analysis	Updated Price	Percent Change	Weight	Updated Index Component Analysis
Material Item 1	$ 25.00	SF	8.0%	0.0800	$ 28.00	12.00%	8.0%	0.0896
Material Item 2	$ 90.00	CY	16.0%	0.1600	$ 95.00	5.56%	16.0%	0.1689
Material Item 3	$ 1.25	SF	13.0%	0.1300	$ 1.50	20.00%	13.0%	0.1560
Material Item 4	$ 44.00	SF	5.0%	0.0500	$ 45.00	2.27%	5.0%	0.0511
Material Item 5	$ 0.55	LB	16.0%	0.1600	$ 0.65	18.18%	16.0%	0.1891
Material Item 6	$ 6.25	SF	5.0%	0.0500	$ 6.00	-4.00%	5.0%	0.0480
Labor Item 1	$ 36.00	HR	6.0%	0.0600	$ 40.00	11.11%	6.0%	0.0667
Labor Item 2	$ 27.00	HR	11.0%	0.1100	$ 31.00	14.81%	11.0%	0.1263
Labor Item 3	$ 45.00	HR	9.0%	0.0900	$ 48.00	6.67%	9.0%	0.0960
Labor Item 4	$ 23.00	HR	11.0%	0.1100	$ 28.00	21.74%	11.0%	0.1339
			100.0%	1.0000			100.0%	1.1256
						Index Adjustment =		12.56%

Figure 4.2 Hypothetical example of index calculation approach.

tioning of the pricing determines the validity and viability of the index.

Calculating output or price indexes requires an ongoing assessment of contractor/subcontractor prices in-place for a variety of items of work, ideally for the same building repeatedly procured or bid. The actual calculation process will be similar to that of the input index, but because of the nature of the index, the number of components will generally be very limited.

An article in *Engineering News Record* (ENR; March 26, 2001), which discusses the recent drop in lumber prices, highlights the difference between the two types of indexes:

> The annual rate of escalation of the (ENR) Building Cost Index has fallen from a peak of 4% last May to just 0.2% this month. Other indexes that measure labor and material input costs also have felt the impact of lower lumber prices. Marshall & Swift estimates that the annual inflation rate measured by its construction cost index will only be 0.7% this April, down from 5% last September. However, cost indexes that track the actual selling price of construction continue to reflect a tight market. The Austin, Turner and Smith Group selling price indexes are up 3.8% for the year, compared to a 1.4% average increase for seven general-purpose and valuation indexes. The 2.4% gap between the two groups of indexes is the widest in several years and is an indication of the markup going on in today's construction market.

This article points out clearly that input pricing that is not a function of supply and demand market conditions can be different from output index pricing, which will reflect supply and demand market conditions.

Indexes can be further subdivided based on whether they are:

- *Temporal*, meaning that they are intended to measure change over time.
- *Geographical*, meaning that they are intended to measure changes that occur from location to location.
- *Combined*, some that measure both.

Available Input Cost Indexes

Input cost indexes available as sources are described in the following subsections.

Engineering News Record

This weekly publication, quoted previously, produces a quarterly cost report and two indexes, the Construction Cost Index (CCI) and the Building Cost Index (BCI). The former was established in 1921 and was designed as a general-purpose tool to chart basic cost trends. It is a weighted aggregate index of the prices of constant quantities of structural steel, portland cement, lumber, and common labor. This hypothetical market basket was valued at $100 using 1913 prices.

The original use of common labor as part of the CCI was intended to reflect wage rate activity for all construction workers. In the 1930s, however, wage and fringe benefit rates climbed much faster in percentage terms for common laborers than for skilled tradesmen. ENR, therefore, introduced its BCI in 1938 to weigh the impact of skilled labor trades on construction costs.

The BCI labor component is the average union wage rate, plus fringes, for carpenters, bricklayers, and structural steelworkers. The materials component is the same as that used in the CCI.

Both indexes are designed to indicate basic underlying trends of construction costs in the United States. Therefore, components are based on construction materials less influenced by local conditions. ENR chose steel, lumber, and cement because they have a stable relationship to the U.S. economy and price structure. The proportions are as follows:

CCI	BCI
Common labor: 79 percent	Skilled labor: 63 percent
Steel: 11 percent	Steel: 20 percent
Lumber: 9 percent	Lumber: 15 percent
Cement: 1 percent	Cement: 2 percent

ENR also regularly publishes the material prices for 20 major cities in the United States. However, as ENR itself admitted, "…the use of just a few cost components makes indexes for individual cities more vulnerable to source changes and misquoted prices. These aberrations tend to average out for the 20-city indexes."

Neither index is adjusted for productivity, managerial efficiency, labor market conditions, contractor overhead and profit, or other intangible cost factors. Figure 4.3 shows an excerpt of the ENR BCI with a history of its value from 1978 to October 2001.

R. S. Means Company

R. S. Means Company is the producer of several well-known cost data books covering all aspects of construction. The Means index is based on a composite building that represents current design standards and practices. The composite building is

BUILDING COST INDEX HISTORY (1915-2001)

HOW ENR BUILDS THE INDEX: 66.38 hours of skilled labor at the 20-city average of bricklayers, carpenters and structural ironworkers rates, plus 25 cwt of standard structural steel shapes at the mill price prior to 1996 and the fabricated 20-city price from 1996, plus 1.128 tons of portland cement at the 20-city price, plus 1,088 board-ft of 2 x 4 lumber at the 20-city price.

	JAN	FEB	MAR	APR	MAY	JUN	JUL	AUG	SEP	OCT	NOV	DEC	ANNUAL AVG
1978	1609	1617	1620	1621	1652	1663	1696	1705	1720	1721	1732	1734	1674
1979	1740	1740	1750	1749	1753	1809	1829	1849	1900	1900	1901	1909	1819
1980	1895	1894	1915	1899	1888	1916	1950	1971	1976	1976	2000	2017	1941
1981	2015	2016	2014	2064	2076	2080	2106	2131	2154	2151	2181	2178	2097
1982	2184	2198	2192	2197	2199	2225	2258	2259	2263	2262	2268	2297	2234
1983	2311	2348	2352	2347	2351	2388	2414	2428	2430	2416	2419	2406	2384
1984	2402	2407	2412	2422	2419	2417	2418	2428	2430	2424	2421	2408	2417
1985	2410	2414	2406	2405	2411	2429	2448	2442	2441	2441	2446	2439	2428
1986	2440	2446	2447	2458	2479	2493	2499	2498	2504	2511	2511	2511	2483
1987	2515	2510	2518	2523	2524	2525	2538	2557	2564	2569	2564	2589	2541
1988	2574	2576	2586	2591	2592	2595	2598	2611	2612	2612	2616	2617	2598
1989	2615	2608	2612	2615	2616	2623	2627	2637	2660	2662	2665	2669	2634
1990	2664	2668	2673	2676	2691	2715	2716	2716	2730	2728	2730	2720	2702
1991	2720	2716	2715	2709	2723	2733	2757	2792	2785	2786	2791	2784	2751
1992	2784	2775	2799	2809	2828	2838	2845	2854	2857	2867	2873	2875	2834
1993	2886	2886	2915	2976	3071	3066	3038	3014	3009	3016	3029	3046	2996
1994	3071	3106	3116	3127	3125	3115	3107	3109	3116	3116	3109	3110	3111
1995	3112	3111	3103	3100	3096	3095	3114	3121	3109	3117	3131	3128	3111
1996	3127	3131	3135	3148	3161	3178	3190	3223	3246	3284	3304	3311	3203
1997	3332	3333	3323	3364	3377	3396	3392	3385	3378	3372	3350	3370	3364
1998	3363	3372	3368	3375	3374	3379	3382	3391	3414	3423	3424	3419	3391
1999	3425	3417	3411	3421	3422	3433	3460	3474	3504	3505	3498	3497	3456
2000	3503	3523	3536	3534	3558	3553	3545	3546	3539	3547	3541	3548	3540
2001	3545	3536	3542	3541	3547	3572	3625	3605	3597	3602			

Base: 1913=100. Indexes revised for March, April and May 2000

Figure 4.3 Excerpt of the ENR building cost index.

composed from a mixture of the following building types:

Factory, 1-story
Office, 2–4 story
Store, retail
Town Hall, 2–3 story
High school, 2–3 story
Hospital, 4–8 story
Parking Garage
Apartment, 1–3 story
Hotel/Motel, 2–3 story

The components of the index consist of 66 commonly used construction materials, specific labor-hours for 21 building trades, and specific days of equipment rental for 6 types of construction equipment. The material and equipment costs are updated quarterly by gathering quotations from 719 cities in the United States and Canada. The labor costs are based on the most recently negotiated labor wage rates for the 21 trades. From this data a national average can be calculated, which is based on the results obtained for 30 major U.S. cities.

Like the ENR index, the Means index does not take into consideration productivity variations between cities or trades, managerial efficiency, market conditions, automation, restrictive union practices, unique local requirements, or regional variations due to specific building codes. Figure 4.4 presents an excerpt of R. S. Means's Construction Cost Indexes.

The Hanscomb/Means Report

This newsletter, which is a joint publication of Hanscomb Inc. and R. S. Means, provides international

Means Construction Cost Indexes ©2001

CSI DIV. NO.	JULY 1, 2001 ITEM	30 CITY AVERAGE			NEW YORK, NY			CHICAGO, IL		
		MAT.	INST.	TOTAL	MAT.	INST.	TOTAL	MAT.	INST.	TOTAL
01590	EQUIPMENT RENTAL	.0	112.4	112.4	.0	131.5	131.5	.0	105.5	105.5
02300	EARTHWORK	121.7	115.3	116.1	186.1	147.9	152.7	112.9	104.2	105.3
02400, 02450	TUNNELING & LOAD-BEARING ELEMENTS	100.8	111.1	106.5	96.6	122.3	111.0	100.5	116.5	109.4
02700	BASES & PAVEMENTS	138.1	113.1	134.3	178.9	135.8	172.4	148.8	117.9	144.1
02500, 02600	UTILITY SERVICES & DRAINAGE	118.2	126.6	118.9	114.7	215.4	123.3	110.4	168.7	115.3
02800	SITE IMPROVEMENTS	111.9	113.8	112.8	104.3	132.6	117.8	101.1	130.7	115.2
02900	PLANTING	122.7	116.0	119.3	174.6	162.6	168.4	76.4	105.5	91.4
02	SITE CONSTRUCTION	123.3	115.3	117.2	168.9	148.6	153.2	110.4	105.0	106.2
03100	CONCRETE FORMS & ACCESSORIES	121.5	125.5	125.0	133.1	221.1	209.2	125.2	165.5	160.1
03200	CONCRETE REINFORCEMENT	115.3	124.9	120.7	121.2	229.8	182.3	109.5	202.8	162.0
03300	CAST-IN-PLACE CONCRETE	136.5	121.7	130.1	172.8	202.1	185.4	154.6	158.5	156.3
03400	PRECAST CONCRETE	119.2	118.6	119.1	160.7	162.8	161.0	123.6	144.8	126.5
03	CONCRETE	127.0	123.7	125.3	159.2	212.9	186.3	136.4	168.3	152.5
04050	BASIC MASONRY MATERIALS & METHODS	135.4	123.9	129.6	162.2	198.3	180.3	146.2	158.8	152.5
04200	MASONRY UNITS	125.7	126.1	126.0	136.5	215.1	184.5	116.8	167.9	148.0
04400	STONE	137.4	126.2	129.8	153.4	214.6	195.2	130.4	167.6	155.8
04	MASONRY	126.8	126.0	126.3	139.3	213.9	185.0	119.8	167.2	148.8
05100	STRUCTURAL METAL FRAMING	123.9	120.7	122.7	140.0	173.9	152.1	118.3	152.0	130.4
05200, 05300	METAL JOISTS & DECKING	134.4	119.9	128.5	147.0	169.4	156.1	129.1	149.6	137.5
05500	METAL FABRICATIONS	100.0	128.7	105.3	100.0	209.1	120.3	100.0	189.1	116.5
05	METALS	128.1	120.5	125.2	140.4	171.9	152.3	123.3	151.7	134.0
06100	ROUGH CARPENTRY	121.9	125.5	124.2	144.7	223.6	195.5	122.0	164.6	149.5
06200	FINISH CARPENTRY	176.2	126.1	169.8	180.0	227.5	186.1	184.9	166.1	182.5

06 WOOD & PLASTICS	141.9	125.6	133.0	157.7	223.8	193.7	145.1	164.7	155.8
07100 DAMPPROOFING & WATERPROOFING	105.2	126.1	121.6	111.9	227.5	202.4	102.6	166.1	152.3
07200, 07800 THERMAL, FIRE & SMOKE PROTECTION	109.8	124.4	114.5	116.4	218.4	148.9	107.3	164.8	125.7
07400, 07500 ROOFING & SIDING	143.7	119.1	130.5	148.3	172.0	160.9	148.9	149.9	149.4
07600 FLASHING & SHEET METAL	112.6	129.7	125.6	112.6	210.8	187.1	112.6	158.8	147.6
07 THERMAL & MOISTURE PROTECTION	119.4	123.7	121.4	124.5	200.4	159.8	119.3	158.8	137.7
08100 - 08300 DOORS & FRAMES	114.8	127.7	117.6	107.1	220.6	132.3	115.9	179.6	130.0
08800, 08900 GLAZING & GLAZED CURTAIN WALLS	147.3	126.5	138.0	174.2	207.4	189.0	140.8	176.2	156.6
08 DOORS & WINDOWS	125.2	127.1	125.6	121.6	219.1	144.8	130.1	176.4	141.1
09200 PLASTER & GYPSUM BOARD	153.9	126.1	134.7	159.3	227.5	206.4	153.4	166.1	162.2
09300, 09400 TILE & TERRAZZO	115.1	122.9	118.6	145.5	201.9	171.0	98.0	161.3	126.6
09500, 09800 CEILINGS & ACOUSTICAL TREATMENT	112.1	126.1	121.1	117.4	227.5	188.5	107.3	166.1	145.3
09600 FLOORING	116.6	124.3	118.4	115.0	204.8	136.1	99.0	161.7	113.7
09700, 09900 WALL FINISHES, PAINTS & COATINGS	119.5	125.0	122.7	116.8	197.7	163.3	95.5	168.3	137.3
09 FINISHES	119.5	125.1	122.3	128.9	216.1	173.3	105.8	164.9	135.9
10000 - 14000 TOTAL DIV, 10000 - 14000	141.3	128.8	138.5	141.3	194.0	153.1	141.3	158.1	145.0
150 - 152,154 PLUMBING: PIPING, FIXTURES & EQUIPMENT	119.1	128.4	123.4	119.1	213.3	162.4	119.1	155.0	135.6
15300,13900 FIRE PROTECTION/SUPPRESSION	90.3	130.2	115.6	90.3	206.8	164.1	90.3	155.2	131.4
15500 HEAT GENERATION EQUIPMENT	129.3	128.4	128.9	131.2	207.7	161.4	129.4	161.1	141.9
15600 - 15800 AIR CONDITIONING & VENTILATION	156.1	128.0	153.5	156.1	210.8	161.0	156.1	161.0	156.5
15 MECHANICAL	124.4	128.8	126.3	124.6	211.3	162.4	124.4	155.7	138.0
16 ELECTRICAL	107.8	131.2	123.0	119.8	229.9	191.5	109.0	172.9	150.7
01 - 16 WEIGHTED AVERAGE	124.9	125.4	125.1	134.4	204.7	168.4	123.8	157.7	140.1
BASED ON JAN. 1, 2001	103.4	101.3	102.3	111.3	165.4	137.7	102.5	127.4	114.6

Figure 4.4 Example of R.S. Means's Construction Cost Indexes.

construction intelligence. "The Hanscomb/Means Report (HMR)" is issued eight times annually and includes a Quarterly International Construction Cost Index. "The HMR" also includes In-Country Profiles, Building Type Cost Comparisons, Procedural/Contractual Issues Reports, and Country and Regional Overviews. Figure 4.5 contains an excerpt of the Hanscomb/Means Index, as excerpted from a recent report.

Table 2: Historic Price Change						Table 3: Tax Rates (Effective March 1999)	
	1st Quarter 1997	3rd Quarter 1997	1st Quarter 1998	3rd Quarter 1998	1st Quarter 1999	VAT, GST, etc. Rates	
EUROPE						EUROPE	
Austria	97.4	97.4	100.9	102.1	102.4	Austria	15 %
Belgium	103.0	103.8	105.7	106.5	107.8	Belgium	21 %
Denmark	107.8	111.0	110.3	111.9	115.2	Denmark	25 %
Finland	112.2	117.8	121.1	126.1	135.6	Finland	22 %
France	105.2	105.9	106.8	107.9	108.4	France	20.6 %
Germany	98.8	96.8	101.6	102.3	101.6	Germany	16 %
Great Britain	107.4	113.7	119.4	121.0	125.3	Great Britain	17.5 %
Greece	116.9	121.6	124.9	129.9	131.7	Greece	18 %
Ireland	119.6	126.7	123.9	125.7	130.1	Ireland	12.5 %
Italy	105.1	143.2	143.2	110.4	113.2	Italy	20 %
Netherlands	101.1	103.6	103.2	104.3	106.9	Netherlands	17.5 %
Norway	107.8	110.5	111.0	114.4	116.0	Norway	23 %
Poland	145.3	156.6	187.2	195.0	205.0	Poland	22 %
Portugal	113.5	116.4	119.5	121.9	123.3	Portugal	17 %
Russia	113.8	113.8	117.5	118.6	111.6	Russia	20 %
Spain	103.7	104.4	108.1	108.8	111.5	Spain	16 %
Sweden	104.5	106.1	107.3	108.6	110.5	Sweden	25 %
Switzerland	102.2	102.5	105.2	106.2	107.3	Switzerland	7 %
Turkey	289.4	387.8	549.8	687.2	945.6	Turkey	15 %
AMERICAS						AMERICAS	
Brazil	n/a	n/a	n/a	n/a	n/a	Brazil	12-17 %
Canada	104.7	106.8	108.4	109.2	111.1	Canada	7 %
Mexico	177.1	190.4	199.3	209.2	227.2	Mexico	15 %
U.S.A.	109.2	110.9	113.8	115.5	117.5	U.S.A.	8.75 %
PACIFIC						PACIFIC	
Australia	111.9	114.7	124.5	128.2	132.1	Australia	5-30 %
Japan	95.5	93.5	96.5	96.0	94.8	Japan	5 %
Malaysia	105.7	112.1	126.9	133.9	123.9	Malaysia	5 %
New Zealand	107.8	106.2	107.8	106.2	107.2	New Zealand	12.5 %
Thailand	105.6	113.6	128.9	138.5	135.3	Thailand	10 %

Figure 4.5 Hanscomb/Means Index.

Cost-Estimating Tools

U.S. Department of Commerce

Two construction-related indexes are published by the U.S. Department of Commerce. The Composite Fixed-Weighted Index is a ratio of the annual value of new construction put-in-place in current dollars to comparable values in 1992. The index reflects change in price only. The Implicit Price Deflator is a similar index but reflects market conditions as well as price. Both are published monthly, and both reflect the national picture and do not break out individual cities.

Bureau of Reclamation

Known colloquially as BuRec, the Bureau of Reclamation, based in Denver, Colorado, publishes on a quarterly basis cost indexes for 34 different types of dam and water projects under its jurisdiction. It also publishes a general property index that measures costs for office and maintenance buildings associated with its projects. How the agency gathers or standardizes its data is not documented.

Factory Mutual Engineering

Factory Mutual Engineering, an organization based in Norwood, Massachusetts, produces semiannually a weighted aggregate cost index based on the wage rates of eight trades and costs of seven materials. The weight of the factors in the index is derived from an analysis of construction inputs to five typical industrial buildings, ranging from a one-story steel-framed warehouse to a multistory reinforced-concrete building. The index is an average of 164 locations across the United States. The organization also computes indexes for residential construction and industrial process machinery and equipment.

Handy Whitman

Originally published in 1934, the Handy Whitman index, published semiannually, is a six-region average index for a reinforced-concrete building. Published by Whitman, Requardt and Associates in Baltimore, Maryland, the index reflects materials prices for ready-mix concrete, lumber, steel bars, brick, concrete block, and wages for laborers and six skilled trades. The firm also publishes indexes for electric, gas, and water utilities.

Lee Saylor, Inc.

Lee Saylor Inc. publishes a monthly index based on information compiled by the Wallers Group in Sacramento, California; it provides two indexes: The first is the labor-material cost index that weighs labor and materials at 54 percent and 46 percent, respectively. The labor factor is based on quotes for nine trades (carpenters, bricklayers, iron workers, laborers, operating engineers, plasterers, plumbers, electricians, and teamsters) in 16 cities. The materials factor reflects 23 materials (aluminum sheet, bricks, concrete, PVC pipe, etc.) in 20 cities. The index can be subdivided by type of building—concrete, steel, or wood framing. The second index is the subcontractor index, which expresses an unweighted composite of in-place unit prices for 21 materials (acoustic tile, brick, gypsum wall board [GWB], ductwork, etc.); it is really a price index.

Department of Defense Area Cost Factors

The DOD publishes annually a list of Area Cost Factors (ACF) used to adjust costs geographically for program estimates. The ACF indexes are used as a guide for preparation and review of military construction and family housing budget cost estimates. The ACF of individual locations reflects a relative comparison to the ACF of 1.00 for the national average of 96 base cities (two cities per state in the continental United States). The ACF index lists the combination factors of local construction costs of labor, material, and equipment (LME), and seven other matrix factors such as weather, climate, seismic, mobilization, overhead and profit, labor availability, and labor productivity. The ACF indexes were not intended for annual comparisons. Furthermore, the construction community would likely question the use of internally generated index. An excerpt of the ACF is contained in Figure 4.6.

Available Output Price Indexes

The output price indexes that can be used as sources are described in the following subsections.

The Austin Company

Published quarterly in Cleveland, Ohio, the Austin Company's index is based on pricing in major industrial areas for two hypothetical projects: a 116,760 square-foot steel-framed industrial structure and an 8,325 square-foot office building. Estimates are based on labor and basic material costs including sitework, electrical, mechanical, HVAC, and process services. The specific methods for obtaining estimates and/or bids are not available.

Fru-Con Corporation

The index published monthly by the Fru-Con Corporation of Baldwin, Missouri, is based on an average industrial building in the St. Louis, Missouri, region, priced with the contractor's current material

TABLE B
AREA COST FACTOR INDICES
April 10, 2001

<u>**PART I - U.S. LOCATIONS**</u>

STATE		LOCATION	ACF INDEX
ALABAMA			0.85
		MOBILE	0.84
		MONTGOMERY	0.86
	(A)	ANNISTON ARMY DEPOT	0.84
	(A)	FORT MCCLELLAN	0.84
	(A)	FORT RUCKER	0.81
	(AF)	MAXWELL AIR FORCE BASE	0.86
	(N)	MOBILE AREA	0.84
	(A)	REDSTONE ARSENAL	0.86
ALASKA			1.59
		ANCHORAGE	1.49
		FAIRBANKS	1.69
	(N)	ADAK NAVAL STATION	2.35
	(AF)	CLEAR AIR FORCE BASE	1.88
	(AF)	EIELSON AIR FORCE BASE	1.69
	(AF)	ELMENDORF AIR FORCE BASE	1.49
	(A)	FORT GREELY	1.88
	(A)	FORT RICHARDSON	1.49
	(A)	FORT WAINWRIGHT	1.69
	(AF)	SHEMYA AIR FORCE BASE	2.42
ARIZONA			0.98
		FLAGSTAFF	0.98
		TUSCON	0.98
	(AF)	DAVIS MONTHAN AIR FORCE BASE	1.01
	(A)	FORT HUACHUCA	1.00
	(AF)	LUKE AIR FORCE BASE	0.98
	(A)	NAVAJO ARMY DEPOT	0.96
	(N)	YUMA MCAS	1.16
	(A)	YUMA PROVING GROUND	1.12
ARKANSAS			0.87
		FORT SMITH	0.85
		PINE BLUFF	0.89
	(A)	FORT CHAFFEE	0.84
	(AF)	LITTLE ROCK AIR FORCE BASE	0.83
	(A)	PINE BLUFF ARSENAL	0.89

Figure 4.6 Example of Department of Defense area cost factors.

and labor costs. Adjustments are made for changes in construction materials and building methods. The index is weighted using different percentages of labor, concrete, mortar, clay products, lumber, plastics, metals, paint, and glass. This index is obviously most beneficial for anyone contemplating a project in St. Louis.

Turner Construction Company

The Turner Construction Company, based in New York City, is one of the largest building contractors in the United States. It publishes quarterly an index based on actual selling prices that reflect current experience on labor rates, materials prices, labor productivity, management and plant efficiency, and competitive conditions. The company tracks these costs across the country, so the index is an average of all the areas canvassed. The index can, therefore, be a useful indicator of the national market, but it does not have a regional or city component that can be broken out and identified separately.

Smith Group

The Smith Group, an architecture/engineering firm based in Detroit, Michigan, publishes an index monthly that expresses actual in-place project costs. It uses building materials costs, freight rates, and skilled and unskilled labor rates. It also factors labor efficiency and premiums, bidding competition, contractor profit margins, and overhead. The weighting method is the result of reviewing actual contractor schedules of values over several years. The index is based on 60 percent labor and 40 percent material. It is not clear what building types are used, whether the same building plans are bid year after year, or how the data is standardized.

Marshall & Swift

From its Los Angeles, California, office, Marshall & Swift produces monthly an index that is an average of 100 U.S. cities combined into various regional, district, and national indexes. These indexes can be further subdivided into building types, as follows:

Fire-proofed steel
Reinforced concrete
Masonry
Wood
Preengineered steel frame

Selected materials, labor rates, taxes, business factors, and the cost of construction funds are factored into the indexes. Marshall & Swift also has regional indexes that include major cities.

E. H. Boeckh Company

Now a subsidiary of Marshall & Swift, just described, E. H. Boeckh is based in Milwaukee, Wisconsin. Its index covers 11 building types in 213 cities throughout the United States. It lists costs for 115 elements in each location—19 building trades, 89 materials, and 7 tax and insurance elements. Boeckh researches both union and merit shop wage rates, and the index uses the prevailing wage for a specific location. The index also combines five types of commercial and industrial buildings, to produce an average index.

Determining Which Index to Use: Cost versus Price

It is a challenge to determine which type of index to use when adjusting project costs. If a cost index such as Means or ENR will be applied, then a further adjustment may need to be made for differences in market conditions between locations. A price index can be applied, which in theory accounts for both recorded cost increases and market-applied increases (or decreases).

The following lists present national averages for selected cost and price indexes for the period January 2000 to January 2001:

Source	2000–2001 change
R. S. Means	+2.8%
Engineering News Record CCI: 20-city cost	+2.4%
Engineering News Record BCI: 20-city cost	+1.1%
Commerce Department: fixed, weighted	+4.1%
BuRec: general buildings	+0.4%
Handy-Whitman: general buildings	+1.6%
Lee Saylor, Inc.: material/labor	+3.6%
Average of the above	**+2.3%**

Published Construction Price Indexes

Source	2000–2001 change
Commerce Department: price deflator	+ 3.8%
Turner: general building	+ 4.1%
The Austin Co. (industrial)	+ 4.3%
Lee Saylor, Inc.; subcontractor	+ 8.4%
Smith Group: general	+ 3.0%
Average of the above	**+ 4.7%**

The variances in the above figures indicate the difficulty of applying an index to adjust for changes for a specific location and for differences in time. R. S. Means has possibly the most comprehensive set of indexes, covering numerous locations. However, as mentioned earlier, Means indexes track costs only, and cost indexes measure changes in material costs and labor and equipment rates only without necessarily reflecting supply and demand market issues. Further, the city cost indexes published by Means are only relative to a national average and are primarily used to compare costs between cities, although the indexes can be used to track cost changes in a particular city. ENR also has city-specific indexes but again these track only costs, not prices. Variations between indexes obviously exist. For the time period January 2000 and January 2001, ENR's index for Chicago, for example, increased by 3.8 percent, while R. S. Means increased by 2.48 percent.

Price indexes could potentially provide a more accurate comparison since they reflect both market conditions and the overall cost of construction. However, for a price index to be predictably accurate, the same project, or certainly very similar projects, would have to be repeatedly used for the analysis. Otherwise, discrepancies created by design differences, project size, building owner, and type of construction could skew the results. Clearly, the application of cost indexes requires careful judgment to assure that results are sensible and correct.

Applying Cost Indexes: Examples

Cost indexes can be applied in a number of different ways. For example, costs can be adjusted for variations:

➤ In the same city for different years
➤ In different cities for the same year
➤ In different cities for different years
➤ For given cities to a national average

The basic formula is as follows:

$$\text{Revised Cost} = \frac{(\text{Base Cost}) \times (\text{Revised Index})}{\text{Base Index}}$$

For example, let's look at an elementary school bid in St. Louis, Missouri, in July 1999, priced at $102.20 per square foot. What would the same design cost in Chicago, Illinois in 2001?

Cost Index: St. Louis July 1999 106.3
Chicago October 2001 130.8

Calculation: $\dfrac{\$102.20 \times 130.8}{106.3} = \$125.75$

Some cost indexes, such as Means Historical Construction Cost Indexes, may also be used to forecast costs by averaging annual index changes over any number of past years and then using the average over that period to calculate future costs. This process, known as *linear regression,* can be demonstrated hypothetically as follows:

Five-year history:
1996	100.2
1997	103.1
1998	105.4
1999	108.0
2000	110.7

Average increase over the five years
2.5% per year

Customizing Cost Indexes

Recently, there has been an effort in the federal government to examine cost increases that occur through inflation/escalation and to examine methods to exclude inflation from price offers and bidding. This issue is particularly important for projects of long duration, especially longer than three years.

A major renovation project in the Washington, D.C., area developed a method to adjust negotiated contract prices for economic changes that occur during the contract period. The method utilized an index based on a market basket consisting of material items and units of labor representative of the construction under consideration. The index is intended to reflect changes in overall construction cost by reflecting changes in the pricing of these items. Prices are monitored over time such that a percentage change in the index over the previous period of time would be applied to the contract to adjust contract prices for an equivalent period of time in the future. The intent of indexing for price changes is to remove some of the risk from those making offers and, thereby, secure more competitive offers.

Referencing Published Cost Information

No matter how sophisticated an organization is, there is always a need to use and reference standardized cost information. There are numerous sources available.

Table 4.1 contains sources for published cost information available as of 2001, along with the Web addresses and main telephone numbers. No attempt has been made to comment on the quality and reliability of the data. Additional information is available on the Association for the Advancement of Cost Engineering (AACE) Web site (www.aace.org).

Developing and Maintaining Cost Data Files

The effective utilization of historical cost information has been an industry objective for many years. In the early 1970s, the American Institute of archi-

Table 4.1

Published Cost Information Sources

Company	Contact Information
R. S. Means Company, Inc.	http://www.rsmeans.com 1-800-334-3509
Richardson Engineering Services, Inc.	http://www.resi.net/IndexBody.htm 480-497-2062
Craftsman Book Company, Inc.	http://www.craftsmanbook.com 1-800-829-8123
Saylor Publications, Inc.	http://www.saylor.com 1-800-624-3352
Bni Building News	http://www.bni-books.com 1-888-264-7483
Marshall & Swift	http://www.marshallswift.com/index.asp 1-800-451-2367
Frank R. Walker Company	http://www.frankrwalker.com 1-800-458-3737

tects (AIA) in conjunction with the General Services Administration (GSA) initiated the development of the system called MASTERCOST. The intent was to categorize and collect project information in a comprehensive manner such that architects and other designers could extract this information and use it for both budgeting purposes and for benchmarking in comparison to other projects. This ambitious program never achieved any degree of implementation for a number of reasons. The task of collecting and correctly interpreting the information using the then-limited capabilities of computers proved to be a daunting task. Concomitantly, the economy took a turn downward, making it more difficult to find funding for the project. Ultimately, it was abandoned.

Nonetheless, the principles behind the MASTERCOST effort remain viable today as does the need for the information. Publishers such as R. S. Means Company have helped to provide useful cost information to the construction industry in terms of project histories and modeling systems that are available. However, there is still no substitute for an organization categorizing and maintaining information on its own projects. It is actually rather alarming that an industry as large as the construction industry would have such a dearth of available information. As an industry, we simply do not have the ability to clearly state what it has cost to build buildings and other facilities; therefore, it is not surprising that we have such difficulty predicting the cost of facilities and buildings.

In terms of effort, it is not that difficult to collect project information and put it into a usable form. What is difficult is finding time to do it. Actual project cost information becomes available to designers and owners at the very end of the design process. No one likes to categorize cost information solely on the basis of estimates; everyone would prefer to have the cost information based on actual contract costs. Is it possible—and if so how—to gather actual contract cost information and make it usable?

The first difficulty that should be overcome again raises the issue discussed in Chapters 2 and 3: the format of the information. It is not feasible in the long run to utilize cost information in the Master-Format 16-division structure. As explained, it is very difficult, if not impossible, to compare similar projects made up of dissimilar materials and methods.

Any system of historical cost information would have to be grouped around an elemental format such as UNIFORMAT. Unfortunately, most historical information provided in schedules of values and breakdowns is in the 16-division format. What's the answer?

It is relatively easy to develop and utilize simple spreadsheets that will allow conversion of Master-Format-based information into UNIFORMAT structure as long as the MasterFormat structure is subdivided to allow for the breakout. Forms can be subdivided into 16 divisions and is further subdivided within each division according to major UNIFORMAT components. This makes it possible for contractors to submit costs in a format they are comfortable with, and at the same time allow for the completion of the UNIFORMAT costs.

Using this type of method, it becomes possible to extract schedule-of-values information and create historical data on project using UNIFORMAT. An example of the result of this complete approach is given in Figure 4.7. Figures 4.8 and 4.9 provide the backup in MasterFormat and UNIFORMAT to demonstrate how Figure 4.7 could be created. Note that Figure 4.7 is a building cost-model type format, and in addition to the cost figures and UNIFORMAT, a breakdown is also included of other parametric measures for each major system.

These measures give an additional method of interpretation of the costs of the facility. For example, the exterior wall costs per gross building area is approximately $7 per square foot, but the cost per wall square foot is approximately $17 per square foot for 31,000 square feet of wall. Another example is the HVAC cost that is approximately $13.50 per square

BUILDING COST SUMMARY

Project Description:	Elementary School, Virginia - Example 1					Bid Date:	11/96
Project Type:	School					Construction time(Months):	14
Gross Building Area:(GSF)	77,200					Market Conditions:	good

SYSTEM / ELEMENT DESCRIPTION	UNIFORMAT REFERENCE	TOTAL COST	COST PER GSF	% OF BUILDING	ELEMENTAL ANALYSIS			
					MEASURE	UNIT	VALUE	COST/UNIT
BUILDING:		b	b / GSF	b / 27			c	b / c
1 Foundations	(A10)	506,192	6.56	9.3%	Ground Floor Area	SF	77,200	6.56
2 Standard Foundations	(A1010)	302,142	3.91	5.6%	Ground Floor Area	SF	77,200	3.91
3 Other Foundations	(A1020)	-	-	0.0%	Ground Floor Area	SF	77,200	-
4 Slab on Grade	(A1030)	204,050	2.64	3.8%	Ground Floor Area	SF	77,200	2.64
5 Basement Construction	(A20)	-	-	0.0%	Ground Floor Area	SF	77,200	-
6 Substructure—Subtotal	(A)	506,192	6.56	9.3%	Ground Floor Area	SF	77,200	6.56
7 Superstructure	(B10)	400,900	5.19	7.4%	Gross Bldg. Area	SF	77,200	5.19
8 Exterior Enclosure	(B20)	537,917	6.97	9.9%	Gross Enclosure Area	SF	31,000	17.35
9 Roofing	(B30)	273,275	3.54	5.0%	Roof Surface Area	SF	80,000	3.42
10 Shell—Subtotal	(B)	1,212,092	15.70	22.3%	Gross Bldg. Area	SF	77,200	15.70
11 Interior Construction	(C10)	560,523	7.26	10.3%	Gross Bldg. Area	SF	77,200	7.26
12 Stairs	(C20)	-	-	0.0%	Gross Bldg. Area	SF	77,200	-
13 Interior Finishes	(C30)	394,833	5.11	7.3%	Gross Bldg. Area	SF	77,200	5.11
14 Interiors—Subtotal	(C)	955,356	12.38	17.6%	Gross Bldg. Area	SF	77,200	12.38
15 Conveying Systems	(D10)	7,288	0.09	0.1%	Total No. of Stops	EA	1	7,288
16 Plumbing	(D20)	447,800	5.80	8.2%	No. of Fixtures	EA	150	2,985
17 HVAC	(D30)	1,049,400	13.59	19.3%	Tons (or MBH)	EA	200	5,247
18 Fire Protection	(D40)	151,800	1.97	2.8%	Protected Area	SF	77,200	1.97
19 Electrical	(D50)	859,866	11.14	15.8%	Gross Bldg. Area	SF	77,200	11.14
20 Electrical Service & Distribution	(D5010)	182,120	2.36	3.4%	Connected KW	KW	650	280
21 Lighting & Branch Wiring	(D5020)	286,132	3.71	5.3%	Gross Bldg. Area	SF	77,200	3.71
22 Communications & Security	(D5030)	205,778	2.67	3.8%	Gross Bldg. Area	SF	77,200	2.67
23 Other Electrical Systems	(D5040)	185,836	2.41	3.4%	Gross Bldg. Area	SF	77,200	2.41
24 Services—Subtotal	(D)	2,516,154	32.59	46.3%	Gross Bldg. Area	SF	77,200	32.59
25 Equip. & Furnishings—Subtotal	(E)	211,210	2.74	3.9%	Gross Bldg. Area	SF	77,200	2.74
26 Spec. Construct. & Demo—Subtotal	(F)	28,500	0.37	0.5%	Gross Bldg. Area	SF	77,200	0.37
27 **TOTAL BUILDING**		$ 5,429,504	$ 70.33	100.0%	Accommodation Units	EA	750	$ 7,239
28 **SITEWORK & UTILITIES:**		-						
29 Site Preparation	(G10)	467,598	6.06	8.6%	Gross Site Area	SF	600,000	0.78
30 Site Improvements	(G20)	85,122	1.10	1.6%	Gross Site Area	SF	600,000	0.14
31 Site Mechanical Utilities	(G30)	301,500	3.91	5.6%	Gross Site Area	SF	600,000	0.50
32 Site Electrical Utilities	(G40)	-	-	0.0%	Gross Site Area	SF	600,000	-
33 Other Site Construction	(G50)	-	-	0.0%	Gross Site Area	SF	600,000	-
34 **TOTAL SITEWORK & UTILITIES:**	(G)	854,220	11.07	15.7%	Gross Site Area	SF	600,000	1.42
35 General Conditions, Overhead & Profit @ 5.1%		322,647	4.18	5.9%				
36 **TOTAL FACILITY COST - CURRENT**		$ 6,606,371	$ 85.57	121.7%	Accommodation Units	EA	750	$ 8,808
37 Contingency @		-	-	0.0%				
38 Escalation @		-	-	0.0%				
39								
40 **TOTAL FACILITY COST - PROJECTED**		$ 6,606,371	$ 85.57	121.7%	Accommodation Units	EA	750	$ 8,808

Parameters:		Measure	Value	Area Analysis:	Area (SF)
1	Gross Bldg. Area	SF	77,200		
2	Ground Floor Area	SF	77,200	Basement	-
3	Gross Enclosure Area	SF	31,000	Ground Floor	77,200
4	Percent Fenestration	%	12%	Upper Floors	
5	Roof Surface Area	SF	80,000	Penthouses	
6	Total No.of Conveying Stops	STOPS	1	Other Areas	-
7	Tons Cooling (or MBH Htg)	TONS	200		
8	No. of Plumbing Fixtures	EA	150	Gross Floor Area	77,200
9	Fire Protected Area	SF	77,200		
10	Connected KW	KW	650		
11	Accommodation Units	EA	750		
12	Floor to Floor Height (Avg.)	LF	12		
13	Gross Site Area	SF	600,000		
14	Gross Bldg. Area/ Accommodation Units	SF/EA	103		-

Figure 4.7 Building cost summary prepared from historical information.

Project _____ **Architect** _____ **Project No.** _____
Owner _____ **Contractor** _____ **Date** _____

Item Description	UNIFORMAT Ref.	Item Amount
1 GENERAL REQUIREMENTS		
a. Mobilization & initial expenses	(Total)	(44,629)
b. Site overhead & fee	(Total)	367,276
		322,647
2 SITEWORK		
b. Subsurface investigation & clearing	(G10)	54,128
c. Site & building demolition	(G10)	
d. Building elements demolition	(F20)	
e. Grading & earthwork (site)	(G10)	413,470
f. Excavation & backfill (foundations)	(A1010)	
g. Excavation & backfill (basement)	(A2010)	
h. Fill below grade slab	(A1030)	
i. Rock excavation	(A1020)	
Pile foundations		
Shoring		
Underpinning		
Site drainage		
Foundation drainage		
Dewatering		
Paving, landscaping		
Off-site work		
Railroad, marine		
3 CONCRETE		
a.–f. Conc. forms		
g.–j. Conc. fin		
Precast conc		
Cementitious decks		
4 MASONRY		
a. Masonry foundations	(A1010)	409,659
b. Masonry basement walls	(B10)	96,553
c. Masonry exterior walls	(B10)	664,462
d. Masonry interior partitions	(C20)	14,500
e. Interior paving & finish	(C1030)	
f. Exterior paving & masonry (site work)	(G20)	775,495
5 METALS		
a. Structural steel in foundations	(A1010)	
b. Structural steel framing	(B10)	363,300
c. Metal joists & decking	(B10)	
d. Metal stairs	(C20)	
e. Misc. & ornamental metal (building)	(C1030)	
f. Misc. & ornamental metal (site work)	(G20)	363,308

Item Description	UNIFORMAT Ref.	Item Amount
6 WOOD & PLASTICS		
a. Rough carpentry (framing & decking)	(B10)	37,600
b. Rough carpentry interior wall	(B2010)	
c. Rough carpentry (partitions)	(C1010)	
d. Rough carpentry (roof, other than framing & decking)	(B30)	
f. Heavy timber & prefab. structural wood	(B10)	
f. Exterior wood siding & trim	(B2010)	59,200
h. Fin. carpentry, millwork & cabinet work	(C1030)	
h. Wood paneling	(C30)	
i. Wood stairs	(C20)	
j. Plastic fabrications	(C1030)	96,800
7 THERMAL & MOISTURE PROTECTION		
9 FINISHES		
a. Lath & plaster (exterior)	(B2010)	17,889
b. Lath & plaster (interior)	(C30)	39,500
c. Gypsum wallboard partitions	(C1010)	
d. Gypsum wallboard finishes	(C3010)	
e. Tile & terrazzo	(C30)	84,167
f. Acoustical ceilings & treatment	(C3030)	73,250
g. Wood flooring	(C3020)	
h. Resilient flooring	(C3020)	72,856
i. Carpeting	(C3020)	125,060
j. Exterior coatings	(B2010)	
k. Interior special flooring & coatings	(C3020)	
l. Interior painting & wall covering	(C3010)	412,722

Item Description	UNIFORMAT Ref.	Item Amount
10 SPECIALTIES		
a. Chalkboards & tackboards	(C1030)	30,549
b. Compartments & cubicles	(C1010)	8,660
c. Signs & supergraphics	(C1010)	12,100
d. Partitions	(C1010)	
e. Lockers	(E20)	650
f. Toilet, bath, wardrobe accessories	(C1030)	14,700
g. Sun control devices	(B2010)	
h. Access flooring	(C3020)	496
i. Miscellaneous specialties	(C1030)	2,297
j. Flagpoles	(G20)	69,452
		205,240
11 EQUIPMENT (specify)	(E10)	1,649,000

16 ELECTRICAL

Item Description	UNIFORMAT Ref.	Item Amount
a. Utilities & serv. ent. to 5 ft. of bldg.	(G40)	
b. Substations & transformers	(D5010)	182,120
c. Distribution & panel boards	(D5010)	202,020
d. Lighting fixtures	(D5020)	
e. Branch wiring & devices	(D5020)	84,112
f. Special electrical systems	(D5040)	185,836
g. Communications	(D5030)	205,778
h. Electric heating	(D5040)	859,866
	TOTAL $	**6,606,371**

189

Figure 4.8 Completed MasterFormat schedule of values.

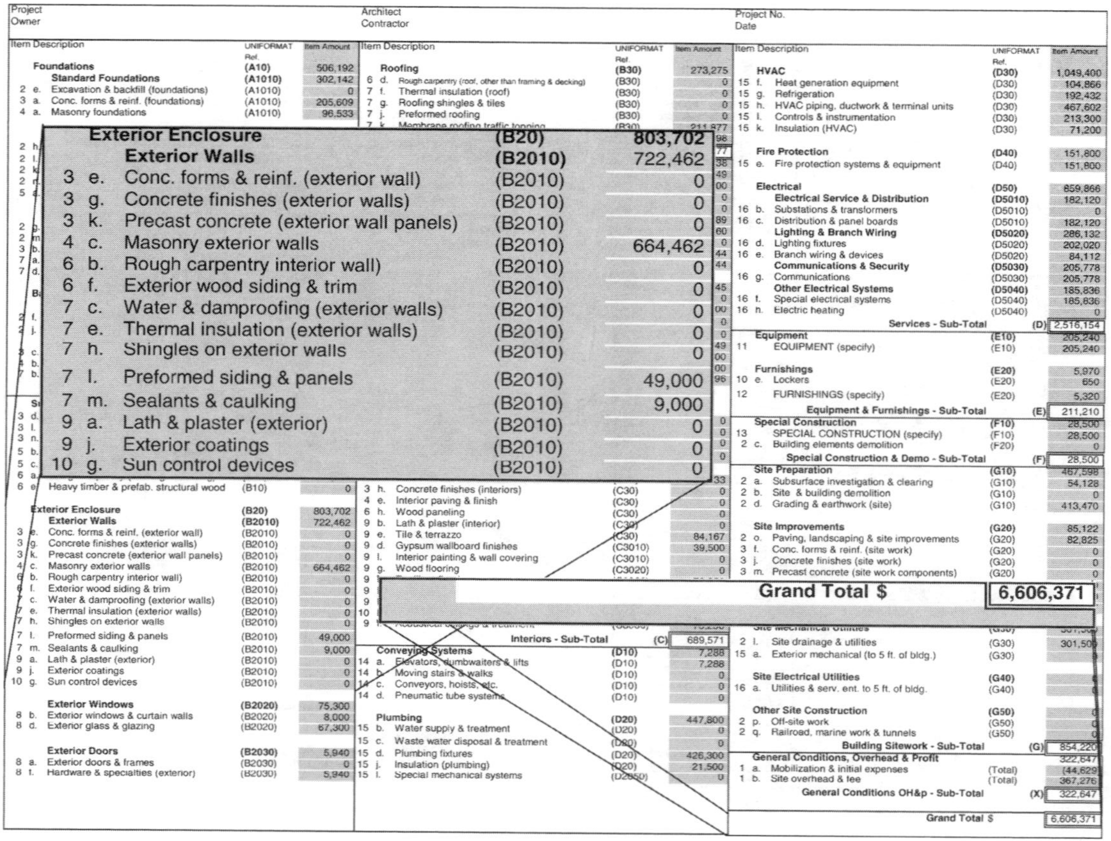

Figure 4.9 Completed UNIFORMAT schedule of values.

foot, and a little over $5,000 per installed ton of A/C (200 tons). These measures are extremely useful as both a check and budgeting device. The importance of measuring and collecting this information cannot be overstated.

Comparable historical costs can be obtained from several published sources, including R. S. Means, as shown in Figure 3.20 (page 110).

Doing Computer-Assisted Estimating

Numerous computer-assisted estimating programs are available for installation on personal computers. No consensus has formed on a superior program, as the choice is a highly personal one dependent on how it will be used. For example, an installing subcontractor will not have the same interests or needs as a general contractor, or for that matter, a designer. And it is important to point out that many of these programs have been designed for contractors, hence have limited benefit to a designer, cost consultant, or owner.

Most users probably will make the move to computer-aided cost estimating step-by-step, typically in these increments:

- ► Simple word processing and calculating programs
- ► Spreadsheet programs
- ► Estimating organization and analytical systems
- ► Database programs
- ► Digitizer programs
- ► Computer-assisted design (CAD) integrated systems

Spreadsheets and word processors offer total flexibility for formatting and estimating approach, but the opportunity for mathematical and other errors is relatively high. Software that is designed for cost estimating will generally limit the ability to define the approach and formatting of the estimate, but there are fewer opportunities for mathematical and other errors.

Full implementation of CAD-integrated systems is still a long way off. It will require the designer to utilize object-oriented CAD. While this will have long-term benefits to the designer, it is more time-consuming to prepare documents using object-oriented CAD.

Some larger design firms and owners and contractors have developed their own computer packages, in many cases, at great expense. If an organization can afford to develop its own software, of course it can prove highly beneficial. But, often, the amount of money necessary to develop an in-house software program is significantly more than anybody reasonably can estimate. The point is, care should be exercised before undertaking such development.

Estimating Software Vendors

Many software vendors produce estimating programs; a good place to begin the investigation into sources is by calling those named on the following partial list.

Building System Design (BSD)	1-800-875-0047
G2, Inc.	1-800-657-6312
Management Computer Controls (MC2)	1-800-225-5622
Timberline Software Corp.	1-800-628-6583
US COST, Inc.	1-800-955-1385
Winestimator, Inc.	1-800-950-2374
Design 4/Cost, DC&D Technologies, Inc.	1-800-685-9555
Talisman Partners PACES System	1-303-771-3103

It's also a good idea to visit the AACE Web site for further information (www.aace.org).

R. S. Means also offers a very useful service called DemoSource that allows a user to investigate various software programs online, at www.rsmeans.com/demo.

Conclusions

This chapter presented the importance of acquiring good information, how to obtain cost data, and how to work with cost information within your organization. Published sources of cost information were identified, and specific techniques were presented to organize and assemble historical cost information.

Chapters 1 through 4 provided the essential background, concepts, and methodology that make up the cost management process. Essentially, these represent the tools in the toolbox. The next chapter presents an organized approach to coordinating and applying these tools as part of an overall cost management approach. Particular focus will be on the early planning and conceptual/schematic phases of the development of a project, but the entire design and construction process will be addressed. Additional information on the impact of alternate delivery methods will also be presented. Particular focus will be on integrating and coordinating cost management into the overall project delivery process.

Cost Management Methodology

5

Cost estimating, value engineering, and life-cycle costing are all useful tools, as are the numerous sources of information and methods used to analyze the information they produce. Cost management is the application of all these tools within an overall project management structure. It is an organized and focused application intended to address project challenges while remaining sensitive to how decisions interrelate. The objective of cost management is to maintain a balance and alignment of scope, user/owner expectations, and budget from the outset and over time. To explain how to achieve that objective, the key topics addressed in this chapter are:

- ▶ Integrating the cost management process
- ▶ Budgeting and cost planning
- ▶ Managing costs during design
- ▶ Implementing construction phase cost management
- ▶ Understanding the impact of delivery methods on cost management

This chapter also addresses how to utilize these tools effectively as part of the overall cost management approach to help assure that owner demands for more effective cost management are satisfied.

Integrating the Cost Management Process

An essential principal of effective cost management is the integration of cost management into the overall design and delivery process. If cost management is treated as an afterthought of design and construction decisions, then it is, effectively, "reactive management," a practice that makes it difficult to achieve good value in decision making. Therefore, integrating cost management into the overall delivery process is the first step of effective cost management. Figure 5.1 presents a chart that depicts the overall integrated cost management approach. Figures 5.1(a) to 5.1(c) present the process as applied to Planning and Programming; Concept Development and Schematic Design; and Design Development and Construction Documents, respectively. The process is based on several key principles:

Developing a Realistic Budget
- ▸ Developing a budget that connects and aligns scope and expectations is the first and perhaps most important step in the process.
- ▸ Any budget should be subdivided into the disciplines that control decisions within the overall design.
- ▸ Each discipline should have an individual budget, as well as key parameters and drivers of their respective budget. Management of the

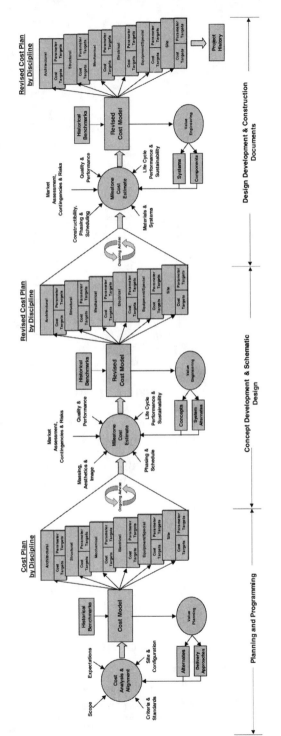

Figure 5.1 Integrated cost management approach.

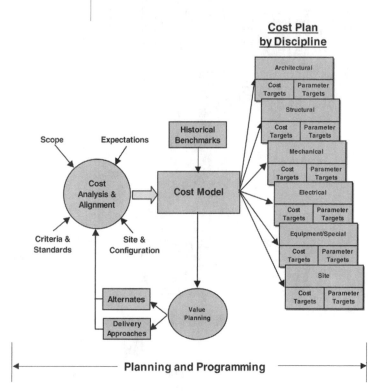

Figure 5.1(a) Integrated cost management approach (Planning and Programming).

process focuses on these key parameters and drivers, as well as the budget for the discipline.

Obtaining Advice and Cost Input on an Ongoing Basis

➤ Decisions should be reviewed for cost implications as they are made.

➤ Reviewing the cost implications of decisions on an ongoing basis requires that cost management input be provided on an ongoing basis; it cannot be removed from the design process.

Setting Accurate Milestone Estimates

➤ Estimates are prepared at the conclusion of each major phase of design and may require reconciliation among several parties.

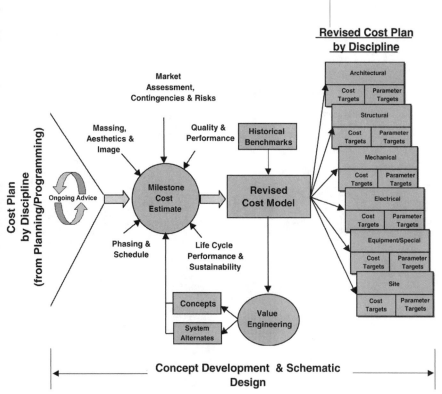

Figure 5.1(b) Integrated cost management approach (Concept Development and Schematic Design).

- ▶ A final reconciled estimate results in the redistribution and reassessment of the budget assigned to each discipline in an updated cost plan.

- ▶ The process starts again and becomes progressively more detailed at each phase of design.

- ▶ Historical cost analysis and benchmarking can provide an additional measure of confidence and justification for the estimates.

Implementing Value Engineering as a Cost Management Tool

- ▶ VE can be utilized both as an optimization tool and as a means to maintain alignment among competing design issues.

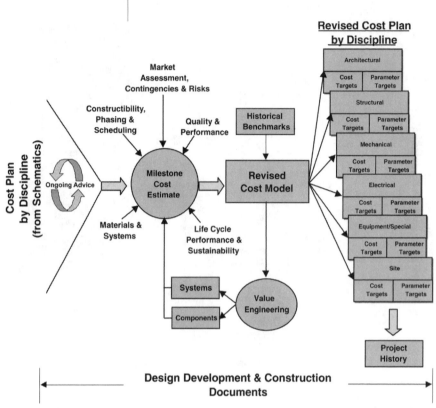

Figure 5.1(c) Integrated cost management approach (Design Development and Construction Documents).

▶ Sound, team-based value engineering is an indispensable tool for maintaining alignment, effecting change, and making adjustments, without compromising critical aspects of the design.

▶ VE focus should narrow as the design develops, adjusting from conceptual issues to detailed issues, materials, and systems.

Being Sensitive to Life-cycle Costs and Sustainability

▶ Industry professionals need to pay closer attention to life-cycle performance in facility design.

- An organized approach, in conjunction with proper economics, should be taken to address issues of energy efficiency, sustainability, and reliability.
- Life-cycle costing is a recognized method of properly comparing competing alternatives during the development of the design and, hence, should be included as an important component of ongoing cost advice.

Planning Sensibly for Risk and Contingencies

- Contingency planning is an essential element of overall cost management and should be addressed early in the process and diligently managed throughout the process.
- Risk management is an important tool for understanding how to establish contingencies and for focusing attention on important aspects of the design.
- As the design progresses, risks and contingencies will minimize but will likely remain part of the process.

Focusing on Cost Drivers

- Focusing on the key cost drivers is achieved by identifying individual cost targets for each discipline and key parameter targets for each discipline.
- The effort involves a constant balancing process, and recognizes that meeting overall cost targets may require a certain amount of trade-offs and adjustments between disciplines.
- Details are important but attention should focus on "big picture" issues.

Planning, Programming, and Budgeting

Budgeting and cost planning together comprise the first step in the process of cost management that starts during planning and programming [see Figure 5.1(a)]. The importance of effective budgeting cannot be overstated; simply put, if the budget is flawed in any way, it is highly unlikely that the design process can repair those flaws without substantial effort. In the long run, investing the time and effort it takes to draw up a realistic budget will be rewarded many times over the life of the project.

What are the characteristics of a sound budget? The answer is fourfold:

> *The budget is the single most important figure prepared over the life of the project.* It sets the stage for all future activities and will be remembered by all those who participated in its development and those who received it for financial purposes. Memories are long when it comes to budgets.

> *A budget may have many uses.* Often, a project cannot be initiated without a budget. In many cases, major macro-level financial alternatives will be calculated on the basis of budget input; and return on investment (ROI) calculations may hinge on budget investment.

> *A budget contains sufficient definition and documentation for comparison and analysis during the life of the project.* A budget that is insufficiently defined will lead to confusion and, potentially, arguments over what the actual basis of the budget was and is. Therefore, it is essential that the basis of all significant budgetary decisions be clearly and accurately defined and documented.

➤ *Conversely, the characteristics of an unsound budget reflect a lack of documentation and, in many cases, an overly optimistic determination of what is financially reasonable.* This may include selecting as a baseline for a budget facilities that do not represent actual programmatic requirements of facilities in the future, or where changing expectations are not reflected in budgetary requirements. In other words, unsound budgets are almost always misaligned.

How long it takes to prepare a budget will vary from the private sector to the public sector and often within each sector. Driving influences on public sector budgeting often have more to do with financial appropriations than they do with project necessities. The federal government uses a variety of budgetary documents, many of which are intended for congressional review and oversight. Figure 5.2 provides an example of what the Defense Department uses as an appropriation method. It shows the cover sheet of what is commonly referred to as a 1391 document; it provides background and discussion of the requirements of the project and may be prepared on a very conceptual level or be backed up by as much as 35 percent design. All projects that flow through the Defense Department are budgeted and reviewed using the 1391.

The General Services Administration (GSA) prepares what is called a Program Development Study (PDS; formerly, a Prospectus Development Study) as a basis of budgeting and defining projects for the federal government. The PDS defines the scope and requirements of federal projects, in particular federal courthouses that represent some of the most complicated projects built by GSA. The PDS is prepared on

1. Component	FY 2002 MILITARY CONSTRUCTION PROGRAM		2. Date
NAVY			3/21/2000

3. Installation and Location/UIC: N00210	4. Project Title
RTC GREAT LAKES, IL	INFRASTRUCTURE PHASE 1

5. Program Element	6. Catagory Code	7. Project Number	8. Project Cost
	851.10	746	6,900

9. COST ESTIMATES

Item	U/M	Quantity	Unit Cost	Cost ($000)
INFRASTRUCTURE PHASE 1		-	-	-
SUPPORTING FACILITIES	LS	-	-	6,510
SPECIAL CONSTRUCTION FEATURES	LS	-	-	(2,750)
ELECTRICAL	LS	-	-	(900)
MECHANICAL UTILITIES	LS	-	-	(2,280)
PAVING AND SITE IMPROVEMENT	LS	-	-	(580)
DEMOLITION	LS	-	-	-

SUBTOTAL	-	-	-	6,510
Contingency (0.0%)	-	-	-	-

TOTAL CONTRACT COST	-	-	-	6,510
Supervision Inspection & Overhead (6.0%)	-	-	-	390

TOTAL REQUEST	-	-	-	6,900
EQUIPMENT FROM OTHER APPROPRIATIONS		-	(NON-ADD)	-

Guidance Unit Cost Analysis

Category Code	U/M	Guidance Cost	Guidance Size	Project Scope	Size Factor	Area Cost Factor	Unit Cost
851.10 N/A		0	0	0	0	0	0

Not available. This work is supporting facilities only.

10. Description of Proposed Construction

    This project supports the program to recapitalize existing RTC facilities. This is the first of three phases for the overall project. It will modify utility systems at RTC Great Lakes and extend roads and utility systems to serve 57 acres of adjacent property being acquired from the Veterans Administration for new facility construction. This project provides roads on the VA land and includes a vehicular and pedestrian underpass below the existing railroad, sanitary and storm sewer systems, extension of the low pressure potable water system from RTC, overhead electrical power distribution, street lighting, and a conduit system for

(Continued On DD 1391C)

DD 1 Dec 76 Form **1391**

Page No. 2

Figure 5.2 Example of a 1391 budgeting document.

                                                Cost Management Methodology

the basis of either GSA form 3596, for new construction, or form 3597, for major renovations.

The process is initiated with a space request that defines the basic requirements of a GSA tenant in terms of types of space. Once a space request has been received from clients, or a change to the space has been identified, the GSA regional office undertakes a *feasibility study*. The feasibility study identifies basic requirements, analyzes project alternatives, evaluates alternative delivery methods, and recommends preferred solutions. The feasibility study is generally based upon several prior studies (such as seismic, building condition assessment, historic, environmental, or hazardous materials) that provide the basis for defining the scope and costs of alternatives. If the project is deemed to have further merit, a PDS is undertaken. The PDS is intended to:

- ▶ Establish project scope requirements

- ▶ Set an initial implementation strategy

- ▶ Establish the project budget

- ▶ Provide cost estimates for tenant improvements (TI) that may be paid directly by the tenant

- ▶ Define and establish GSA financial viability for the project, including income stream projections, since GSA's "income" is in the form of rent paid by the federal tenant

The prospectus is a two- or three-page synopsis of the PDS prepared by GSA to request congressional funding for the project. The document outlines the space need, scope, schedule for execution, overall projected project budget, and dollar amount requested for funding in the current fiscal year. After the PDS and prospectus have been prepared, the project will be considered for evaluation and inclusion in the annual GSA fiscal budget request. The final GSA budget request submission is sent to the Office of Management and Budget (OMB) for consideration in the president's budget request to Congress for the Executive Branch. The president's budget request will then be sent to the Hill, where Congress will decide which initiatives will be approved (authorized) and funded (appropriated). Only when a project has been fully authorized and money has been appropriated by Congress does the project begin. Generally, projects proceed through the appropriation cycle twice: once to receive approval and funding for design and site acquisition, and again to receive approval and funding for construction. Figure 5.3 provides an example of the cover sheet from a GSA form 3596 used as part of the PDS process.

Other federal agencies and state and municipal governments have funding processes similar to those used by the Defense Department and by GSA. The process in almost every case requires a budget estimate to be submitted as part of an appropriation process. In some cases, these budgets are developed on the basis of detailed analysis and project investigation; in other cases, projects will be budgeted using historical costs from other similar projects or even on the basis of the unit cost analysis setting limits.

Private sector budgeting techniques may be similar to those of the federal government or very different; for example, those that use a process that is part of an in-depth pro forma analysis wherein the facility being budgeted may be a relatively small portion of the overall pro forma. Figure 5.4 presents a hypothetical pro forma analysis for an office building. In this example, the amount of allocation for construction is a function of desired goals for return on investment and projected income and expenses.

PROJECT COST SUMMARY			
UNIFORMAT SYSTEM ELEMENTS		COST	COST/GSF
A10 Foundations		$0.00	$0.00
A20 Basement Construction		$0.00	$0.00
B10 Superstructure		$0.00	$0.00
B20 Exterior Enclosure		$0.00	$0.00
B30 Roofing		$0.00	$0.00
C05 Interior Construction		$0.00	$0.00
D10 Conveying Systems		$0.00	$0.00
D15 Mechanical		$0.00	$0.00
D50 Electrical		$0.00	$0.00
E05 Equipment & Furnishings		$0.00	$0.00
F05 Special Construction & Demo		$0.00	$0.00
G5 Building Sitework		$0.00	$0.00
Sub Total	A	$0.00	
Excavation		$0.00	
B & O Tax @ 2%	B	$0.00	
Escalation Allowance		$0.00	
Reservations (Art In Arch.) 0.5% @ A+B		$0.00	
Contingency (Construction) 5% @ A+B	C	$0.00	
ECC (A + B + C)	D	$0.00	
EDRC		$0.00	
EMIC		$0.00	
ESC (Est. Site Cost)		$0.00	
ETPC	E	$0.00	
Date Prepared: / /		Estimate Escalation Date: / /	

Jul-99   GSA Form 3596(Updt)

Figure 5.3 Sample GSA Form 3596 as part of a PDS.

Private sector budgeting will often be based on what can reasonably be spent on construction, then be justified by cash flow projections and return on investment expectations. This approach, however, may deliver a budget that proves extremely unrea-

Pro Forma Analysis
Hypothetical Office Building
Interest Rate = 10%
Period (Years) 20

Item	Budget
Total Construction Costs	34,757,000
Indirect Costs	9,249,000
Land Costs	4,480,000
Total Project Cost	48,486,000
Less Mortgage Loan	40,956,000
Equity Investment Required	7,530,000
Gross Income	8,850,000
Operating Costs	3,110,000
Net Income	5,740,000
Less Mortgage Payment (Debt Service)	4,305,000
Before Tax Stabilized Cash Flow	1,435,000
Return on Equity Investment (Simple)	19.1%

Loan Calculation @ 75% of Capitalized Income	40,956,000
PV Factor= 9.5136	

Figure 5.4 Example of a pro forma calculation.

sonable once specific expectations are placed on the project.

When the budget and the expectations of the project are drastically out of balance, the result may be cancellation or abandonment of the project. Industrial organizations that find themselves in this situation may be required to rethink the project or do a reassessment of the cash flow in order to justify the project construction costs. Recently, some of the most complex construction ever undertaken has involved wafer fabrication plants in high-tech businesses. Many of these projects have construction costs that have exceeded $1 billion and have been undertaken on the basis of expectations of sale of product that may change several times over the life of the construction. Recent experience in high-tech projects has shown that the product's competitive life cycle in the market place may be six months or less, in comparison to a typical construction life cycle that may be in excess of two years. It is not surprising that such projects face myriad difficulties.

The point here is that the amount of information available for budgeting or required in the budgeting process may vary quite substantially, as itemized in Figure 5.5. Budgets may be prepared on the basis of completely detailed programs or only on the basis of an approximate accommodation. Likewise, performance and quality expectations may be well defined or be virtually unspecified. Other driving factors, such as the selection of delivery method and project schedule, can vary dramatically.

From the perspective of the cost manager, two issues emerge. The first is the validity of the budget in the first place and the ability to deliver the project within that budget amount. The second is the ability to communicate the expectations of the budget to the eventual design team, regardless of the viability

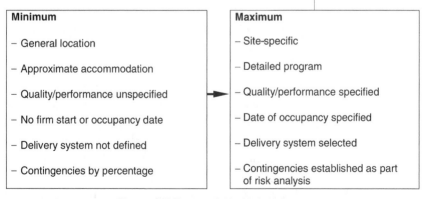

Minimum	Maximum
– General location	– Site-specific
– Approximate accommodation	– Detailed program
– Quality/performance unspecified	– Quality/performance specified
– No firm start or occupancy date	– Date of occupancy specified
– Delivery system not defined	– Delivery system selected
– Contingencies by percentage	– Contingencies established as part of risk analysis

Figure 5.5 Data available for budgeting.

of the budget. For even if the budget is completely attainable given the expectations of the project and scope, if this cannot be accurately communicated to the design team, the project may be substantially jeopardized if the design team makes choices not compatible with budget assumptions.

In order to be successful, then, a good budget should:

➤ *Reflect scope.* The scope should be accurately defined and recorded; it should also reflect proper steps to include grossing factors and other issues driving project size.

➤ *Reflect quality/performance expectations.* Quality and performance expectations should be accurately reflected and documented and be consistent with project issues for comparison purposes.

➤ *Reflect owner's value objectives.* The aspects of quality and performance should reflect those of the owner. It is unreasonable to expect that a high-end project owner will accept moderate or low-end value objectives, or to expect that a modest project owner will be willing to pay for high-end performance objectives. This aspect is not scientific; rather it is reflective of human nature.

➤ *Be achievable and accepted.* The importance of having an achievable budget that has been accepted by the major participants cannot be overstated. Many problem projects in the federal government can be traced to an unrealistic budget that was subsequently rejected at the congressional level. In the private sector, such projects are likewise rejected by executive constituencies such as a board of directors.

➤ *Be defensible.* Budgets may need to be defended in public forums, inside private organizations, or to key constituents. In many instances, realistic budgets for project requirements may not be defensible because they exceed accepted norms or deviate from previous patterns. It may be necessary to anticipate such issues and be prepared to defend a project because of its importance regardless if the project varies from accepted standards.

▶ *Contain adequate reserves.* Defining and including adequate contingencies and reserves is critical. The budgeting process will tend to avoid the definition of contingencies and risks that may be undesirable or may reflect situations that are unlikely. Nevertheless, the budgeting process should reflect what can happen and have a reasonable plan for laying aside reserves in case of unexpected events. Large public and private organizations will expect to expend some monies on projects for unexpected circumstances— which is not to say they will do so on all projects for unexpected circumstances.

▶ *Avoid being "socially acceptable."* Experience has proven repeatedly that a "socially acceptable" budget—that is, the budget everyone *wants* to see—will at best delay the inevitable. Many projects are controversial or contain controversial components or aspects that have an impact on budget and tend to raise cost. In an effort to avoid discord or public debates over these controversial aspects, organizations will opt to exclude them from a budget and present financial figures consistent with everybody's expectations but that perhaps are not reflective of the actual needs of the project.

▶ *Avoid playing it too safe.* The opposite of the socially acceptable budget is the budget that

WARNING

A "socially acceptable" budget—that is, the budget everyone wants to see—will at best delay the tries to cover all the bases, containing contingencies, extras, and allowances for every conceivable circumstance. Playing it too safe in this way may doom the project before launch because the costs will be so excessive that there is no probability of going forward. Though it is prudent and sensible to *consider* all potential impacts on a budget, it is not wise to *include* them all in the budget under the premise that they all will occur. The resulting contingency will likely be more than the project can bear and is not necessarily a realistic reflection of what will actually happen.

▶ *Contain a "bridge" to ongoing cost control.* The bridge to ongoing cost control and cost management is that which will allow a realistic budget to result in a successful project. Conversely, an unrealistic budget will prevent an early identification and correction process from beginning. Building this bridge is a critical component of the cost management process. It is a *cost plan* that will be described later in this chapter.

Budgeting Methods

Chapter 4 described a number of estimating methods that can be used in the budgeting process. Most budgets today are based either on historical costs or on some form of feasibility study. The feasibility study (for example, GSA's PDS) in some circumstances can be based on a sizable amount of research, analysis, and predesign effort. From an estimating point of view, the effort involved in preparing an estimate for this type of feasibility study is very similar to the schematic design estimate prepared during the design process; it will be described later in this chapter. The other two methods that can be utilized are the historical cost method and the functional space program method, both of which were described in Chapter 3, and are addressed again in the following subsections.

Historical Cost Method

The historical cost method, as its name implies, relies on project histories to create a database or a collection of information on which future projects will be budgeted. The implementation of this method can be as simple as collecting historical cost per square foot or historical accommodation costs such as cost per garage stall; or the system can be designed to collect detailed project histories categorized by elements, or possibly by trades, for later retrieval. As a general rule, the historical method works best with projects whose programs and functional requirements are similar. Schools are excellent examples of the type of project where the historical cost method can be utilized as a basis for budgeting future projects.

When using this method, it is important to ensure that the historical costs collected are complete and representative of the total scope of the project; in use, it is essential that the process take into account economic shifts and market conditions between the time that the referenced project was bid and constructed and the time of utilization. These techniques were described in Chapter 3.

As an example, consider the sample project presented in Figure 5.6, an elementary school located in the Virginia suburbs of the Washington, D.C., area. This school, bid in November 1996, consisted of 77,200 square feet and supported 750 students. The cost-accumulation methods shown previously in

TIP

It is important to ensure that the historical costs collected are complete and representative of the total scope of the project.

Figures 4.8 and 4.9, demonstrate how a schedule of values can be utilized as a basis of historical costs. These forms could be utilized to prepare the example in Figure 5.6. Extending the process another step would be to create a complete data file for multiple projects of a similar program. Figures 5.7(a) and (b) summarize five similar elementary school projects collected over a five-year period from 1993 to 1997.

Individual costs were adjusted for inflation (calculated at 3 percent per year) and for market conditions (6 percent was added for "excellent" market conditions; 6 percent was deducted for "poor" market conditions). Note that although this is a mathematical process, a great deal of judgment is involved, and there are no absolute or correct approaches. The point is, a cost manager is expected to adjust and modify costs as necessary to represent realistic conditions. Obviously, it would be unreasonable not to adjust for inflation, just as it would be unreasonable to treat abnormal market conditions existing at the time of bidding as representative of those at the time of the study.

This historical data file can be used for budgeting new projects. Consider the following sample budgetary problem of an elementary school:

- ▶ Gross floor area equals 65,000 square feet.

- ▶ Footprint area equals 65,000 square feet.

- ▶ Exterior closure area equals 25,000 square feet.

- ▶ Roof area equals 67,000 square feet.

- ▶ Bid date equals April 2001.

- ▶ Construction equals 14 months.

Selecting from the sample projects contained in the database, the information presented in Figure 5.8 is a potential result of the budgeting process. The

BUILDING COST SUMMARY

Project Description:	**Elementary School, Virginia - Example 1**		Bid Date:	11/96
Project Type:	**School**		Construction time(Months):	14
Gross Building Area:(GSF	77,200		Market Conditions:	good

	SYSTEM / ELEMENT DESCRIPTION	UNIFORMAT REFERENCE	TOTAL COST	COST PER GSF	% OF BUILDING	ELEMENTAL ANALYSIS MEASURE	UNIT	VALUE	COST/UNIT
	BUILDING:		b	b / GSF	b / 27			c	b / c
1	Foundations	(A10)	506,192	6.56	9.3%	Ground Floor Area	SF	77,200	6.56
2	Standard Foundations	(A1010)	302,142	3.91	5.6%	Ground Floor Area	SF	77,200	3.91
3	Other Foundations	(A1020)	-	—	0.0%	Ground Floor Area	SF	77,200	-
4	Slab on Grade	(A1030)	204,050	2.64	3.8%	Ground Floor Area	SF	77,200	2.64
5	Basement Construction	(A20)	-	—	0.0%	Ground Floor Area	SF	77,200	-
6	Substructure—Subtotal	(A)	506,192	6.56	9.3%	Ground Floor Area	SF	77,200	6.56
7	Superstructure	(B10)	400,900	5.19	7.4%	Gross Bldg. Area	SF	77,200	5.19
8	Exterior Enclosure	(B20)	537,917	6.97	9.9%	Gross Enclosure Area	SF	31,000	17.35
9	Roofing	(B30)	273,275	3.54	5.0%	Roof Surface Area	SF	80,000	3.42
10	Shell—Subtotal	(B)	1,212,092	15.70	22.3%	Gross Bldg. Area	SF	77,200	15.70
11	Interior Construction	(C10)	560,523	7.26	10.3%	Gross Bldg. Area	SF	77,200	7.26
12	Stairs	(C20)	-	—	0.0%	Gross Bldg. Area	SF	77,200	-
13	Interior Finishes	(C30)	394,833	5.11	7.3%	Gross Bldg. Area	SF	77,200	5.11
14	Interiors— Subtotal	(C)	955,356	12.38	17.6%	Gross Bldg. Area	SF	77,200	12.38
15	Conveying Systems	(D10)	7,288	0.09	0.1%	Total No. of Stops	EA	1	7,288
16	Plumbing	(D20)	447,800	5.80	8.2%	No. of Fixtures	EA	150	2,985
17	HVAC	(D30)	1,049,400	13.59	19.3%	Tons (or MBH)	EA	200	5,247
18	Fire Protection	(D40)	151,800	1.97	2.8%	Protected Area	SF	77,200	1.97
19	Electrical	(D50)	859,866	11.14	15.8%	Gross Bldg. Area	SF	77,200	11.14
20	Electrical Service & Distribution	(D5010)	182,120	2.36	3.4%	Connected KW	KW	650	280
21	Lighting & Branch Wiring	(D5020)	286,132	3.71	5.3%	Gross Bldg. Area	SF	77,200	3.71
22	Communications & Security	(D5030)	205,778	2.67	3.8%	Gross Bldg. Area	SF	77,200	2.67
23	Other Electrical Systems	(D5040)	185,836	2.41	3.4%	Gross Bldg. Area	SF	77,200	2.41
24	Services—Subtotal	(D)	2,516,154	32.59	46.3%	Gross Bldg. Area	SF	77,200	32.59
25	Equip. & Furnishings—Subtotal	(E)	211,210	2.74	3.9%	Gross Bldg. Area	SF	77,200	2.74
26	Spec. Construct. & Demo—Subtotal	(F)	28,500	0.37	0.5%	Gross Bldg. Area	SF	77,200	0.37
27	**TOTAL BUILDING**		$ 5,429,504	$ 70.33	100.0%	Accommodation Units	EA	750	$ 7,239
28	**SITEWORK & UTILITIES:**		-						
29	Site Preparation	(G10)	467,598	6.06	8.6%	Gross Site Area	SF	600,000	0.78
30	Site Improvements	(G20)	85,122	1.10	1.6%	Gross Site Area	SF	600,000	0.14
31	Site Mechanical Utilities	(G30)	301,500	3.91	5.6%	Gross Site Area	SF	600,000	0.50
32	Site Electrical Utilities	(G40)	-	—	0.0%	Gross Site Area	SF	600,000	-
33	Other Site Construction	(G50)	-	—	0.0%	Gross Site Area	SF	600,000	-
34	**TOTAL SITEWORK & UTILITIES:**	(G)	854,220	11.07	15.7%	Gross Site Area	SF	600,000	1.42
35	General Conditions, Overhead & Profit @	5.1%	322,647	4.18	5.9%				
36	**TOTAL FACILITY COST - CURRENT**		$ 6,606,371	$ 85.57	121.7%	Accommodation Units	EA	750	$ 8,808
37	Contingency	@	-	—	0.0%				
38	Escalation	@	-	—	0.0%				
39									
40	**TOTAL FACILITY COST - PROJECTED**		$ 6,606,371	$ 85.57	121.7%	Accommodation Units	EA	750	$ 8,808

	Parameters:	Measure	Value		Area Analysis:	Area (SF)
1	Gross Bldg. Area	SF	77,200			
2	Ground Floor Area	SF	77,200		Basement	—
3	Gross Enclosure Area	SF	31,000		Ground Floor	77,200
4	Percent Fenestration	%	12%		Upper Floors	
5	Roof Surface Area	SF	80,000		Penthouses	
6	Total No.of Conveying Stops	STOPS	1		Other Areas	—
7	Tons Cooling (or MBH Htg)	TONS	200			
8	No. of Plumbing Fixtures	EA	150		Gross Floor Area	77,200
9	Fire Protected Area	SF	77,200			
10	Connected KW	KW	650			
11	Accommodation Units	EA	750			
12	Floor to Floor Height (Avg.)	LF	12			
13	Gross Site Area	SF	600,000			
14	Gross Bldg.Area/Accommod Unit	SF/EA	103			

Figure 5.6 Sample school historical file.

BUILDING COST SUMMARY - ALL PROJECTS (Adjusted to April 2001)

Project Description:	Elementary Schools	Bid Date	11/96		8/95		10/93	
Project Type:	School	Constr Time	14		15		14	
		Market	good		good		excellent	

SYSTEM / ELEMENT DESCRIPTION	UNIFORMAT REFERENCE	Example 1 TOTAL COST	Adjusted $/sf by:	Example 2 TOTAL COST	Adjusted $/sf by:	Example 3 TOTAL COST	Adjusted $/sf by:
BUILDING:		b	1.14	b	1.18	b	1.32
1 Foundations	(A10)	506,192	7.47	485,255	6.83	397,823	7.80
2 Standard Foundations	(A1010)	302,142	4.46	277,228	3.90	219,741	4.31
3 Other Foundations	(A1020)	-	-	-	-	-	-
4 Slab on Grade	(A1030)	204,050	3.01	208,027	2.93	178,081	3.49
5 Basement Construction	(A20)	-	-	-	-	-	-
6 Substructure—Subtotal	(A)	506,192	7.47	485,255	6.83	397,823	7.80
7 Superstructure	(B10)	400,900	5.92	408,714	5.75	291,566	5.72
8 Exterior Enclosure	(B20)	537,917	7.94	504,529	7.10	391,216	7.67
9 Roofing	(B30)	273,275	4.03	278,601	3.92	198,747	3.90
10 Shell—Subtotal	(B)	1,212,092	17.89	1,191,845	16.78	881,529	17.28
11 Interior Construction	(C10)	560,523	8.27	571,448	8.04	346,508	6.79
12 Stairs	(C20)	-	-	-	-	-	-
13 Interior Finishes	(C30)	394,833	5.83	483,034	6.80	258,438	5.07
14 Interiors—Subtotal	(C)	955,356	14.10	1,054,482	14.84	604,946	11.86
15 Conveying Systems	(D10)	7,288	0.11	7,430	0.10	5,300	0.10
16 Plumbing	(D20)	447,800	6.61	456,528	6.43	325,675	6.38
17 HVAC	(D30)	1,049,400	15.49	1,283,824	18.07	763,206	14.96
18 Fire Protection	(D40)	151,800	2.24	154,759	2.18	110,401	2.16
19 Electrical	(D50)	859,866	12.69	859,866	12.10	859,866	16.86
20 Electrical Service & Distribution	(D5010)	182,120	2.69	185,670	2.61	132,452	2.60
21 Lighting & Branch Wiring	(D5020)	286,132	4.22	291,709	4.11	208,098	4.08
22 Communications & Security	(D5030)	205,778	3.04	209,789	2.95	149,658	2.93
23 Other Electrical Systems	(D5040)	185,836	2.74	189,458	2.67	135,155	2.65
24 Services—Subtotal	(D)	2,516,154	37.14	2,762,407	38.89	2,064,449	40.47
25 Equip. & Furnishings—Subtotal	(E)	211,210	3.12	215,327	3.03	153,609	3.01
26 Spec. Construct. & Demo—Subtotal	(F)	28,500	0.42	29,055	0.41	20,727	0.41
27 **TOTAL BUILDING**		$5,429,504	80.14	$5,738,371	80.78	$4,123,083	80.83
28 **SITEWORK & UTILITIES:**		-		-		-	
29 Site Preparation	(G10)	467,598	6.90	657,181	9.25	375,979	7.37
30 Site Improvements	(G20)	85,122	1.26	99,695	1.40	88,977	1.74
31 Site Mechanical Utilities	(G30)	301,500	4.45	353,117	4.97	242,426	4.75
32 Site Electrical Utilities	(G40)	-	-	-	-	-	-
33 Other Site Construction	(G50)	-	-	-	-	-	-
34 **TOTAL SITEWORK & UTILITIES:**	(G)	854,220	12.61	1,109,993	15.63	707,382	13.87
35 General Conditions, Overhead & Profit @ 5.1%		322,647	4.76	351,639	4.95	248,027	4.86
36 **TOTAL FACILITY COST - CURRENT**		$6,606,371	97.51	$7,200,003	101.36	$5,078,492	99.56
37 Contingency @							
38 Escalation @		-	-	-	-	-	-
40 **TOTAL FACILITY COST - PROJECTED**		$6,606,371	97.51	$7,200,003	101.36	$5,078,492	99.56
41 **TOTAL FACILITY COST/SF - PROJECTED**		$ 85.57	97.51	$ 85.71	101.36	$ 75.24	99.56

Parameters:		Measure	Value		Value		Value	
1	Gross Bldg. Area	SF	77,200		84,000		67,500	
2	Ground Floor Area	SF	77,200		84,000		67,500	
3	Gross Enclosure Area	SF	31,000		33,731		28,000	
4	Percent Fenestration	%	12%		12%		15%	
5	Roof Surface Area	SF	80,000		87,047		69,948	
6	Total No.of Conveying Stops	STOPS	1		1		1	
7	Tons Cooling (or MBH Htg)	TONS	200		240		200	
8	No. of Plumbing Fixtures	EA	150		160		130	
9	Fire Protected Area	SF	77,200		84,000		67,500	
10	Connected KW	KW	650		750		600	
11	Accommodation Units	EA	750		800		600	
12	Floor to Floor Height (Avg.)	LF	12		12		12	
13	Gross Site Area	SF	600,000		750,000		580,000	
14	Gross Bldg. Area per Acc. Unit	SF/EA	103		105		113	

Figure 5.7(a) Example of historical project files (projects 1 to 3).

BUILDING COST SUMMARY - ALL PROJECTS (Adjusted to April 2001)

Project Description: **Elementary Schools**	Bid Date	1/97		9/94		Adjusted	Adjusted			
Project Type: **School**	Constr Time	14		16		Average	Average			
	Market	good		good		of All	of All			
SYSTEM / ELEMENT DESCRIPTION	UNIFORMAT REFERENCE	Example 4 TOTAL COST	Adjusted $/sf by:	Example 5 TOTAL COST	Adjusted $/sf by:	($/SF)	($/Parameter)			
		b	1.13	b	1.21					
BUILDING:										
1 Foundations	(A10)	561,768	8.13	385,840	7.01	7.45	Ground Floor Area	74,780	SF	7.45
2 Standard Foundations	(A1010)	348,071	5.04	230,305	4.18	4.38	Ground Floor Area	74,780	SF	4.38
3 Other Foundations	(A1020)	-	-	-	-	-	Ground Floor Area	74,780	SF	-
4 Slab on Grade	(A1030)	213,698	3.09	155,535	2.82	3.07	Ground Floor Area	74,780	SF	3.07
5 Basement Construction	(A20)	-	-	-	-	-	Ground Floor Area	74,780	SF	-
6 Substructure—Subtotal	(A)	561,768	8.13	385,840	7.01	7.45	Ground Floor Area	74,780	SF	7.45
7 Superstructure	(B10)	461,841	6.69	305,582	5.55	5.92	Gross Bldg. Area	74,780	SF	5.92
8 Exterior Enclosure	(B20)	563,351	8.16	360,819	6.55	7.48	Gross Enclosure Area	30,646	SF	18.25
9 Roofing	(B30)	329,125	4.77	208,301	3.78	4.08	Roof Surface Area	77,492	SF	3.94
10 Shell—Subtotal	(B)	1,354,317	19.61	874,703	15.88	17.49	Gross Bldg. Area	74,780	SF	17.49
11 Interior Construction	(C10)	587,025	8.50	405,890	7.37	7.80	Gross Bldg. Area	74,780	SF	7.80
12 Stairs	(C20)	-	-	-	-	-	Gross Bldg. Area	74,780	SF	-
13 Interior Finishes	(C30)	413,501	5.99	361,149	6.56	6.05	Gross Bldg. Area	74,780	SF	6.05
14 Interiors—Subtotal	(C)	1,000,526	14.49	767,040	13.93	13.84	Gross Bldg. Area	74,780	SF	13.84
15 Conveying Systems	(D10)	7,633	0.11	5,555	0.10	0.11	Total No. of Stops	1	EA	7,901
16 Plumbing	(D20)	468,973	6.79	341,331	6.20	6.48	No. of Fixtures	144	EA	3,365
17 HVAC	(D30)	1,099,017	15.91	799,895	14.53	15.79	Tons (or MBH)	208	EA	5,689
18 Fire Protection	(D40)	158,977	2.30	115,708	2.10	2.20	Protected Area	74,780	SF	2.20
19 Electrical	(D50)	859,866	12.45	859,866	15.62	13.94	Gross Bldg. Area	74,780	SF	13.94
20 Electrical Service & Distribution	(D5010)	190,731	2.76	138,819	2.52	2.64	Connected KW	660	KW	299
21 Lighting & Branch Wiring	(D5020)	344,610	4.99	218,101	3.96	4.27	Gross Bldg. Area	74,780	SF	4.27
22 Communications & Security	(D5030)	269,384	3.90	156,852	2.85	3.13	Gross Bldg. Area	74,780	SF	3.13
23 Other Electrical Systems	(D5040)	194,623	2.82	141,652	2.57	2.69	Gross Bldg. Area	74,780	SF	2.69
24 Services—Subtotal	(D)	2,594,466	37.57	2,122,355	38.54	38.52	Gross Bldg. Area	74,780	SF	38.52
25 Equip. & Furnishings—Subtotal	(E)	221,196	3.20	193,191	3.51	3.17	Gross Bldg. Area	74,780	SF	3.17
26 Spec. Construct. & Demo—Subtotal	(F)	29,848	0.43	21,724	0.39	0.41	Gross Bldg. Area	74,780	SF	0.41
27 **TOTAL BUILDING**		$5,762,121	83.44	$4,364,853	79.27	80.89	Accommodation Units	700	EA	$8,675
28 **SITEWORK & UTILITIES:**			-		-					
29 Site Preparation	(G10)	482,827	6.99	527,489	9.58	8.02	Gross Site Area	620,000	SF	0.96
30 Site Improvements	(G20)	87,894	1.27	71,129	1.29	1.39	Gross Site Area	620,000	SF	0.17
31 Site Mechanical Utilities	(G30)	311,319	4.51	214,147	3.89	4.51	Gross Site Area	620,000	SF	0.55
32 Site Electrical Utilities	(G40)	-	-	-	-	-	Gross Site Area	620,000	SF	-
33 Other Site Construction	(G50)	-	-	-	-	-	Gross Site Area	620,000	SF	-
34 **TOTAL SITEWORK & UTILITIES:**	(G)	882,041	12.77	812,765	14.76	13.93	Gross Site Area	620,000	SF	1.68
35 General Conditions, Overhead & Profit @	5.1%	341,154	4.94	265,852	4.83	4.87				-
36 **TOTAL FACILITY COST - CURRENT**		$6,985,316	101.15	$5,443,470	98.86	99.69	Accommodation Units	700	EA	$10,692
37 Contingency	@	-	-	-	-	-				-
38 Escalation	@	-	-	-	-	-				-
40 **TOTAL FACILITY COST - PROJECTED**		$6,985,316	101.15	$5,443,470	98.86	99.69	Accommodation Units	700	EA	$10,692
41 **TOTAL FACILITY COST/SF - PROJECTED**		$ 89.21	101.15	$ 81.37	98.86	99.69	-			

Parameters:	Measure	Value	Value	Value
1 Gross Bldg. Area	SF	78,300	66,900	74,780
2 Ground Floor Area	SF	78,300	66,900	74,780
3 Gross Enclosure Area	SF	32,500	28,000	30,646
4 Percent Fenestration	%	12%	15%	13%
5 Roof Surface Area	SF	81,140	69,326	77,492
6 Total No. of Conveying Stops	STOPS	1	1	1
7 Tons Cooling (or MBH Htg)	TONS	200	200	208
8 No. of Plumbing Fixtures	EA	150	130	144
9 Fire Protected Area	SF	78,300	66,900	74,780
10 Connected KW	KW	700	600	660
11 Accommodation Units	EA	750	600	700
12 Floor to Floor Height (Avg.)	LF	12	12	12
13 Gross Site Area	SF	600,000	570,000	620,000
14 Gross Bldg. Area per Acc. Unit	SF/EA	104	112	107

Figure 5.7(b) Example of historical project files (projects 4 to 5 and summary).

BUDGET COST ESTIMATE WORKSHEET

PROJECT: Elementary School Budget Exercise

			Brief Description of Building:
Building Type: Elementary School			One Level Elementary School with connected wings.
Location: Washington D.C. Area			
Architect:			Budget Analysis
Bid Date: Apr-01			
Construction Time: 14 Months			
Classification No:			
Client:			
Index:			
Market Conditions: Good			

	Area	No.		
			Average Story Height	12 FT
Basement Area	0	SF	Footprint at Grade	65000 SF
Ground Floor Area	65000	SF	Perimeter Length at Grade	2000 LF
Upper Floors Area	0	SF	Basement Wall Area	0 SF
Penthouses, etc.	0	SF	Fenestration Area	25000 SF
Gross floor area	65000	SF	Roof Area	67000 SF
			Partition Area	78000 SF
			No. of Plumbing Fixtures	135 EA
			Accommodation Units	650 EA

	COST ANALYSIS System	Elemental Quantity		Elemental Rate	Amount	$/SF	%	OUTLINE SPECIFICATION
A10	Substructure	65000	SF	7.50	$ 487,500	$ 7.50	6.8%	Slab on grade
A20	Basement Construction	0	SF	-	$ -	$ -	0.0%	None
B10	Superstructure	65000	SF	6.00	$ 390,000	$ 6.00	5.5%	Steel framed
B20	Exterior Closure	25000	SF	18.50	$ 462,500	$ 7.12	6.5%	Brick veneer on masonry
B30	Roofing	67000	SF	4.00	$ 268,000	$ 4.12	3.7%	Built up
C	Interiors	65000	SF	14.00	$ 910,000	$ 14.00	12.7%	Primarily masonry partitions
D10	Conveying	0	STOP	-	$ -	$ -	0.0%	None
D20	Plumbing	135	EA	3,400	$ 459,000	$ 7.06	6.4%	Standard fixtures
D30	HVAC	200	TON	5,700	$ 1,140,000	$ 17.54	15.9%	Four pipe system
D40	Fire Protection	65000	SF	2.20	$ 143,000	$ 2.20	2.0%	Standard
D50	Electrical	65000	SF	16.00	$ 1,040,000	$ 16.00	14.5%	Power , Lighting & special systems
E	Equipment & Furnishings	65000	SF	3.50	$ 227,500	$ 3.50	3.2%	Includes kitchen, excludes lockers
G	Sitework	600000	SF	1.50	$ 900,000	$ 13.85	12.6%	Included for reference
	General Conditions O&P	%		6%	$ 385,650	$ 5.93	5.4%	Based on Schedule of Values Gen Cond
	Escalation			Incl	$ -	$ -	0.0%	Included in prices
	Contingency			5%	$ 340,658	$ 5.24	4.8%	Predesign figure based on bid prices
								Cost per Accommodation Unit
	TOTALS				$ 7,153,808	$ 110.06	100.0%	$ 11,006

Calculations and Notes:

Figure 5.8 Sample elementary school budget.

form provides a simple method of recording assumptions and calculating the estimate. Since the database contained cost per square foot by building element, as well as a cost-per-parameter measure, those involved in the budgeting process can look at building elements by their primary driver as well as by the overall cost per square foot of the facility. In Figure 5.8, the section titled Outline Specification is useful for recording the assumptions for the project; it is also useful if each project assigned to the history data file properly records these major outline specifications. This will facilitate the process of adjustment. For the sample, most budgeting numbers are taken from the "adjusted average" column of Figure 5.7(b) if there is no reason to think that a variation is necessary. For example, Substructure was calculated at $7.50 per square foot, which is close to the average of the projects. Two areas were adjusted slightly to accommodate changes that had taken place in the design of schools relative to those in the database. These two areas are electrical and HVAC, reflecting the increased use of high-tech equipment and computers in schools, which increase the watts per square foot load electrically and cooling load mechanically. Thus, judgment was applied to increase both of these figures approximately 10 percent to reflect these design differences. This process would continue across other building elements if there were reasonable evidence of a need of change.

Two other situations require attention. General conditions overhead and profit will generally, on a project of this magnitude, exceed 15 percent. But, because the historical projects were based on schedule-of-values information, as reported by contractors, this category will tend to be undervalued because profit is seldom identified in schedules of values and instead, is usually spread among the trades. Estimates prepared using this database will have to make comparable assumptions. The alternate would be to modify the database. Escalation is not added in this case, because the database itself was adjusted to the bid date of April 2001; and because figures were based on bids, any escalation at the midpoint of construction is already included in the bid information.

The last issue is contingency. Normally, predesign estimates would include contingency in the range of 10 to 15 percent to as much as 20 percent when the estimates are based on estimated costs. Since the five projects all used bid information as a basis of cost, the contingency that would be added would be a function of a program-related contingency, rather than an estimate-related contingency. This is a difficult subject for many people in the industry because contingency and the amount of contingency added obviously have significant effects on the budget. For these projects, adding a contingency of over 5 percent would probably be excessive unless there were significant programmatic risks that had not been identified or were considered to be variable.

The point of the exercise is to demonstrate that historical cost information can be used for budgetary purposes. This will require great care when cataloging the historical information, adjusting the historical information for time and market, and then utilizing information to adjust project-specific conditions when they vary from the norm in the database. Furthermore, it becomes evident that other parameter information can be useful for the designers of record for budgeting guidance and assumptions.

It is also possible to utilize historical information by building elements when comparing projects that are dissimilar but that may contain similar building elements, for example, wall systems. This, however, requires a good deal of knowledge of the historical projects and of the likely choices of building elements of the project under study. Published cost information can also be useful in the budgeting process as a means of overall comparison and as a cross-check on the building elements. As a general rule, mixing and matching can be a tricky proposition.

Functional Area Method

The functional area method provides a mechanism for preparing budgets while reflecting actual project programs. One of the risks of the historical method just discussed is accommodating program differences from project to project. The previous example used elementary school projects that had extremely similar programs and proportions between program elements. The functional area method requires the definition of program components that can vary in their proportion to each other.

As described in Chapter 3, there are two basic functional program approaches. The first is based on the overall program mix by space type on a cost-per-square-foot basis, and the second separates the budget into core and shell and tenant fitout. Figure 5.9 presents recent cost information by functional area published by GSA; Figure 5.10 contains grossing factors suggested for use by GSA and adjusting net programs to gross building area.

The basic methodology for applying this technique is as follows:

Construction Unit Costs

Item	Space Type	English Units		
		Low Cost $/GSF	**Typical** $/GSF	High Cost $/GSF
1	General Office	$124	**$130**	$151
2	Office (Enhanced Finish Buildings - Courthouses)	$140	**$147**	$173
3	ST-1 General Storage	$76	**$107**	$140
4	ST-2 Inside Parking	$59	**$70**	$76
5	Outside Parking (Garage Structure)	$31	**$35**	$40
6	ST-3 Warehouse	$77	**$85**	$101
7	SP-1A Laboratories	$175	**$176**	$236
8	SP-1B Private Toilets, Clinics, Health Facilities/Child Care	$168	**$173**	$176
9	SP-2 Food Service	$155	**$169**	$192
10	SP-3A Structurally Changed Areas	$168	**$188**	$207
11	SP-3B Courtrooms	$206	**$228**	$248
12	SP-4 Automatic Data Processing	$171	**$185**	$222
13	SP-5A Conference and Classroom Training	$137	**$149**	$165
14	SP-5B Judicial Hearing Rooms, Small Courtrooms	$191	**$213**	$233
15	SP-5C Judicial Chambers	$162	**$164**	$181
16	SP-6 Light Industrial	$109	**$117**	$128

Figure 5.9 GSA GCCRG suggested unit costs.

1. *Establish overall building construction cost by multiplying known gross area quantities of involved space types with corresponding unit costs.* This unit cost approach has been established because little design information is usually available in the early planning phase of a project. Geographical cost variations can be addressed by applying a construction cost index (CCI) multiplier. Unit costs can also adjusted for special conditions, such as seismic conditions. Other known space factors may also be applied, if appropriate. Further adjustment is possible by adding itemized costs for a project's known special features.

2. *Use space unit costs to represent a range of possible extremes.* Within this range, indicated "typical" unit costs are suitable for most applications, usually associated with midrise construction (5–9 stories). Space unit costs should be

	Type of Space	Efficiency Factors*		
		Low	Typical	High
	General Office - All Open Plan	0.72	**0.75**	0.78
	General Office - Equal Mix Plan	0.68	**0.72**	0.76
	General Office - Closed Plan	0.67	**0.70**	0.73
ST-1	General Storage	0.76	**0.81**	0.86
ST-2	Inside Parking	0.82	**0.86**	0.90
	Outside Parking (Garage Structure)	0.85	**0.89**	0.92
SP-1A	Laboratories	0.50	**0.58**	0.66
SP-1B	Priv.Toilets/Clinics/Health/Child Care	0.54	**0.61**	0.68
SP-2	Food Service	0.63	**0.68**	0.72
SP-3A	Structurally Changed Areas	0.70	**0.74**	0.78
SP-3B	Courtrooms	0.60	**0.65**	0.70
SP-4	Automated Data Processing	0.60	**0.65**	0.70
SP-5A	Conference and Classroom Training	0.60	**0.65**	0.70
SP-5B	Judicial Hearing Rms./Sm. Courtrooms	0.60	**0.65**	0.70
SP-5C	Judicial Chambers	0.60	**0.65**	0.70
SP-6	Light Industrial	0.86	**0.89**	0.92
Other		–	–	–
Other		–	–	–

*Space efficiency ranges include support space requirements.

Figure 5.10 GSA's GCCRD suggested grossing factors by space type.

adjusted for known factors and conditions that would increase or decrease unit costs. Unit costs can be higher with smaller building size, urban construction, small floorplates, enhanced finishes, increased use of partitions for closed offices, and moderate high-rise construction (10–20 stories). Conversely, low-rise construction (1–4 stories), increased floor areas, and large building gross areas tend to reflect economies of scale, which can reduce space unit costs.

3. *Apply unit costs to gross building areas.* Typically, gross areas are estimated from occupiable space needs that are defined within housing

plan documents. Within indicated ranges, "typical" space efficiencies are appropriate for most project applications. However, if the building configuration is clear, consider low-range efficiencies for moderate high-rise construction, for small space areas, or for small floorplate buildings; consider high-efficiency values for low-rise construction, for large space areas, or for large floorplate buildings.

4. *Based on a housing plan/space needs assessment, indicate occupiable square-foot or square-meter requirements for the project and all impacted building areas.* Group similar space type assignments into common unit cost categories, as listed within Figure 5.9. Convert to gross areas, as appropriate, using space-efficiency values as shown in Figure 5.10.

5. *Assess the general character and massing requirements.* Consider levels of finishes, known programming needs, floorplate size, building height, and so on. Use these assessments to establish a rationale for selecting within space efficiency and unit cost ranges.

6. *Identify any other known space factor(s) that would increase all space types uniformly.* For example, enhanced security or the application of innovative "showcase" technologies would fall into this category.

7. *Escalate these costs to the desired reference date.* GSA's unit costs include escalation allowances for construction period: As such, escalation should not consider construction duration.

8. *Consider whether special building requirements and/or equipment are needed to support proposed tenant operations.* If so, add these costs separately.

9. *Combine space cost estimates with special requirements costs (item 8 above) to establish the estimated construction costs.*

Consider the following example: As part of a portfolio planning assessment, a new federal building and courthouse is being considered for Raleigh, North Carolina. From the housing plan, the following summary of space needs has been set, with values in square feet. The site has not been determined, so no constraints in floorplate layout are assumed. Also, no special requirements are known to exist that would influence project cost.

Space Type	Occupied Area in Square Feet
General Office	150,000
General Storage	2,450
Inside Parking (102 spaces)	35,900
Private Toilets	800
Clinics, Health Care	900
Child Care	2,400
Food Service	5,800
Structurally Changed Area	3,000
Courtrooms	24,000
Automated Data Processing	10,580
Conference/Classroom Training	6,500
Judicial Hearing Rms.	4,000
Small Courtrooms	8,000
Judicial Chambers	18,000
Total	*272,330*

Using the techniques as described and the unit costs presented in Figure 5.9 and the grossing factors presented in Figure 5.10, a budget could be prepared for this hypothetical facility. Figure 5.11 details the calculation.

It is interesting to note that the project total cost per square foot is $124, which is probably lower than

GENERAL CONSTRUCTION COST ANALYSIS

Project Name:	Submission or Purpose:		GCCRG Issue Date:
New Federal Building Courthouse	Planning Cost Analysis - New Construction Alternative		10/01/97
City, State	Applied GCCRG Location:	Annual Const. Esc. Rate:	Cover Sheet Analysis Date:
Raleigh, North Carolina	North Carolina	2.30%	GCCRG Cost Index: 0.80 — 12/15/97
Estimator:	Organization Symbol:	Telephone Number:	Estimate Date For Specials:
John Doe	XPCP	(202) 501-0000	Seismic Zone Factor: 1.00 — 12/25/97
Portfolio Management Coordinator:	Organization Symbol:	Telephone Number:	Desired Reference Date:
Steve Smith	XPLX	(202) 501-1321	Other Space Factor: 1.00 — 01/01/01

Space Types (Directly Involved or Impacted)	Area Occupiable	Area Efficiency	Area Gross	Unit Cost From GCCRG Table	Space Cost For Location & Factors On GCCRG Date	Space Cost Escalated To Reference Date
General Office (Equal Mix Plan)	150,000	72%	208,333	$130.00	$21,667,000	$23,331,000
Office (Within Enhanced Finish Building)	0	0%	0	$0.00	$0	$0
ST-1 General Storage	2,450	81%	3,025	$107.00	$259,000	$279,000
ST-2 Inside Parking	35,900	86%	41,744	$70.00	$2,338,000	$2,518,000
Outside Parking (Garage Structure)	0	0%	0	$0.00	$0	$0
ST-3 Warehouse	0	0%	0	$0.00	$0	$0
SP-1A Laboratories	0	0%	0	$0.00	$0	$0
SP-1B Priv.Toilets/Clinics/Health/Child Care	4,100	61%	6,721	$173.00	$930,000	$1,001,000
SP-2 Food Service	5,800	68%	8,529	$169.00	$1,153,000	$1,242,000

					Special Costs	Special Costs
					On Estimate Date	Escalated To Reference Date
SP-3A Structurally Changed Areas	3,000	74%	4,054	$178.00	$577,000	$621,000
SP-3B Courtrooms	24,000	65%	36,923	$228.00	$6,735,000	$7,252,000
SP-4 Automated Data Processing	10,580	65%	16,277	$185.00	$2,409,000	$2,594,000
SP-5A Conference and Classroom Training	6,500	65%	10,000	$149.00	$1,192,000	$1,284,000
SP-5B Judicial Hearing Rms./Sm. Courtrooms	12,000	65%	18,462	$213.00	$3,146,000	$3,388,000
SP-5C Judicial Chambers	18,000	65%	27,692	$164.00	$3,633,000	$3,912,000
SP-6 Light Industrial	0	0%	0	$0.00	$0	$0
Other	0	0%	0	$0.00	$0	$0
Other	0	0%	0	$0.00	$0	$0

Note: Unit Costs and Efficiency Factors Provide for Building Support Space. Site Development Costs Are Also Proportioned Within Space Unit Costs.
Space Unit Costs Reflect: Contingencies (Design & Construction), General Conditions/Profit, Art-In-Architecture And Other Reservations.

| Space Totals | 272,300 OSF | | 381,800 GSF | | $44,039,000 | $47,422,000 |

Overall Building Space Efficiency   =   70%   (Without Parking)
    =   71%   (With All Indicated Parking)

Special Requirements	Quantity	Units	Unit Cost	Const. Cont. & Reserv.	Special Costs	Special Costs
			On Estimate Date	On Estimate Date	On Estimate Date	Escalated To Reference Date
	0		$0	$0	$0	$0
Special Totals					$0	$0

Note: Special Requirements Unit Costs Include Location Effects, Design Contingency, and General Conditions/Profit.
Special Requirements Unit Costs Do Not Include Construction Contingencies, Art-In-Architecture, Or Other Reservations.

Total Estimated Construction Cost	$47,422,000
Building Unit Cost ($/GSF)	$124

Figure 5.11 Example of GCCRC calculation.

would be expected for a federal courthouse (even as based on the benchmark of 1998 for the example). However, a quick inspection of the housing program indicates that a sizable portion is interior parking, whose average cost per square foot is quite low in comparison to a fully finished building, thereby depressing the overall cost per square foot. Also, over 50 percent of the program is general office space, which likewise depresses the average cost per square foot.

Core and Shell Plus Tenant Functional Area Method

The current model used in the GCCRG can produce a separate estimate for core and shell and for tenant fit-out. Furthermore, this model can also produce a UNIFORMAT estimate as a cost plan resulting from the use of the model. This process is essential in connecting a space or functional area method with a cost plan. Figure 5.12 presents the summary of the model using the housing plan in the previous example as a basis, but updating the estimate to May 2002. Additionally, Figure 5.13 presents the UNIFORMAT summary of estimate indicating the contribution to the total cost plan of each space type, as well as the total cost plan that can be used as a starting point for the design process. Figure 5.14 presents a summary of this cost plan and indicates how core and shell and tenant can be separated, then eventually merged into a single estimate.

One of the inherent difficulties of working with a functional space program is caused by the fact that the assumptions over the core and shell can vary substantially from building to building, even within the confines of repetitive building types. Moreover, the model and the accuracy of the model are highly dependent on these assumptions and the flexibility

Cost Management Methodology

GCCRG Comparator Estimate
Summary by Space Classification
Hanscomb Inc
12/19/01

Project: Example Project

Print All | Print | Print Table

Print Buttons

#	SPACE TYPE	Program Area OSF	Space Efficiency Override	Space Efficiency Default	Space Efficiency Used	Gross Area	Base Shell Cost Per GSF	Base Shell Cost Per OSF	Base Shell Constr Costs	Fitout Cost Per GSF	Fitout Cost Per OSF	Fitout Costs	Total Cost Per GSF	Total Cost Per OSF	Total Constr Costs
1	OFFICE (TYPICAL)	150,000		72%	72%	208,333	94.80	131.66	19,749,701	$23.80	$33.05	$4,958,046	118.60	164.72	$24,707,747
2	OFFICE - ENHANCED	0		70%	70%	0	0.00	0.00	0	$0.00	$0.00	$0	0.00	0.00	$0
	OFFICE - OPEN PLAN	0		75%	75%	0	0.00	0.00		$0.00	$0.00	$0	0.00	0.00	$0
3	ST-1 GENERAL STORAGE	2,450		81%	81%	3,025	80.81	99.76	244,418	$17.44	$21.53	$52,744	98.25	121.29	$297,161
4	ST-2 INSIDE PARKING	35,900		86%	86%	41,744	64.36	74.83	2,686,536	$0.00	$0.00	$0	64.36	74.83	$2,686,536
6	ST-3 WAREHOUSES			89%	89%	0	0.00	0.00	0	$0.00	$0.00	$0	0.00	0.00	$0
7	SP-1A LABORATORIES			58%	58%	0	0.00	0.00	0	$0.00	$0.00	$0	0.00	0.00	$0
8	SP-1B PRIVATE TOILETS, CLINIC HEALTH FACILITIES, DAY CARE	4,100		61%	61%	6,721	90.44	148.27	607,898	$66.72	$109.37	$448,418	157.16	257.64	$1,056,316
9	SP - 2 FOOD SERVICE	5,800		68%	68%	8,529	122.47	180.10	1,044,594	$31.53	$46.37	$268,974	154.00	226.48	$1,313,567
10	SP - 3A STRUCTURALLY CHANGED AREAS	3,000		74%	74%	4,054	127.09	171.74	515,220	$40.93	$55.31	$165,941	168.02	227.05	$681,161
11	SP - 3B COURTROOMS	24,000		65%	65%	36,923	96.66	148.71	3,569,153	$112.93	$173.74	$4,169,762	209.60	322.45	$7,738,915
12	SP - 4 AUTOMATIC DATA PROCESSING	10,580		65%	65%	16,277	123.65	190.24	2,012,722	$45.77	$70.42	$745,047	169.43	260.66	$2,757,769
13	SP - 5A CONFERENCE AND CLASSROOM TRAINING	6,500		65%	65%	10,000	109.91	169.09	1,099,054	$28.04	$43.15	$280,445	137.95	212.23	$1,379,500
14	SP - 5B JUDICIAL HEARING ROOMS, SMALL COURTROOMS	12,000		65%	65%	18,462	98.08	150.89	1,810,725	$97.19	$149.52	$1,794,191	195.27	300.41	$3,604,916
16	SP - 5C JUDICIAL CHAMBERS	18,000		65%	65%	27,692	99.31	152.78	2,750,036	$69.93	$107.58	$1,936,423	169.23	260.36	$4,686,459
17	SP - 6 LIGHT INDUSTRIAL	0		89%	89%	0	0.00	0.00	0	$0.00	$0.00	$0	0.00	0.00	$0
	Total	272,330			71%	381,761	$94.54	$132.52	$36,090,056	$38.82	$64.42	$14,819,991	$133.36	$186.94	$50,910,047

Statistics:

Cost Date Benchmark = May-02	Location Factor = 0.80	Additional Adjustment Factor 1.00	Renovation - Demolition (Yes/No) no
Contingency = 0%	Inflation Rate = 3.1%	Type of Construction (New/Reno) new

Figure 5.12
Example of core
and shell
budgeting
approach.

229

GCCRG Comparator Estimate
Hanscomb Inc

Construction Cost Summary - Total Cost
Example Project

10/14/01

Category	1 Office Typical	3 ST-1 Gen Stor	4 ST-2 Inside Park	8 SP-1B Private	9 SP-2 Food	10 SP-3A Struct Chg	11 SP-3B Courts	12 SP-4 ADP	13 SP-5A Conf/Trng	14 SP-5B Jud Hrng	16 SP-5C Chambers	Total Cost	Total Cost/Gsf
01 FOUNDATIONS	**361,524**	**5,638**	**138,156**	**2,838**	**14,910**	**1,104**	**13,248**	**35,406**	**17,394**	**7,718**	**11,530**	**609,467**	**1.60**
011 STANDARD FOUNDATIONS	361,524	5,638	138,156	2,838	14,910	1,104	13,248	35,406	17,394	7,718	11,530	609,467	1.60
012 SPECIAL FOUNDATIONS	0	0	0	0	0	0	0	0	0	0	0	0	0.00
02 SUBSTRUCTURE	**161,876**	**2,349**	**833,372**	**19,511**	**6,639**	**13,764**	**97,964**	**12,720**	**7,765**	**44,453**	**89,155**	**1,289,568**	**3.38**
021 SLAB ON GRADE	161,876	2,349	50,061	5,772	6,639	8,334	28,501	12,720	7,765	13,503	26,084	323,602	0.85
022 BASEMENT EXCAVATION	0	0	540,168	6,528	0	2,580	33,001	0	0	14,704	29,964	626,943	1.64
023 BASEMENT WALLS	0	0	243,144	7,212	0	2,851	36,463	0	0	16,246	33,107	339,023	0.89
03 SUPERSTRUCTURE	**3,669,089**	**71,868**	**565,045**	**126,688**	**150,137**	**49,375**	**643,094**	**394,263**	**175,477**	**286,764**	**584,080**	**6,715,880**	**17.59**
031 FLOOR CONSTRUCTION	3,061,066	63,090	559,974	107,584	124,899	42,478	543,668	346,632	146,456	241,316	493,588	5,730,750	15.01
032 ROOF CONSTRUCTION	470,769	6,785	0	14,754	19,581	5,121	76,706	36,407	22,433	35,324	69,862	757,743	1.98
033 STAIR CONSTRUCTION	137,255	1,993	5,072	4,351	5,656	1,776	22,720	11,224	6,588	10,123	20,630	227,387	0.60
04 EXTERIOR CLOSURE	**3,044,315**	**44,636**	**0**	**82,038**	**124,641**	**33,079**	**419,504**	**245,603**	**146,154**	**215,846**	**382,250**	**4,738,066**	**12.41**
041 EXTERIOR WALLS	1,737,392	25,662	0	60,690	71,149	24,519	316,261	143,429	83,422	130,616	287,252	2,880,392	7.55
042 EXTERIOR DOORS AND WINDOWS	1,306,923	18,975	0	21,348	53,492	8,560	103,243	102,174	62,732	85,230	94,998	1,857,674	4.87
05 ROOFING	[illegible]	[illegible]	[illegible]	[illegible]	[illegible]	[illegible]	[illegible]	[illegible]	[illegible]	[illegible]	[illegible]	**629,876**	**1.65**
051 ROOFING	[illegible]	[illegible]	[illegible]	[illegible]	[illegible]	[illegible]	[illegible]	[illegible]	[illegible]	[illegible]	[illegible]	629,876	1.65
06 INTERIOR CONS	[illegible]	[illegible]	[illegible]	[illegible]	[illegible]	[illegible]	[illegible]	[illegible]	[illegible]	[illegible]	[illegible]	**11,583,559**	**30.34**
061 PARTITIONS	[illegible]	[illegible]	[illegible]	[illegible]	[illegible]	[illegible]	[illegible]	[illegible]	[illegible]	[illegible]	[illegible]	3,238,606	8.48
062 INTERIOR FINISH	[illegible]	[illegible]	[illegible]	[illegible]	[illegible]	[illegible]	[illegible]	[illegible]	[illegible]	[illegible]	[illegible]	8,107,974	21.24
063 SPECIALTIES	[illegible]	[illegible]	[illegible]	[illegible]	[illegible]	[illegible]	[illegible]	[illegible]	[illegible]	[illegible]	[illegible]	236,978	0.62
07 CONVEYING SYS	[illegible]	[illegible]	[illegible]	[illegible]	[illegible]	[illegible]	[illegible]	[illegible]	[illegible]	[illegible]	[illegible]	**1,404,055**	**3.68**
071 ELEVATORS	[illegible]	[illegible]	[illegible]	[illegible]	[illegible]	[illegible]	[illegible]	[illegible]	[illegible]	[illegible]	[illegible]	1,404,055	3.68
072 ESCALATORS	[illegible]	[illegible]	[illegible]	[illegible]	[illegible]	[illegible]	[illegible]	[illegible]	[illegible]	[illegible]	0	0	0.00
08 MECHANICAL	[illegible]	[illegible]	[illegible]	[illegible]	[illegible]	[illegible]	[illegible]	[illegible]	[illegible]	[illegible]	[illegible]	**7,849,311**	**20.56**
081 PLUMBING	[illegible]	[illegible]	[illegible]	[illegible]	[illegible]	[illegible]	[illegible]	[illegible]	[illegible]	[illegible]	[illegible]	1,866,586	4.89
082 HVAC	[illegible]	[illegible]	[illegible]	[illegible]	[illegible]	[illegible]	[illegible]	[illegible]	[illegible]	[illegible]	[illegible]	4,874,772	12.77
083 FIRE PROTECTIC	[illegible]	[illegible]	[illegible]	[illegible]	[illegible]	[illegible]	[illegible]	[illegible]	[illegible]	[illegible]	[illegible]	1,107,954	2.90
084 SPECIAL MECHA	[illegible]	[illegible]	[illegible]	[illegible]	[illegible]	[illegible]	[illegible]	[illegible]	[illegible]	[illegible]	0	0	0.00
09 ELECTRICAL	[illegible]	[illegible]	[illegible]	[illegible]	[illegible]	[illegible]	[illegible]	[illegible]	[illegible]	[illegible]	[illegible]	**4,220,581**	**11.06**
091 SERVICE AND D	[illegible]	[illegible]	[illegible]	[illegible]	[illegible]	[illegible]	[illegible]	[illegible]	[illegible]	[illegible]	[illegible]	1,114,602	2.92
092 LIGHTING AND P	[illegible]	[illegible]	[illegible]	[illegible]	[illegible]	[illegible]	[illegible]	[illegible]	[illegible]	[illegible]	[illegible]	1,746,816	4.58
093 SPECIAL ELECTRICAL SYSTEMS	405,466	3,675	42,064	14,972	16,120	11,516	426,713	185,861	36,900	102,702	113,174	1,359,163	3.56
10 GENERAL CONDITIONS AND PROFIT	**2,758,962**	**32,726**	**317,874**	**119,131**	**148,392**	**59,943**	**895,886**	**312,385**	**155,324**	**400,425**	**536,595**	**5,737,643**	**15.03**
102 GENERAL CONDITIONS	1,439,101	17,070	165,806	62,140	77,403	31,267	467,302	162,943	81,018	208,865	279,893	2,992,809	7.84
104 OVERHEAD AND PROFIT	1,319,861	15,656	152,068	56,991	70,990	28,676	428,583	149,442	74,305	191,559	256,702	2,744,834	7.19
11 EQUIPMENT	**201,043**	**2,919**	**5,453**	**28,065**	**193,155**	**32,703**	**1,936,629**	**15,483**	**60,092**	**701,485**	**57,567**	**3,234,595**	**8.47**
111 FIXED AND MOVEABLE EQUIPMENT	0	0	5,453	0	184,475	0	0	[illegible]	[illegible]	[illegible]	[illegible]	[illegible]	0.56
112 FURNISHINGS	201,043	2,919	0	28,065	8,680	32,703	1,936,629	[illegible]	[illegible]	[illegible]	[illegible]	[illegible]	7.91
113 SPECIAL CONSTRUCTION	0	0	0	0	0	0	0	0	0	0	0	0	0.00
12 SITEWORK	**1,636,036**	**24,009**	**115,677**	**89,628**	**67,640**	**35,238**	**319,133**	**127,545**	**60,310**	**175,519**	**246,712**	**2,897,446**	**7.59**
121 SITE PREPARATION	61,772	897	8,435	4,648	2,529	1,891	20,326	4,825	3,108	11,526	12,916	132,872	0.35
122 SITE IMPROVEMENTS	1,249,451	18,397	66,796	57,578	51,831	22,320	245,573	97,352	41,611	135,393	158,809	2,145,111	5.62
123 SITE UTILITIES	324,814	4,716	40,446	27,401	13,279	11,026	53,234	25,368	15,590	28,601	74,987	619,463	1.62
124 OFFSITE WORK	0	0	0	0	0	0	0	0	0	0	0	0	0.00
TOTAL CONSTRUCTION ESTIMATE	**24,707,747**	**297,161**	**2,686,536**	**1,056,316**	**1,313,567**	**681,161**	**7,738,915**	**2,757,769**	**1,379,500**	**3,604,916**	**4,686,459**	**50,910,047**	**133.36**

Category	1 Office Typical	3 ST-1 Gen Stor	4 ST-2 Inside Park
03 SUPERSTRUCTURE	**3,669,089**	**71,868**	**565,045**
031 FLOOR CONSTRUCTION	3,061,066	63,090	559,974
032 ROOF CONSTRUCTION	470,769	6,785	0
033 STAIR CONSTRUCTION	137,255	1,993	5,072
04 EXTERIOR CLOSURE	**3,044,315**	**44,636**	**0**
041 EXTERIOR WALLS	1,737,392	25,662	0
042 EXTERIOR DOORS AND WINDOWS	1,306,923	18,975	0

50,910,047	133.36

Figure 5.13 Cost plan example from GCCRG.

Hanscomb, Inc.
10/17/01
Construction Cost Summary - Total
Example Project

Category	Total Cost	Cost/Gsf	Total Cost	Cost/Gsf	Total Cost	Cost/Gsf
01 FOUNDATIONS	0	0.00	700,967	1.84	700,967	1.84
02 SUBSTRUCTURE	0	0.00	1,483,173	3.89	1,483,173	3.89
03 SUPERSTRUCTURE	0	0.00	7,724,144	20.23	7,724,144	20.23
04 EXTERIOR CLOSURE	0	0.00	5,449,398	14.27	5,449,398	14.27
05 ROOFING	0	0.00	724,440	1.90	724,440	1.90
06 INTERIOR CONSTRUCTION	7,802,153	20.44	5,417,876	14.19	13,220,029	34.63
07 CONVEYING SYSTEMS	0	0.00	1,614,847	4.23	1,614,847	4.23
08 MECHANICAL	1,387,417	3.63	7,640,322	20.01	9,027,739	23.65
09 ELECTRICAL	2,351,971	6.16	2,502,251	6.55	4,854,222	12.72
10 GENERAL CONDITIONS AND PROFIT	2,001,360	5.24	4,583,916	12.01	6,585,276	17.25
11 EQUIPMENT	3,371,726	8.83	348,483	0.91	3,720,210	9.74
12 SITEWORK	0	0.00	3,332,444	8.73	3,332,444	8.73
TOTAL CONSTRUCTION ESTIMATE	16,914,627	44.31	41,522,262	108.77	58,436,890	153.07

Figure 5.14 Cost plan example from GCCRG: summary.

231

and sensitivity of these assumptions. When GSA reviewed and benchmarked previously constructed federal courthouses, it was determined that in many instances the projected figures from the GCCRG were low in comparison to built facilities. On inspection, it became apparent that many of these differences were a function of core and shell construction rather than tenant fit-out, and that many aspects of the previous model were significantly deficient in predicting proper core and shell costs. This has led GSA to update the GCCRG approach to separate core and shell from tenant fit-out into two processes for budgeting. Eventually, GSA will utilize a modified functional space approach with separate core and shell and tenant fit-out elements. This process is still under development and is expected to be released for general use in early 2002.

That said, the overall approach is consistent with the process of separating core and shell from tenant fit-out. It is necessary to define accurately what is included in core and shell and what is included in tenant fit-out. No universal industry standard has emerged. GSA is addressing this issue and expects to publish a standards guideline in 2002.

Assessing Escalation, Market Factors, and Risks

Chapter 3 fully discussed how to assess escalation, market factors, and other risks associated with the project. In terms of the subject of this chapter, dealing with these issues is a challenge, in particular when preparing an initial budget well in advance of the actual construction work.

Some published information is available that can help the cost manager predict escalation based on projections of general economy inflation. One source is the Office of Management and Budget (OMB). OMB is responsible for providing direction to federal agencies regarding budgetary issues, including potential inflation/escalation. Figure 5.15 is an extract of a report produced in August 2001 that updated some previous information from the year and presented projected inflation as well as projected change in gross domestic product. Note that as of August 2001, projections past 2002 included a 2.5 percent change per year for inflation. OMB tends to make projections of inflation that are linear or continuous after one or two years. Considering that there are very few in this industry who make projections beyond one year, this is not surprising. Using a source such as OMB at least provides a dependable basis and defensible starting point relative to projecting future conditions.

Predicting market risks is a considerably more difficult circumstance because in almost every case, market conditions fluctuate in cyclical patterns. Therefore, in the middle of a boom period projecting forward, it is difficult to predict a likely down pattern within two to three years. The first and most important thing that any cost manager can do is to document assumptions clearly and to base judgments on reasonable and dependable sources of information.

Unfortunately, any predictions probably will be wrong and out of phase with actual circumstances, and hindsight will regard the assumptions critically. This is why documenting assumptions is important: it is not necessarily the accuracy of any projection that is critical, it is the ability to adjust a project's cost for known conditions once they occur. It may be appropriate, as some owners do, to define a market contingency as a hedge against an

ECONOMIC ASSUMPTIONS [1]
(Calendar years; dollar amounts in billions)

	Actual		Projections									
	2000	2001	2002	2003	2004	2005	2006	2007	2008	2009	2010	2011
Gross Domestic Product (GDP):												
Levels, dollar amounts in billions:												
Current dollars	9,963	10,364	10,937	11,575	12,228	12,880	13,553	14,263	15,009	15,794	16,619	17,488
Real, chained (1996) dollars	9,318	9,474	9,776	10,122	10,468	10,800	11,133	11,476	11,829	12,194	12,569	12,956
Chained price index (1996 = 100), annual average	107	109.5	111.9	114.3	116.8	119.2	121.7	124.3	126.9	129.5	132.2	135
Percent change, fourth quarter over fourth quarter:												
Current dollars	5.8	4.2	5.8	5.5	5.2	5.2	5.2	5.2	5.2	5.2	5.2	5.2
Real, chained (1996) dollars	3.4	1.7	3.5	3.4	3.1	3.1	3.1	3.1	3.1	3.1	3.1	3.1
Chained price index (1996 = 100)	2.3	2.4	2.2	2.1	2.1	2.1	2.1	2.1	2.1	2.1	2.1	2.1
Percent change, year over year:												
Current dollars	7.1	4	5.5	5.8	5.6	5.3	5.2	5.2	5.2	5.2	5.2	5.2
Real, chained (1996) dollars	5	1.7	3.2	3.5	3.4	3.2	3.1	3.1	3.1	3.1	3.1	3.1
Chained price index (1996 = 100)	2.1	2.3	2.2	2.2	2.1	2.1	2.1	2.1	2.1	2.1	2.1	2.1
Incomes, billions of current dollars:												
Corporate profits before tax	926	796	969	1,020	1,104	1,164	1,182	1,202	1,224	1,254	1,291	1,337
Wages and salaries	4,769	4,989	5,272	5,621	5,951	6,270	6,572	6,888	7,224	7,589	7,969	8,370
Other taxable income [2]	2,281	2,372	2,418	2,507	2,589	2,693	2,788	2,887	2,994	3,107	3,226	3,326
Consumer Price Index (all urban): [3]												
Level (1982–84 = 100), annual average	172.3	178	182.7	187.4	192	196.8	201.8	206.8	212	217.3	222.7	228.3
Percent change, fourth quarter over fourth quarter	3.4	3.2	2.6	2.5	2.5	2.5	2.5	2.5	2.5	2.5	2.5	2.5
Percent change, year over year	**3.4**	**3.3**	**2.7**	**2.5**	**2.5**	**2.5**	**2.5**	**2.5**	**2.5**	**2.5**	**2.5**	**2.5**
Unemployment rate, civilian, percent:												
Fourth quarter level	4	4.8	4.7	4.7	4.6	4.6	4.6	4.6	4.6	4.6	4.6	4.6
Annual average	4	4.6	4.8	4.7	4.6	4.6	4.6	4.6	4.6	4.6	4.6	4.6
Federal pay raises, January, percent:												
Military [4]	4.8	3.7	4.6	3.9	3.9	3.9	3.9	3.9	3.9	3.9	3.9	3.9
Civilian [5]	4.8	3.7	3.6	3.9	3.9	3.9	3.9	3.9	3.9	3.9	3.9	3.9
Interest rates, percent:												
91-day Treasury bills [6]	5.8	3.8	3.9	4.3	4.3	4.3	4.3	4.3	4.3	4.3	4.3	4.3
10-year Treasury notes	6	5.2	5.2	5.2	5.2	5.2	5.2	5.2	5.2	5.2	5.2	5.2

ADDENDUM: [7]

Gross Domestic Product (GDP):

Levels, dollar amounts in billions:												
Current dollars	9,873	10,278	10,846	11,479	12,126	12,772	13,440	14,144	14,884	15,662	16,481	17,343
Real, chained (1996) dollars	9,224	9,385	9,685	10,027	10,370	10,699	11,028	11,368	11,719	12,080	12,451	12,835
Chained price index (1996 = 100), annual average	107	109.5	111.9	114.4	116.8	119.3	121.8	124.3	126.9	129.5	132.2	135
Percent change, fourth quarter over fourth quarter:												
Current dollars	5.3	4.2	6	5.8	5.5	5.2	5.2	5.2	5.2	5.2	5.2	5.2
Real, chained (1996) dollars	2.8	1.8	3.7	3.5	3.4	3.1	3.1	3.1	3.1	3.1	3.1	3.1
Chained price index (1996 = 100)	2.4	2.4	2.2	2.2	2.1	2.1	2.1	2.1	2.1	2.1	2.1	2.1
Percent change, year over year:												
Current dollars	6.5	4.1	5.5	5.8	5.6	5.3	5.2	5.2	5.2	5.2	5.2	5.2
Real, chained (1996) dollars	4.1	1.7	3.2	3.5	3.4	3.2	3.1	3.1	3.1	3.1	3.1	3.1
Chained price index (1996 = 100)	**2.3**	**2.3**	**2.2**	**2.2**	**2.1**	**2.1**	**2.1**	**2.1**	**2.1**	**2.1**	**2.1**	**2.1**
Incomes, billions of current dollars:												
Corporate profits before tax	845	714	870	916	991	1,045	1,061	1,079	1,099	1,125	1,159	1,200
Wages and salaries	4,837	5,085	5,374	5,730	6,066	6,391	6,699	7,022	7,363	7,735	8,123	8,532
Other taxable income [2]	2,236	2,341	2,387	2,476	2,558	2,661	2,755	2,855	2,961	3,074	3,193	3,293

[1] Based on information available as of June 2001.

[2] Rent, interest, dividend and proprietor's components of personal income.

[3] Seasonally adjusted CPI for all urban consumers.

[4] Percentages apply to basic pay only; additional rank-specific adjustments are proposed for 2002; adjustments for housing and subsistence allowances will be determined by the Secretary of Defense.

[5] Overall average increase, including locality pay adjustments.

[6] Average rate (bank discount basis) on new issues within period.

[7] Assumptions adjusted to reflect revised historical series for GDP and incomes released by the Bureau of Economic Analysis in July 2001.

Figure 5.15 Extract of OMB projections (August 2001).

upward swing in the market. Refer back to Chapter 2, Figure 2.14 (page 46), which presented the swinging market conditions that occurred between 1982 and 2001: there was as much as a 15-percent swing from a "fair market value" to the actual bids received for projects. If a tight market is anticipated, then, holding aside a 5 to 10 percent market contingency would appear to be a prudent move. Conversely, the advance of a down market could return to the owner as much as a 15 percent benefit and reduce bid costs against estimates. While it is not recommended that 15 percent be deducted from a project cost, it is a good idea to have reasonably implementable options defined in advance so that if the market turn down and bids are desirable, the owner is in a position to take advantage.

On very complicated projects or programs, it may be advisable to perform a formal risk analysis for the project that includes a complete range estimate with contingency analysis. The risk of the up or down market is one aspect of the range estimate and of the risk assessment. (Refer to Chapter 3 for a discussion of risk analysis and range estimating.) One way or the other, identifying options that can be elected or declined without adverse impacts to the project is a prudent way to proceed. When options are considered as part of the overall design from the outset of a project, they can be included efficiently and coordinated properly with minimum risk. Experience has shown that implementing changes of significant magnitude late in a project without having considered those changes during the design leads to coordination problems, higher costs, and schedule delays, not to mention the high probability of expensive and divisive change orders.

Value Planning

It may be feasible and desirable at the conclusion of planning and programming to consider conducting a value engineering study. The purpose of the value engineering study, usually termed *value planning*, is to consider basic alternates and their impact on budget, scope, and expectations, and to address with some degree of confidence the issue of alignment. Some organizations, including the Naval Facilities Engineering Command (NAVFAC), consider this an important step in achieving alignment and providing eventual direction to the design team of record. Whether this step is considered to be the final step of planning and programming or the initial step of design process is irrelevant. Function Analysis Concept Development (FACD) is a process conducted for NAVFAC. The process is applied to many NAVFAC projects as part of the early design process and, in particular, is utilized for design-build projects and for preparing requests for proposals (RFPs) for such projects.

Benchmarking

Whether as an input to the value-planning session or as a separate activity, a benchmarking process can be extremely valuable in the initial budgeting process and as a means to verify the validity of the planning and programming phase. Benchmarking could involve a simple comparison to similar facilities or a comprehensive review and evaluation of the project's program and expected cost relative to other projects. An added advantage of benchmarking is that a positive correlation with other projects may increase the confidence of those who control the actual financing of a project. For example, congressional approval of federal projects will often be followed by a benchmarking process either through an independent source or through such organizations as GAO. Regardless, the objective is to determine that the budget being assigned to a project represents a sensible, appropriate, and defensible figure.

Managing Costs during Design

Once the design process has been initiated, and scope, expectations, and a budget have been prepared, it's time to start the design process.

Converting a Budget into a Cost Plan

Referring again to Figure 5.1 (page 197) and to Figure 5.1(a) (page 198), the key aspect of initiating the design process is the development of a comprehensive cost plan. The cost plan follows after planning and programming; it apportions the budget by discipline so that each has a clear directive as to individual scope and the budget attached to it. Along with costs, a series of parameters is defined to establish the scope of each discipline and to allow for progress tracking and assessment, along with cost information. For example, structural design could be assessed a target number of pounds of steel per square foot (assuming a steel-based design) that is consistent with expectations for live loading and spans and other structural drivers such as seismic conditions and blast requirements. This cost plan would be the basic cost management tool for the life of the project.

As an example, consider an apartment complex for which the initial budgeting goals and objectives have been converted into a cost plan that subdivides the entire budget into disciplines and with a series of parameters guiding the eventual design of the apartments in the complex (see Figure 5.16). Selected drivers include:

- Overall gross area equals 53,780 square feet.
- Gross enclosure area equals 28,000 square feet.
- HVAC costs equal $365,000.
- Electrical costs equal $615,000.
- Contingency equals 10 percent.
- Escalation factor equals 5 percent (included separately, not as part of the overall summary sheet).

For this example, we'll assume that market conditions are expected to remain favorable and that construction time for the apartment building is scheduled to be completed in eight months. (This example is expanded in the design development section of this chapter.)

To repeat, the purpose of the cost plan is to communicate assumptions in advance of the start of design so that members of each discipline clearly understand their individual tasks. Moreover, these assumptions should be documented in a way that allows for future comparison.

Managing Conceptual and Schematic Design Phase Costs

The conceptual and schematic design phase of a project is when the initial design is developed to represent form, shape, and general massing, and when building systems and materials are selected.

The key steps to follow during the conceptual and schematic design phases are as follows:

BUILDING COST SUMMARY

Project Description:	**Apartment - Cost Plan**		Bid Date:	1/02
Project Type:	**Apartments**		Construction time(Months):	8
Gross Building Area:(GSF	53,783		Market Conditions:	good

SYSTEM / ELEMENT DESCRIPTION	UNIFORMAT REFERENCE	TOTAL COST	COST PER GSF	% OF BUILDING	ELEMENTAL ANALYSIS MEASURE	UNIT	VALUE	COST/UNIT
		b	b / GSF	b / 27			c	b / c
BUILDING:								
1 Foundations	(A10)	240,137	4.46	5.3%	Ground Floor Area	SF	19,103	12.57
2 Standard Foundations	(A1010)	113,356	2.11	2.5%	Ground Floor Area	SF	19,103	5.93
3 Other Foundations	(A1020)	-	-	0.0%	Ground Floor Area	SF	19,103	-
4 Slab on Grade	(A1030)	126,781	2.36	2.8%	Ground Floor Area	SF	19,103	6.64
5 Basement Construction	(A20)	-	-	0.0%	Ground Floor Area	SF	19,103	-
6 Substructure - Sub-Total	(A)	240,137	4.46	5.3%	Ground Floor Area	SF	19,103	12.57
7 Superstructure	(B10)	488,315	9.08	10.7%	Gross Bldg. Area	SF	53,783	9.08
8 Exterior Enclosure	(B20)	517,563	9.62	11.3%	Gross Enclosure Area	EA	28,213	18.34
9 Roofing	(B30)	203,544	3.78	4.5%	Roof Surface Area	SF	22,733	8.95
10 Shell - Sub-Total	(B)	1,209,421	22.49	26.4%	Gross Bldg. Area	SF	53,783	22.49
11 Interior Construction	(C10)	892,023	16.59	19.5%	Gross Bldg. Area	SF	53,783	16.59
12 Stairs	(C20)	17,129	0.32	0.4%	Gross Bldg. Area	SF	53,783	0.32
13 Interior Finishes	(C30)	382,936	7.12	8.4%	Gross Bldg. Area	SF	53,783	7.12
14 Interiors - Sub-Total	(C)	1,292,089	24.02	28.2%	Gross Bldg. Area	SF	53,783	24.02
15 Conveying Systems	(D10)	100,941	1.88	2.2%	Total No. of Stops	EA	3	33,647
16 Plumbing	(D20)	585,757	10.89	12.8%	No. of Fixtures	EA	296	1,979
17 HVAC	(D30)	367,641	6.84	8.0%	Tons (or MBH)	EA	90	4,085
18 Fire Protection	(D40)	161,911	3.01	3.5%	Protected Area	SF	53,783	3.01
19 Electrical	(D50)	615,904	11.45	13.5%	Gross Bldg. Area	SF	53,783	11.45
20 Electrical Service & Distribution	(D5010)	190,912	3.55	4.2%	Connected KW	KW	269	710
21 Lighting & Branch Wiring	(D5020)	309,983	5.76	6.8%	Gross Bldg. Area	SF	53,783	5.76
22 Communications & Security	(D5030)	82,149	1.53	1.8%	Gross Bldg. Area	SF	53,783	1.53
23 Other Electrical Systems	(D5040)	32,860	0.61	0.7%	Gross Bldg. Area	SF	53,783	0.61
24 Services - Sub-Total	(D)	1,832,154	34.07	40.1%	Gross Bldg. Area	SF	53,783	34.07
25 Equip. & Furnishings - Sub-Total	(E)	-	-	0.0%	Gross Bldg. Area	SF	53,783	-
26 Spec. Construct. & Demo - Sub-Total	(F)	-	-	0.0%	Gross Bldg. Area	SF	53,783	- -
27 **TOTAL BUILDING**		$ 4,573,801	$ 85.04	100.0%	Accommodation Units	EA	95	$ 48,145
28 **SITEWORK & UTILITIES:**								
29 Site Preparation	(G10)	85,395	1.59	1.9%	Gross Site Area	SF	85,500	1.00
30 Site Improvements	(G20)	318,971	5.93	7.0%	Gross Site Area	SF	85,500	3.73
31 Site Mechanical Utilities	(G30)	102,394	1.90	2.2%	Gross Site Area	SF	85,500	1.20
32 Site Electrical Utilities	(G40)	7,402	0.14	0.2%	Gross Site Area	SF	85,500	0.09
33 Other Site Construction	(G50)	-	-	0.0%	Gross Site Area	SF	85,500	-
34 **TOTAL SITEWORK & UTILITIES:**	(G)	514,163	9.56	11.2%	Gross Site Area	SF	85,500	6.01
35 General Conditions, Overhead & Profit @	11.0%	559,676	10.41	12.2%				
36 **TOTAL FACILITY COST - CURRENT**		$ 5,647,640	$ 105.01	123.5%	Accommodation Units	EA	95	$ 59,449
37 Contingency @	10.0%	564,764	10.50	12.3%				
38 Escalation @		-	-	0.0%				
40 **TOTAL FACILITY COST - PROJECTED**		$ 6,212,404	$ 115.51	135.8%	Accommodation Units	EA	95	$ 65,394

Parameters:		Measure	Value	Area Analysis:	Area (SF)
1	Gross Bldg. Area	SF	53,783		
2	Ground Floor Area	SF	19,103	Basement	-
3	Gross Enclosure Area	SF	28,213	Ground Floor	19,103
4	Percent Fenestration	%	11%	Upper Floors	34,680
5	Roof Surface Area	SF	22,733	Penthouses	
6	Total No.of Conveying Stops	STOPS	3	Other Areas	-
7	Tons Cooling (or MBH Htg)	TONS	90		
8	No. of Plumbing Fixtures	EA	296	Gross Floor Area	53,783
9	Fire Protected Area	SF	53,783		
10	Connected KW	KW	269		
11	Accommodation Units	EA	95		
12	Floor to Floor Height (Avg.)	LF	9		
13	Gross Site Area	SF	85,500		

Figure 5.16 Example of a cost plan for an apartment project.

> **Defining Terms**
>
> For the purposes of this discussion, conceptual design refers to the initial phases of design, which generally involve multiple design approach considerations. Schematic design is defined here as the design phase following the determination of the basic scheme. The distinction between conceptual and schematic estimating is significant only in that the conceptual phase will potentially consider several schemes, whereas the schematic phase will generally be based on only one scheme.

1. *Solicit advice on an ongoing basis.* Beginning with the initial design concept and throughout the decision-making process, it is important to solicit input regarding costs. The advice you seek should highlight major issues for future consideration and help to determine whether additional expertise is necessary to effectively evaluate cost aspects of critical components.

2. *Establish a milestone estimate.* A milestone estimate should be set at the conclusion of conceptual design (assuming multiple concepts are being considered) or at the conclusion of schematic design after a basic concept has been selected. The purpose of the estimate is to establish an overall cost for the schematic design under consideration and to verify the individual costs of components and systems that have been allocated to each discipline.

3. *Assess market conditions, contingencies, and escalation.* An assessment of market conditions should be conducted to predict conditions at the time of bidding/pricing for the project, in conjunction with an evaluation of contingencies, escalation, and the impact of any major

risks that have been identified. Figure 5.17 presents an example of GSA market survey requirements and its current guidelines. It is important that the design team participate in the development of this estimate and verify the major assumptions being made. The design team should not assume that the estimator/cost manager will be interpreting every aspect of the design as the design team intended.

4. *Revise the cost plan.* The eventual estimate will also detail the key parameters that have been defined for each discipline, along with their individual cost allocations. All of this leads to a revision of the cost plan/cost model, to collect and summarize the estimate overall and to compare it with the previous cost plan for the purpose of evaluating status and progress.

5. *Conduct a value engineering study.* As part of the overall cost management process it is strongly recommended that a value engineering study be conducted at the conclusion or near the conclusion of the schematic design phase. The purpose of the study is to evaluate the basic concept being considered and to review the major system alternatives that have been defined. The VE study can be an important aspect of the final revision of the cost plan and the eventual development of the cost plan for the next phase of design.

6. *Account for life-cycle costing and sustainability.* The necessity of considering capital costs is obvious; it is an ongoing part of any process. But to be successful today it is also necessary to consider the impact of life-cycle costs and sustainability in the developing design. This step doesn't necessarily require doing an in-depth analysis, especially at the conceptual/

11. Application. As may be required within design programming documents and for every project anticipated to have an ECCA greater than $10,000,000, a Market Survey shall be conducted to verify that projected unit costs are appropriate and to assure that project delivery assumptions of materials and labor availability are reasonable.

12. Survey Approach. The A-E shall visit the site and local market areas to determine the following:

    o Availability of major materials to be in the project
    o Capability of local fabricators, precast yards, concrete plants, etc.
    o Availability of labor crafts necessary for the project
    o Availability of special erection equipment
    o Anticipated capacity of local contractors during bidding period
    o Special conditions that might influence bidding
    o Local escalation experience
    o Site accessibility

13. Report content. Submit a written report (the Market Survey) which shall include:

    o Who was contacted
    o Where they are located with respect to site
    o When contact was made
    o Why they were contacted
    o What information was obtained
    o A summary assessment with specific recommendations

14. Scheduling. The survey must be conducted before the Design Development (Tentatives) submission to enable the A-E sufficient time to address/revise design, incorporate bid alternates, change construction schedule, or whatever else might be necessary to assure project feasibility.

Figure 5.17 Excerpt of market survey requirements for GSA.

schematic design phase, but certainly any decisions being made should be investigated in the context of their impact on life-cycle costs. Figure 5.18 presents an analysis conducted on the Merchants Exchange Building for the National Park Service in Philadelphia to help decide whether the historic structure could be renovated and reused or new space had to be procured. The analysis indicated that many of the costs necessary to renovate and reuse the historic structure were also necessary to privatize the facility. In addition, alternate rental

Life-Cycle Cost Analysis
General Purpose Worksheet

Study Title: Lease Build Analysis - Government Office Bldg.
Discount Rate: 6.3% Date: 1/28/98
Life Cycle (Yrs.): 30

		Alternative 1 Renovate Historic Facility		Alternative 2 Lease Space From GSA		Alternative 3 Renovate Current Space	
Initial/Collateral Costs		Estimated Costs	Present Worth	Estimated Costs	Present Worth	Estimated Costs	Present Worth
A.	Work in MEB						
B.	Hazardous Materials Removal & Structural Rehab	5,509,000	5,509,000	5,509,000	5,509,000	5,509,000	5,509,000
C.	Historic Preservation	2,255,258	2,255,258				
D.	Basic Program Needs	6,930,742	6,930,742				
E.	Lease Space - Interior Fitout- Basic Program Needs			500,000	500,000		
F.	Work in Current Space (3-Buildings)						
G.	Hazardous Materials Removal & Structural Rehab	2,490,000	2,490,000	2,490,000	2,490,000	2,490,000	2,490,000
H.	Historic Preservation					1,170,000	1,170,000
I.	Basic Program Needs - Construct., Fees, Sup. & Mods.					8,610,000	8,610,000
J.	- Moving & Swing Space Cost					1,450,000	1,450,000
	Total Initial/Collateral Costs	$17,185,000	$17,185,000	$8,499,000	$8,499,000	$19,229,000	$19,229,000
	Difference				$8,686,000		($2,044,000)

Replacement/Salvage (Single Expenditures)		Year	PW Factor	Estimated Costs	Present Worth		Estimated Costs	Present Worth
A.	Major Replacements	10	0.543	358,750	194,742		323,000	175,336
B.	Major Replacements	15	0.400	717,500	286,961		646,000	258,365
C.	Major Replacements	20	0.295	861,000	253,710		775,200	228,428
D.	Major Replacements	25	0.217	1,076,250	233,658		969,000	210,374
E.								
F.								
G.								
H.								
I.								
J.								
	Total Replacement/Salvage Costs				$969,072			$872,502

INITIAL / COLLATERAL COSTS

REPLACEMENT / SALVAGE COSTS

Annual Costs		Differential Escal. Rate	PW Factor						
A. Lease annual cost per OSF									
B. 27,000 OSF @	$26.25	2.7%	18.380			708,840	13,028,274		
C. O&M Costs									
D. 30,000 OSF @ $	5.00	2%	16.848	150,000	2,527,207				
E.									
F. 30,000 OSF @ $	4.43	2%	16.848					132,900	2,239,106
G. (equivalent over 28 years)									
H.									
I.									
J.									
Total Annual Costs				$150,000		$708,840		$132,900	
Total Life Cycle Costs (Present Worth)					$2,527,207		$13,028,274		$2,239,106
Total Life Cycle Costs (Present Worth)					$20,681,279		$21,527,274		$22,340,608
Life Cycle Cost PW Difference							($845,996)		($1,659,329)
Discounted Payback (Alt. 2,3,4 vs. Alt. 1)							12.2		70.9
Total Life Cycle Costs - Annualized				Per Year:	$1,551,016	Per Year:	$1,614,462	Per Year:	$1,675,459

ANNUAL COSTS

LIFE CYCLE COSTS

Figure 5.18 Life-cycle cost analysis at schematic design phase.

245

rates were substantially higher than the equivalent rental rate within the renovated facility. Therefore, it was decided, and subsequently justified to Congress, to renovate the MEB.

7. *Benchmark.* Benchmarking efforts initiated under planning and programming provide essential input to the cost management process and to the VE effort. Benchmark comparisons can help determine the validity of the current estimate as well as that of the overall cost management approach. Benchmarking can be done at a level of detail appropriate to the scope and magnitude of the project and to the criticality of the benchmarking effort itself. For extremely large and important projects, such as federal courts, benchmarking is also an important component. Figure 5.19 excerpts a recent benchmarking effort conducted for GSA. The amount of information studied and the degree of effort can be interpreted from the figure.

The cost management tasks undertaken during the conceptual and schematic design phase result in an updated cost plan by discipline, and include updated budgets and parameter targets. Often, it is important to critically compare and adjust discipline budgets in order to maintain overall budget and to retain a proper balance between systems. This process is difficult, and can be contentious, but it is essential if the project is to remain within budget and meet critical expectations.

Managing Design Development Phase Costs

The design development phase [see Figure 5.1(c)] of a project involves advancing the schematic design and developing more definitive design elements for most

Cost Management Methodology

Benchmark Analysis Tables 5.4 - 5.6 Date: 12/1998

Project: Federal Court 1

Recap of Normalized Cost for the Federal Court 1 Courthouse From Tables 4.3b & 5.1.a

	Federal Court 1			Federal Court 2			Federal Court 3		
	Cost of Construction	Total Area (GSF)	$/SF	Cost of Construction	Total Area (GSF)	$/SF	Cost of Construction	Total Area (GSF)	$/SF
Normalized Cost (escalated and area factor)	$76,295,000	633,197 SF	$120.49/GSF	$36,948,000	239,701 SF	$154.14/GSF	$57,299,000	404,277 SF	$141.73/GSF
Normalized Cost (with parking)	$76,295,000	633,197 GSF		$36,948,000	239,701 GSF		$57,299,000	404,277 GSF	
GSF (with parking)									
OSF based on quantity measurement		502,758 OSF			205,152 OSF			314,103 OSF	
Parking Normalized Cost	($5,579,000)			($2,526,000)			($4,654,000)		
Parking GSF using measured average Efficiency %		174,698 GSF			45,678 GSF			159,021 GSF	
Parking OSF based on quantity measurement		138,710 OSF			39,146 OSF			126,899 OSF	
Normalized Cost (without parking)	$70,716,000	458,499 GSF	$154.23/GSF	$34,422,000	194,023 GSF	$177.41/GSF	$52,645,000	245,256 GSF	$214.65/GSF

Table 5.4.a Functioning Courtrooms Provided in Original Bid

	Federal Court 1	Federal Court 2	Federal Court 3
US District Court: Ceremonial	1 EA	1 EA	1 EA
US District Court: Standard	4 EA	3 EA	2 EA
US Circuit Court: Standard	2 EA	1 EA	0 EA
US Magistrate Court: Standard	3 EA	0 EA	2 EA
US Bankruptcy Court: Standard	1 EA	1 EA	2 EA
TOTAL COURTROOMS IN ORIGINAL BID	11 EA	6 EA	7 EA
Normalized Cost (without parking)	$70,716,000	$34,422,000	$52,645,000
$/Courtroom	$6,429,000 /Court	$5,737,000 /Court	$7,521,000 /Court

Table 5.4.b Maximum Courtroom Capacity

	Federal Court 1	Federal Court 2	Federal Court 3
TOTAL EXPANSION COURTROOMS	9 EA	4 EA	3 EA
Cost to fitout courtrooms 10/1/97 pricing	$4,500,000	$2,000,000	$1,500,000
MAXIMUM COURTROOOM CAPACITY	20 EA	10 EA	10 EA
Cost of Courthouse w/max courts in 10/97 $ (without parking)	$75,216,000	$36,422,000	$54,145,000
$/Courtroom	$3,761,000 /Court	$3,642,000 /Court	$5,415,000 /Court

Table 5.6.a Distribution of Project Space

	FC1 OSF	FC1 % OSF w/o Parking	FC1 GSF	FC2 OSF	FC2 % OSF w/o Parking	FC2 GSF	FC3 OSF	FC3 % OSF w/o Parking	FC3 GSF
Total Normalized OSF	502,758 OSF		633,197 GSF	205,152 OSF		239,701 GSF	314,103 OSF		404,277 GSF
Parking Normalized OSF	138,710 OSF		174,698 GSF	39,146 OSF		45,678 GSF	126,899 OSF		159,021 GSF
Total OSF w/o Parking	364,048 OSF		458,499 GSF	166,006 OSF		194,023 GSF	187,204 OSF		245,256 GSF
Courts/Judiciary (Class 11, 14 & 15)	53,848 OSF	15%	67,819 GSF	29,160 OSF	18%	34,081 GSF	25,500 OSF	14%	33,408 GSF
Judicial Office (Class 2)	189,137 OSF	52%	238,208 GSF	91,532 OSF	55%	106,980 GSF	105,651 OSF	56%	138,413 GSF
Regular Office (Class 1)	0 OSF	0%	0 GSF	0 OSF	0%	0 GSF	0 OSF	0%	0 GSF
Other	121,063 OSF	33%	152,473 GSF	45,314 OSF	27%	52,962 GSF	56,053 OSF	30%	73,435 GSF

Table 5.7.b Distribution of Normalized Project Costs Including Maximum Number of Courtrooms

	FC1 Construction Cost & Area	FC1 GSF	FC1 $/SF	FC2 Construction Cost & Area	FC2 GSF	FC2 $/SF	FC3 Construction Cost & Area	FC3 GSF	FC3 $/SF
Normalized Cost w/Parking	$80,346,000		$126.89 /GSF	$38,767,000		$161.73 /GSF	$58,631,000		$145.03 /GSF
Total GSF	633,197 GSF	0 GSF	$31.94 /GSF		0 GSF	$55.30 /GSF		0 GSF	$29.27 /GSF
Parking Normalized Cost	$5,579,000			$2,526,000			$4,654,000		
Courts/Judiciary Cost	$25,458,000	123,307 GSF	$206.46 /GSF	$12,971,000	56,802 GSF	$228.35 /GSF	$13,078,000	47,725 GSF	$274.03 /GSF
Judicial Office Cost	$24,386,000	182,720 GSF	$133.46 /GSF	$12,500,000	84,259 GSF	$148.35 /GSF	$22,465,000	124,096 GSF	$181.03 /GSF
Other Cost	$24,923,000	152,473 GSF	$163.46 /GSF	$10,770,000	52,962 GSF	$203.35 /GSF	$18,434,000	73,435 GSF	$251.03 /GSF

Figure 5.19 Example of detailed benchmark for federal courthouses.

247

of the major building systems. Design development is the last opportunity in the design process to significantly alter the composition of the design without causing a subsequent delay in the project or adding the cost of redesign. Changes during this phase generally need to be accommodated within the form, shape, and massing as defined during the schematic design by adjusting the specific design approaches for each building system.

The steps in the process are very similar to those conducted during schematic design, with the primary difference being that the level of detail is deeper because more information is available and the focus on decision making is narrower and tends to be more focused within each individual discipline. Here are the steps:

1. *Solicit ongoing advice.* Throughout the design development phase it continues to be important to solicit ongoing input regarding decisions as they are being considered. The input during design development will tend to be more detailed; likewise, more decisions will be made than during schematic design. Consequently, it is more urgent that conclusions be drawn. In some circumstances, the general decisions made during schematic design will become more specific choices during this phase. It is also important at this step to record the issues under consideration, as well as the result of recording those issues. Figure 5.20 reproduces an example of a form that can be used for the purpose of recording and presenting issues for ongoing cost analysis.

2. *Establish milestone estimate.* Establishing a milestone estimate at the conclusion of design development is a critical step in the overall cost

VALUE ENHANCED DESIGN	DESIGN INVESTIGATION DOCUMENTATION FORM
	ITEM NUMBER:
PROJECT:	SYSTEM:
LOCATION:	ITEM:
CLIENT:	
DATE:	

STEP 1 - Define Issue / Ideas
ISSUE UNDER CONSIDERATION :

CURRENT APPROACH / DESIGN :

OPTION (S) UNDER CONSIDERATION :

STEP 2 - Investigation, Analysis & Cost Impact
RECOMMENDATION :

ADVANTAGES:

DISADVANTAGES :

Cost Impact : (Recommendation versus Current Approach + Saving (-) Added cost)	Initial Cost $	Present Value of Future O&M Costs $	Total Life Cycle Costs $

Step 3 : Status & Approval

❑ Investigation in process
❑ Recommendation Submitted

*Date Due :*_____

Owner Action :

❑ Accepted
❑ Rejected / Dropped

*Approval Date :*_____

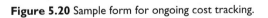
Figure 5.20 Sample form for ongoing cost tracking.

management process. If the estimate is in error and requires adjustment, any significant changes will alter schedule or significantly affect the budget. The purpose of the estimate is to verify the status of the budget, as well as to verify the individual cost of components and systems that have been allocated to each discipline. Figure 5.21 summarizes a cost plan comparison for a recent GSA project. Note that the design development phase (referred to as "tentative design" in GSA) involves the reconciliation of two estimates, one by the design team and one by a construction manager hired by GSA. The design development phase also presents the first opportunity to prepare estimates both in UNIFORMAT and in Master-Format.

3. *Assess market conditions, contingencies, and escalation.* It is important at this stage to update the market survey prepared during schematic design; or, if no survey was prepared, now is the time to do so. It is also important to review the contingencies, escalation, and impact of any major risks that had been identified. It continues to be important that the design team participate in the development of an estimate and verify the assumptions being made for any systems not detailed during design development.

4. *Revise the cost plan.* The eventual estimate will detail the key parameter measures that have been defined for each discipline, along with their individual cost allocations. This requires that a revised cost plan/cost model be drawn, to collect and summarize the estimate and compare it against the previous cost plan for the purpose of evaluating status and progress, keeping in mind that, at this point, the ability to adjust is limited.

Project: GOVERNMENT AGENCY
Location: PHILADELPHIA, PA

Project No: GS
Estimator: HANSCOMB INC

Construction Cost (ECCA) (Level 2)		Concept Budget Est-1 Date: 05/14/96	%	Tentative Budget 1 Est-1 Date: 09/17/97	%	CM-1 Date: 09/18/97	%
01 FOUNDATIONS		1,035,312	2%	1,267,759	3%	1,725,240	3%
02 SUBSTRUCTURE		2,722,423	6%	2,070,874	4%	2,522,385	5%
03 SUPERSTRUCTURE		9,392,566	22%	10,818,279	22%	9,447,036	18%
04 EXTERIOR CLOSURE		3,020,809	7%	3,064,912	6%	4,779,887	9%
05 ROOFING		1,277,017	3%	967,389	2%	992,538	2%
06 INTERIOR CONSTRUCTION		5,771,909	13%	8,975,814	18%	9,914,397	19%
07 CONVEYING SYSTEMS		618,000	1%	618,500	1%	381,000	1%
08 MECHANICAL		7,974,592	18%	9,382,697	19%	9,792,370	19%
09 ELECTRICAL		4,910,362	11%	6,354,995	13%	6,295,981	12%
10 GENERAL CONDITIONS & PROFIT		4,907,988	11%	4,573,893	9%	4,331,174	8%
11 EQUIPMENT		1,094,374	3%	1,008,490	2%	1,120,782	2%
12 SITEWORK/DEMO & HAZMAT ABATEMENT		683,800	2%	1,183,258	2%	1,545,970	3%
SCHEDULE CONTRACT DATE **JULY 1999**							
SUBTOTAL		43,409,152		50,286,860		52,848,760	
DESIGN CONTINGENCY		6,511,373	15%	5,028,686	10%	2,642,438	5%
ESCALATION TO SCHEDULED CONTRACT DATE		2,660,764	6%	1,508,606	3%	3,329,467	6%
Progressive Cost		52,581,289		56,824,152		58,820,665	
Target Cost (ECCA)	56,340,000						
Difference from Target Cost							
Cost per SF	$126.56 /SF	$121.80 /SF		$125.51 /SF		$131.82 /SF	
Cost per SM	$1,362 /M2	$1,310/ M2		$1,350/ M2		$1,418/ M2	
Gross Floor Area	41,361 M2	40,130 M2		42,083 M2		41,479 M2	
Gross Floor Area	445,174 SF	431,719 SF		452,729 SF		446,231 SF	

Figure 5.21 Cost plan update example.

251

5. *Conduct value engineering study.* As part of overall cost management process, it is strongly recommended that a second value engineering study be conducted at the conclusion or near the conclusion of design development, to evaluate the major system alternatives that have been defined. Figures 5.22 and 5.23 reproduce a recommendation of a recent U.S. embassy project that suggested a more durable exterior wall material than the stucco system that was presented with the original design. Figure 5.23 contains the life-cycle cost analysis that helped to justify the selection of the more durable material on the basis of improved life-cycle performance. In this case, there was an additional initial capital cost investment that was paid back in six years according to the assumptions. A companion analysis considered a 10-year replacement cycle for the stucco that still showed the beneficial life-cycle performance but with a longer payback. At the design development stage, constructibility issues should also be considered, particularly for renovation projects.

6. *Account for life-cycle costing/sustainability.* The design development phase is an excellent opportunity to refine decisions based on a consideration of life-cycle cost and sustainability. It becomes extremely important to verify whether a United States Green Buildings Council (USGBC) Leadership in Energy & Environmental Design (LEED) rating is desired, and if so whether the rating is to be bronze, silver, gold, or platinum. Study has shown that attaining these ratings can potentially have a cost impact on the project, in particular for a rating above silver. More information can be obtained on the LEED system,

DEVELOPMENT PHASE	VALUE ENGINEERING PROPOSAL
	Proposal No. AS-18
PROJECT: New Office Building	SYSTEM: Architectural
LOCATION: Overseas Location	ITEM: Consider alternate finish material on the north, east and west walls of the NOB.
CLIENT: US Department of State	
DATE: April 18-21, 2000	

ORIGINAL DESIGN:
The entire north elevation of the NOB (59 m wide x 23 m high) is finished with painted plaster (excluding stone water course).
Parts of the east and west elevations (each 17 m wide x 23 m high) are painted plaster (excluding stone water course).

PROPOSED DESIGN:
- Stone veneer panels in lieu of painted plaster finish on the major building elevations.
  [Alternate: architectural finished concrete if the appropriate concrete skills are locally available]

ADVANTAGES:
- Provides an exterior finish material that is in keeping with the representational image of a U.S. Embassy.
- Low maintenance material; does not require periodic patching and painting that is required by painted plaster.

DISADVANTAGES:
- Higher initial cost; possible impact on project delivery schedule.

DISCUSSION/VERIFICATION:
ISSUES: Representational Image; Maintainability; Life-cycle Costs.
The goal of FBO is to provide buildings that are representational in nature. Although it is understood that painted plaster is a frequently used material in the vicinity of Overseas Location, there is a question if this material is the most appropriate to be used so extensively on the highest profile building in the compound.

There is also a question of the maintainability (life-cycle costs) of plaster veneer in a climate of frequent freeze/thaw cycles. Although plaster veneers is used frequently in the vicinity of Overseas Location, it will require periodic painting and repair. While this may be an acceptable maintenance issue in the private sector in Overseas Location, this periodic maintenance may be disruptive to the activities at the NOB.

Attached are two life cycle cost analyses presenting a seven-year replacement cycle and a ten-year replacement cycle for the stucco. The seven-year cycle indicates a 5.8-year payback and the 10-year cycle indicates a 10.6-year payback cycle. A precise determination of component life is very difficult but the LCC analyses are presented to assist in FBO's value judgment.

LIFE CYCLE COST SUMMARY	COSTS & SAVINGS (PRESENT VALUE)		
	Initial Cost	O&M	Total LCC
Original Design	530,000		
Proposed Design	1,327,000		
Savings	(796,000)		

Figure 5.22 Value engineering proposal for U.S. embassy project.

its certification process, rating system, and project checklist at www.usgbc.org/programs/leed-frames.htm.

7. *Benchmark.* Benchmarking continues to be an important aid in the overall cost management

Life-Cycle Costing – General Purpose Worksheet
NOB Overseas Location, Overseas Location

						Stucco Veneer Exterior Wall (7 Year Cycle)		Stone Veneer Exterior Wall	
Study Title:	Comparison Stucco to Stone Cladding (AS-18)								
Discount Rate :	6.0%	Date:	April 24, 2000			Estimated Costs	Present Worth	Estimated Costs	Present Worth
Life Cycle (Yrs.)	30								

						Estimated Costs	Present Worth	Estimated Costs	Present Worth
INITIAL / COLLATERAL COSTS	**Initial/Collateral Costs**								
	A. North Elevation	Stucco	$ 224	1350 m2		302,400	302,400		
	B. East Elevation	Stucco	$ 224	480 m2		107,520	107,520		
	C. West Elevation	Stucco	$ 224	540 m2		120,960	120,960		
	D. North Elevation	Stone	$ 560	1350 m2				756,000	756,000
	E. East Elevation	Stone	$ 560	480 m2				268,800	268,800
	F. West Elevation	Stone	$ 560	540 m2				302,400	302,400
	G.								
	H.	Total Wall Area =		2370 m2					
	I.								
	J.								
	Total Initial/Collateral Costs					$530,880	$530,880	$1,327,200	$1,327,200
	Difference								($796,320)

			Occurance Year -or- Cycle	Inflation/ Escal. Rate	PW Factor	Estimated Costs	Present Worth	Estimated Costs	Present Worth
REPLACEMENT / SALVAGE COSTS	**Replacement/Salvage (Single Expenditures)**								
	A. Stucco Replacement		7	2%	2.134	743,232	1,586,047		
	B. Stucco Repaint/Refinish		4	2%	3.964	51,002	202,191		
	C. Stone Cleaning		10	2%	1.144			30,601	35,008
	D.								
	E.								
	F.								
	G.								
	H.								
	I.								
	J.								
	Total Replacement/Salvage Costs						$1,788,238		$35,008

				Inflation/ Escal. Rate	PW Factor	Estimated Costs	Present Worth	Estimated Costs	Present Worth
ANNUAL COSTS	**Annual Costs**								
	A. Annual Maintenance			2%	17.458	6,120	106,847	2,040	35,616
	B.								
	C.								
	D.								
	E.								
	F.								
	G.								
	H.								
	I.								
	J.								
	Total Annual Costs					$6,120	$106,847	$2,040	$35,616
	Sub-Total Replacement/Salvage + Annual Costs (Present Worth)						$1,895,085		$70,624
	Difference								

LIFE CYCLE COSTS	**Total Life Cycle Costs (Present Worth)**						$2,425,965		$1,397,824
	Life Cycle Cost PW Difference								$1,028,141
	Payback - Simple Discounted (Added Cost / Annualized Savings)								6.0 Yrs.
	Payback - Fully Discounted (Added Cost+Interest / Annualized Savings)								7.7 Yrs.
	Total Life Cycle Costs - Annualized					Per Year:	$176,244	Per Year:	$101,550

Figure 5.23 LCC Analysis for VE proposal for U.S. embassy project.

process. At the design development stage, benchmarking can provide a cross-check of overall project viability, and may be used to assess individual project components as well. For example, the mechanical system costs on other similar laboratories could be examined for a research laboratory under design as a means of verifying the mechanical design. It is also possible and beneficial to benchmark key facility parameters that are relatively easy to measure and that are not based directly on cost. For example, this laboratory could benchmark the pounds of ductwork per square foot of building area for the laboratories being studied. In this way, it would be possible to determine whether the design was reasonable in comparison to other similar projects, and, if there were a difference, that difference could be explained. The point is, benchmarking can involve parameter verification as well as costs.

Cost management activity during the design development phase again results in an updated cost plan by discipline, and includes updated budgets and parameter targets. Likewise, it is again necessary to critically compare and adjust discipline budgets in order to maintain the overall budget and to retain a proper balance between systems. At this phase, however, the process is even more difficult and contentious than during schematic design because system design has advanced and changes are more difficult to implement; nonetheless, it is essential for the project to remain within budget and continue to meet critical expectations.

Figure 5.24 provides a copy of the updated cost plan for the apartment presented previously, based on the design development estimate. The results indicate that overall costs have increased by approximately $1 million, or a growth of approximately 15 percent. Obviously, this is not an acceptable circumstance because the financial viability of the apartment project is based on projected rental and

BUILDING COST SUMMARY

Project Description:	Apartment - Cost Plan (Updated DD)					Bid Date:		1/02	
Project Type:	**Apartments**					Construction time(Months):		9	
Gross Building Area:(GSF	54,859					Market Conditions:		good	

	SYSTEM / ELEMENT DESCRIPTION	UNIFORMAT REFERENCE	TOTAL COST	COST PER GSF	% OF BUILDING	ELEMENTAL ANALYSIS			
						MEASURE	UNIT	VALUE	COST/UNIT
	BUILDING:		b	b / GSF	b / 27			c	b / c
1	Foundations	(A10)	264,280	4.82	4.9%	Ground Floor Area	SF	19,485	13.56
2	Standard Foundations	(A1010)	124,815	2.28	2.3%	Ground Floor Area	SF	19,485	6.41
3	Other Foundations	(A1020)	–	–	0.0%	Ground Floor Area	SF	19,485	–
4	Slab on Grade	(A1030)	139,465	2.54	2.6%	Ground Floor Area	SF	19,485	7.16
5	Basement Construction	(A20)	–	–	0.0%	Ground Floor Area	SF	19,485	–
6	Substructure—Subtotal	(A)	264,280	4.82	4.9%	Ground Floor Area	SF	19,485	13.56
7	Superstructure	(B10)	537,672	9.80	10.0%	Gross Bldg. Area	EA	54,859	9.80
8	Exterior Enclosure	(B20)	805,117	14.68	15.0%	Gross Enclosure Area	EA	36,437	22.10
9	Roofing	(B30)	224,273	4.09	4.2%	Roof Surface Area	SF	23,188	9.67
10	Shell—Subtotal	(B)	1,567,062	28.57	29.2%	Gross Bldg. Area	SF	54,859	28.57
11	Interior Construction	(C10)	975,989	17.79	18.2%	Gross Bldg. Area	SF	54,859	17.79
12	Stairs	(C20)	18,623	0.34	0.3%	Gross Bldg. Area	SF	54,859	0.34
13	Interior Finishes	(C30)	463,658	8.45	8.6%	Gross Bldg. Area	SF	54,859	8.45
14	Interiors—Subtotal	(C)	1,458,270	26.58	27.1%	Gross Bldg. Area	SF	54,859	26.58
15	Conveying Systems	(D10)	108,966	1.99	2.0%	Total No. of Stops	EA	3	36,322
16	Plumbing	(D20)	633,451	11.55	11.8%	No. of Fixtures	EA	296	2,140
17	HVAC	(D30)	434,263	7.92	8.1%	Tons (or MBH)	EA	90	4,825
18	Fire Protection	(D40)	174,783	3.19	3.3%	Protected Area	SF	54,859	3.19
19	Electrical	(D50)	731,378	13.33	13.6%	Gross Bldg. Area	SF	54,859	13.33
20	Electrical Service & Distribution	(D5010)	206,089	3.76	3.8%	Connected KW	KW	274	751
21	Lighting & Branch Wiring	(D5020)	352,363	6.42	6.6%	Gross Bldg. Area	SF	54,859	6.42
22	Communications & Security	(D5030)	137,454	2.51	2.6%	Gross Bldg. Area	SF	54,859	2.51
23	Other Electrical Systems	(D5040)	35,472	0.65	0.7%	Gross Bldg. Area	SF	54,859	0.65
24	Services—Subtotal	(D)	2,082,841	37.97	38.8%	Gross Bldg. Area	SF	54,859	37.97
25	Equip. & Furnishings—Subtotal	(E)	–	–	0.0%	Gross Bldg. Area	SF	54,859	–
26	Spec. Construct. & Demo—Subtotal	(F)	–	–	0.0%	Gross Bldg. Area	SF	54,859	–
27	**TOTAL BUILDING**		$ 5,372,454	$ 97.93	100.0%	Accommodation Units	EA	95	$ 56,552
28	**SITEWORK & UTILITIES:**								
29	Site Preparation	(G10)	92,184	1.68	1.7%	Gross Site Area	SF	85,500	1.08
30	Site Improvements	(G20)	344,330	6.28	6.4%	Gross Site Area	SF	85,500	4.03
31	Site Mechanical Utilities	(G30)	110,534	2.01	2.1%	Gross Site Area	SF	85,500	1.29
32	Site Electrical Utilities	(G40)	7,991	0.15	0.1%	Gross Site Area	SF	85,500	0.09
33	Other Site Construction	(G50)	–	–	0.0%	Gross Site Area	SF	85,500	–
34	**TOTAL SITEWORK & UTILITIES:**	(G)	555,039	10.12	10.3%	Gross Site Area	SF	85,500	6.49
35	General Conditions, Overhead & Profit @ 11.0%		652,024	11.89	12.1%				
36	**TOTAL FACILITY COST - CURRENT**		$ 6,579,518	$ 119.94	122.5%	Accommodation Units	EA	95	$ 69,258
37	Contingency @ 10.0%		657,952	11.99	12.2%				
38	Escalation @		–	–	0.0%				
39									
40	**TOTAL FACILITY COST - PROJECTED**		$ 7,237,469	$ 131.93	134.7%	Accommodation Units	EA	95	$ 76,184

Parameters:		Measure	Value	Area Analysis:	Area (SF)
1	Gross Bldg. Area	SF	54,859		
2	Ground Floor Area	SF	19,485	Basement	–
3	Gross Enclosure Area	SF	36,437	Ground Floor	19,485
4	Percent Fenestration	%	9%	Upper Floors	35,374
5	Roof Surface Area	SF	23,188	Penthouses	
6	Total No.of Conveying Stops	STOPS	3	Other Areas	–
7	Tons Cooling (or MBH Htg)	TONS	90		
8	No. of Plumbing Fixtures	EA	296	Gross Floor Area	54,859
9	Fire Protected Area	SF	54,859		
10	Connected KW	KW	274		
11	Accommodation Units	EA	95		
12	Floor to Floor Height (Avg.)	LF	9		
13	Gross Site Area	SF	85,500		

Figure 5.24 Updated apartment cost plan: design development.

occupancy rates of the pro forma. The allowable capital expenditure calculated from the pro forma was used to prepare the original cost plan. Figure 5.25 is a graphical representation that enables comparison of previous cost plans. In it, the upper number and each block represent the cost per square foot from the original cost plan at schematic design. The lower figure in each block represents the cost per square foot as estimated. The results indicate a total difference of approximately $16 per square foot, primarily made up of exterior closure at $5 per square foot, HVAC at $1 per square foot, and communications and security at $1 per square foot. In addition, the gross area has increased by slightly over 1,000 square feet. The combination of all these items has resulted in the million-dollar total increase. It is also interesting to note that the parameter measure on the exterior wall in the original cost model represented expectations of 28,200 square feet in comparison to 38,400 square feet as indicated on the cost model assessment. This is a major driver in the differences overall and would be an area of focus by the team as to why the increase occurred. If, in fact, the increase in wall area is necessary to meet project expectations, then in order to remain within budget, other areas would have to be compromised to allow for the overall cost to remain within the budget. It should also be noted that this significant a difference occurring at design development is correctable, though probably not without difficulty.

Managing Costs during the Construction Documents Phase

The construction documents phase of a project involves advancing design development and finaliz-

Apartment - Cost Plan (Updated DD) — Date: October-01 — Phase: Preliminary
Wash D.C. Basis

	Current Construction	+	Contingency @ 10.00%	+	Escalation @ 0.00%	=	Construction @ Bid Date
Target	$105.01		$10.50		$0.00		$115.51
Actual/Estimated	$119.94		$11.99		$0.00		$131.93

Project Location

	GSF	54,859
Bldg Type	NSF	0
Const. Type — Wood Frame	Floors	3
Use Units — 95 Appts		

Apartments

Comparative Ratios:

Parameter	Target	ACT/EST
Cost per Apartment	$65,394	$69,258
Gross Area	53,783	54,859
Exterior Closure SF	28,213	36,437

Legend:
Target (Per Cost Plan)
Actual/Estimated

Node	Target	Actual/Estimated
Building (G)	$95.45	$109.82
Site (G)	$9.56	$10.12

Building breakdown

Component	Target	Actual/Estimated
Structural	$13.54	$14.62
Std. Foundation (A1010)	$2.11	$2.28
Special Foundations (A1020)	$0.00	$0.00
Slab on Grade (A1030)	$2.36	$2.54
Superstructure (B10)	$9.08	$9.80
Architectural	$39.31	$47.33
Ext. Closure (B20)	$9.62	$14.68
Roofing (B30)	$3.78	$4.09
Interiors (C)	$24.02	$26.58
Conveying Sys. (D10)	$1.88	$1.99
Mechanical	$20.74	$22.65
HVAC (D30)	$6.84	$7.92
Plumbing (D20)	$10.89	$11.55
Fire Protection (D40)	$3.01	$3.19
Electrical	$11.45	$13.33
Service & Distribution (D5010)	$3.55	$3.76
Lighting & Branch Wiring (D5020)	$5.76	$6.42
Comm & Security (D5030)	$1.53	$2.51
Other Electrical Sys (D5040)	$0.61	$0.65
Other Construction	$0.00	$0.00
Fixed Equipment (E10)	$0.00	$0.00
Furnishings (E20)	$0.00	$0.00
Special Construction (F10)	$0.00	$0.00
Building Demolition (F20)		
GC, OH & Profit (10)	$10.41	$11.89
Mobilization Expenses (Bond)	$0.00	$0.00
Job Site Overheads	$0.00	$0.00
Demobilization	$0.00	$0.00
Off Expense & Profit	$10.41	$11.89

Site breakdown

Component	Target	Actual/Estimated
Site Preparation (G10)	$1.59	$1.68
Site Improvement (G20)	$5.93	$6.28
Site Utilities (G30,40)	$2.04	$2.16
Other Site Construction (G50)	$0.00	$0.00

Figure 5.25 Cost plan assessment of design development versus schematics.

258

ing design elements for all building systems. This phase represents the last opportunity in the design process to adjust and tune the design. That said, these changes should be kept relatively minor and within the context of the major design decisions already made in order to avoid delays or added design costs.

The steps in the process are nearly identical to those just enumerated for the design development phase [see Figure 5.1(c)], the primary difference being that the level of detail is again deeper, because more information is available and the focus on decision making is narrower and almost completely within individual disciplines. The steps are these:

1. *Solicit ongoing advice.* Throughout the construction documents phase, it continues to be important to request input to the decisions as they are under consideration. The input at this stage will tend to be very detailed and oriented toward design details and specifications. In some cases, the general decisions made during design development will become more specific choices for construction documents, especially in terms of alternates for bidding. The method of recording the issues under consideration, as well as the result of recording of those issues, as previously shown in Figure 5.20, continue to be valuable for ongoing cost analysis.

2. *Establish a milestone estimate.* Setting a milestone estimate both during and at the conclusion of the construction documents phase is an important step in the overall cost management process because these estimates are the last opportunity to change the cost of the project. The purpose of the estimate is to verify the sta-

tus of the budget, as well as to verify the individual cost of components and systems that have been allocated to each discipline. This estimate may be produced either in UNIFORMAT or in MasterFormat with a UNIFORMAT summary.

3. *Assess market conditions, contingencies, and escalation.* It is important during this phase to update the market survey prepared during design development. It is also important to review the considerations of contingencies, escalation, and the impact of any major risks that had been identified. Toward the end of the construction documents phase, contingencies should be approaching zero; if they are not, those contingencies should be clearly identified as to what they represent and how they will be mitigated. It continues to be important that the design team participate in the development of an estimate and verify any continuing assumptions, although these assumptions should be minor because the design is reaching completion. Finalizing the market expectation and evaluating competing projects at bid time are important steps.

4. *Revise cost plan.* The eventual estimate will detail the key parameter measures that have been defined for each discipline, along with their individual cost allocations. This leads to a revised cost plan/cost model that collects and summarizes the estimate overall and compares it against the previous cost plan, to evaluate status and progress. At this point, the ability to adjust is extremely limited. Most likely, the only real opportunities for change will involve bid options.

5. *Conduct value engineering study.* As part of the overall cost management process, it may be

beneficial to conduct an additional value engineering study at or near the conclusion of the construction documents phase for the purposes of evaluating the major system alternatives that have been defined and assessing constructibility issues. Constructibility issues should also be considered in particular for renovation projects. Generally, at the construction documents phase, value engineering studies often focus on significant budget variations, which is generally an unpleasant activity. However, if cost reduction is necessary to meet budget requirements, a value engineering study is a balanced and objective away of achieving the cost reduction while limiting the impact on the design.

6. *Account for life-cycle costing/sustainability.* The construction documents phase offers limited opportunity to refine life-cycle costing and sustainability issues identified during design development. There is, however, an opportunity to refine the LEED rating and to fine-tune aspects of life-cycle performance.

7. *Benchmark.* Benchmarking continues to be an important aid in the overall cost management process. At the construction documents stage, benchmarking can provide a cross-check of overall project viability, and may be used to assess individual project components as well. More often than not, at the construction documents phase, benchmarking is more of a political asset for justifying a given condition than it is a tool for adjustment. Nonetheless, benchmarking can still be a very useful tool.

The cost management activity during the construction documents phase results in a final cost plan by discipline, and includes updated budgets and parameter targets. At this juncture, it is again necessary to critically compare and adjust discipline budgets in order to maintain overall budget and to retain a proper balance between systems. This process becomes even more challenging than the previous two because system design is nearly finalized and changes are difficult to implement. Still, it is essential for the project to remain within budget and continue to meet critical expectations. The basic theme of cost management during this phase is adjusting, fine-tuning, and selecting opportunities for bid options.

Implementing Construction Phase Cost Management

Construction phase cost management consists of two major steps: bid the project and oversee the construction process and any change orders. Collecting historical cost information along the way is another useful process.

Bidding Factors

The bidding process and the input from the cost manager can vary from very little to substantial depending, on the activities of the owner and any of the owner's consultants. Regardless who performs the tasks, however, there are a certain number of very important factors that should be considered for bidding. These are summarized in the following subsections.

Alternate Prices: Additive or Deductive?

Whenever possible, any prices for alternates should be considered as *add alternates*. Why? Because bidding contractors and their subcontractors will consider pricing as a whole as much as possible, because achieving competitiveness is on the whole and not the parts. Generally, deductive alternates will seldom result in full dollar value because the whole is calculated at one level, whereas a deduction is generally calculated at only a partial level. Therefore, whenever possible, it's best to arrange for the base bid condition to be a competitive and complete facility and to regard the add alternates as desirable but not necessary.

An option to achieve a result similar to using deductive alternates is to have add alternates expressed in a priority order. This means that the award of a contract would be based on base bid and all alternates if the total is within an award amount. If it is not within an award amount, then the least important alternate would be excluded and the balance would again be considered using the same process. This method generally allows for award of contract and minimizes complaints from the bidding contractors because of potential arbitrary selection of alternates. The disadvantage is that the owner must prioritize alternates.

Unit Prices: Are They Worth It?

Unit prices can be very useful in the award of initial contract, as well as later as part of any change order negotiation. That said, bidding contractors are not fond of unit prices and will pay little attention to them unless they are part of the eventual award of the contract. One method for dealing with this reluctance is to assign a representative quantity for each unit price and calculate that extension as part of the bid offer. In that way, competitiveness is retained in the unit prices. Caution is required in the number of unit prices used, their veracity for the actual award, and their potential use downstream. The amount of definition necessary to clarify unit prices is another issue.

Cash Allowances: Accuracy Is Essential

Cash allowances in a contract can be useful as a risk-limiting device for the bidders, but if they are not accurate, they can lead to substantial problems downstream. Therefore, the advice is to carefully consider and estimate any cash allowances and ensure they are not used as an excuse to avoid preparing a proper estimate or defining a proper design and specifications.

Cost Breakdowns: Avoid When Possible

Contractors universally dislike cost breakdowns to be submitted with a bid, and not without good reason. Assembling a bid requires a buyout process among a large number of subcontractors and suppliers that can continue for quite some time, leading up to the eleventh hour prior to bid. When a complicated bid form with a complicated cost breakdown is used, it may be very difficult, if not impossible, to assemble all of the subcontractor quotes into the bid form and still make the bid deadline. Typically what happens in this circumstance is that the contractors will fill in the bid form with numbers that may or may not have any bearing on reality but that will add up to the total. Subsequent use of this information is understandably dangerous.

The recommendation is to avoid detailed cost breakdowns if they do not have a valid purpose; if there is a valid purpose for the breakdowns, provide a reasonable amount of time after the submission of the lump sum figure to present them. For small and simple projects, one or two days is usually sufficient; for complicated projects, as much as a week may be necessary to allow the bidders to properly complete the bid breakdowns. The disadvantage of this approach is that the actual bid announcement cannot be made until the bid breakdowns have been received. Furthermore, the contractors will undoubtedly complain about any bid breakdowns regardless of their benefit or use. To minimize this, any requirements for bid breakdowns should be clearly stated in the general requirements of the contract so that it is not a last-minute requirement of the contractor or not perceived as such.

Schedule of Values: Specify the Format

Schedule-of-values information can be very useful for the owner for change order adjustment and for historical information. It is, of course, important to clearly specify the format and level of detail of a schedule of values as part of the general requirements of the contract. This enables the contractors to include in their bid a sum of money to cover the completion of a schedule of values.

The forms presented previously make it possible to establish a schedule of values in a MasterFormat 16-division format with a UNIFORMAT type summary. As with any cost information received from a contractor, care should be taken to assure that costs have been distributed in a reasonable manner and that they have not been significantly "front-loaded" by the contractor. Without proper oversight, it is possible for the contractor to excessively load costs in the early stages of the contract in order to draw more money early. The disadvantage of this tactic is that subsequent aspects of the contract will not have sufficient money tied to them, and should there be problems, the owner would not necessarily have enough money to complete the project.

Change Orders: Specify the Rules

It is critically important to specify as part of a contract the expected method of negotiating and adjusting for change orders. Too often, owners fail to add this information to the initial contract; this causes subsequent change order negotiations to be even more difficult. Change order rules should clearly state exactly how markups will be added for overhead and profit and, in particular, for general conditions at the job site.

Care must be taken to assure that fair markups are paid but that excessive markups are avoided, especially where full-time general conditions resources will also be charged hourly to change orders. Figure 5.26 presents a NAVFAC form used to complete and submit change order proposals. In this case the form is completed with NAVFAC "standard" suggested markups.

Performance Specifications: Change the Focus

Today, performance specifications are more often being included as part of construction contracts. In many respects, doing so is beneficial both to the owner and the contractor, as it allows a focus on performance instead of on specific means and methods. However, because this requires some form of infield verification and, potentially, negotiated pricing, it should be undertaken with great care.

ESTIMATE FOR CHANGE ORDERS (Less than $100,000.00):			Contract #:		
NAVFAC 4330/43 (8/88)			Date:		
CONTRACT TITLE:			Location:		

ROICC OFFICE:

CHANGE DESCRIPTION:

	PRIME CONTRACTOR'S WORK				Revision/Comments:
1 Direct Material			-		
2 Sales Tax on Material	4.5% of line 1	4.5 %	$0.00		
3 Direct Labor			-		
4 Insurance, Taxes, & Fringe Benefits	20% of line 3	20 %	$0.00		
5 Rental Equipment			-		
6 Sales Tax on Rental Equipment	4.5% of line 5	4.5 %	$0.00		
7 Equipment Ownership and Operating Expenses			$0.00		
8 SUBTOTAL (add lines 1-7)				$0.00	
9 Field Overhead	10% of line 8	10 %	$0.00		
10 SUBTOTAL (add lines 8 & 9)				$0.00	
Prime Remarks:					

	SUBCONTRACTOR'S WORK				Revision/Comments:
11 Direct Material			-		
12 Sales Tax on Material	6.0% of line 11	6 %	$0.00		
13 Direct Labor			-		
14 Insurance, Tax, and Fringe Benefits on	24% of line 13	24 %	$0.00		
15 Rental Equipment			-		
16 Sales Tax on Rental Equipment	6.0% of line 15	6 %	$0.00		
17 Equipment Ownership and Operating Expenses					
18 SUBTOTAL (add lines 11-17)				$0.00	
19 Field Overhead	10% of line 18	10 %	$0.00		
20 SUBTOTAL (add lines 18 & 19)				$0.00	
21 Home Office Overhead	03% of line 20	3 %	$0.00		
22 Profit (Weighed guidelines)	10% of line 20	10 %	$0.00		
23 SUBTOTAL (add lines 20 - 22)				$0.00	
Sub's Remarks:					

	SUMMARY				Revision/Comments:
24 Prime Contractor's Work (from line 10)			$0.00		
25 Subcontractor's Work (from line 23)			$0.00		
26 SUBTOTAL (add lines 24 & 25)				$0.00	
27 Prime Overhead on Subcontractor	5% of line 25	5 %	$0.00		
28 Prime Home Office Overhead	3% of line 24	3 %	$0.00		
29 Profit (Weighed guidelines)	10% of line 26	10 %	$0.00	$0.00	
30 SUBTOTAL (add lines 26 & 29)				$0.00	
31 Prime Contractor's Bond Premium	1% of line 30	1 %	$0.00		
32 TOTAL COST (add lines 30 & 31)				$0.00	
Estimate Time Extension and Justification:					

Prime Contractor and Subcontractor's Names:	
Prime:	
Sub:	
Signature & Title of Preparer:	
Name of Preparer:	

Figure 5.26 Sample NAVFAC Form 4330/43: Estimate for Change Orders.

Bid Analysis and Tabulations: Do Tight Numbers Mean Tight Competition?

Once bids have been received, it may be necessary to tabulate the bids and analyze them prior to award. Depending on the rules, regulations, and standards governing the owner, there may be an opportunity for negotiation, or award must be made to the low bidder. It will require finesse and care to find out the number of subcontractors that have bid and how competitive each trade has been.

To help in this regard, it may be possible to contact one of the higher bidders who is out of the running for information and illumination on the subject. Or it may be a good idea to directly contact the subcontractors. Even though they cannot divulge their numbers, they can certainly define their situation and those of their competitors. It is not at all uncommon to discover that what appears to be a very tight bid spread among general contractors is actually the result of limited competition among subcontractors. This happens when all the major trades are shared among the general contractors. The point is, care should be taken in assessing whether tight numbers really represent tight competition.

TIP

It is not at all uncommon to discover that what appears to be a very tight bid spread among general contractors is actually the result of limited competition among subcontractors. Care should be taken in assessing whether tight numbers really represent tight competition.

Progress Payment Control and Progress Assessment: Reporting Earned Value

Based on an established schedule of values, it is possible to assess progress on the entire project using a weighted percentage on a line item basis. This method is often referred to as an *earned value process*, whereby if a particular task is 50 percent complete, then 50 percent of the amount of money associated with that task is payable. There's a great deal of published information on earned value reporting.

Cost-Loaded Schedules: Line by Line

The next level up from using a schedule of values for progress payment control is to use a cost-loaded schedule. This is accomplished by taking each line item on the schedule and attaching a value to it; by monitoring progress on the schedule, the same percentage of schedule progress is applied to payment progress value.

Retainage: Assure Sufficient Funding

The degree of retainage and how retainage is managed is a contentious subject on nearly every project. The purpose of retainage is to assure that sufficient funds are available to carry out any work necessary to achieve substantial completion. Retainage should be assessed on the basis of line items of work, rather than overall work progress. Though retaining funds for this purpose is a prudent idea, doing so requires care, and when work is complete, the funds should be released.

Implementing Cost Reduction Strategies after Bidding

What can be done if bids come in overbudget? First, do not panic and do not finger-point. Then, get the project underway without spending any more money than is absolutely necessary. To that end, follow these steps:

1. *Investigate what actually happened.* There is always a reason for every overrun. It is extremely important to move quickly because time is of the essence. Everybody involved in the project should check their respective "networks" and find out if there's any particular reason for the overage.

2. *Determine the degree of competition that is actually in effect on the project.* The number of prime bidders is obvious and certainly is an indication of the degree of competition. That said, as was previously stated, it is not at all uncommon to see tightly grouped prime bidders *imply* competition when in fact they may all be sharing common subcontractors. Typically, one or two trades may be common to all prime bidders, and those one or two trades may be highly noncompetitive. A good example is control systems for repetitive projects. Specifications for the controls may be written in such a way that only a single bidder can respond. When primes know they are sharing a common bidder and that everybody has the same price, they generally do not seek additional competition. The objective is to ensure that there is adequate competition at a subcontractor level.

3. *Conduct an in-depth and proper analysis of the bids in comparison to the estimate of record.* Subsequently, meet with the bidding contractors and discuss what the source of higher-than-expected prices might be. If it is not possible to meet with the low bidder, it may be possible to meet with one of the higher bidders that is definitely out of the competitive range. This process will sometimes lead to very useful information.

4. *Take action.* It may be possible, depending on rules and regulations governing the process, to negotiate with the apparent low bidder. In general, consider negotiation before taking other steps. Keep in mind that paying a premium as a result of negotiation may be preferable to spending the time and effort to undertake rebidding. If, however, rebidding is

the only option, then it becomes necessary to consider changes to the contract documents as part of the rebidding process. Some potential changes include:

► Review general requirements for schedule and limitations.

► Substitute materials.

► Modify criteria.

► Reduce spare capacity, especially in mechanical and electrical systems.

► Adjust safety factors.

► Transfer risk.

► Improve competition.

► Postpone work not required immediately.

► Reduce scope.

► Reduce quality.

► Do budget transfers (construction budget to other budgets).

► When documents are reissued, assist the bidders by highlighting changes.

Change Order Problems

A number of problems may be encountered in the process of managing change orders. A list of common problems is as follows:

► *The change order is not a bona-fide extra; it is already part of the scope of work but has been presented as a change.* Such a change order often results from misassignments of scope between subcontractors that are passed through by the general contractor. Handling them correctly requires attention to detail in the defined scope of the original documents.

> *The change order may be based on an incorrect scope of work generally in excess of what is actually called for even when a change is legitimate.* This, too, often results from miscommunication of scope between subcontractors.

> *The same change is submitted more than once under different definition or even by different subcontractors.* In some cases, the changes may be legitimate in that they represent work from a common change among different subcontractors.

> *Obtaining a full credit for any change order, in particular when there are "zero cost" change orders.* This will occur under the theory that the owner will be pleased that the change does not cost anything, whereas the owner may be entitled to a substantial credit.

> *Quantities are measured in a number of different ways.* Because there are very few standards in the United States, it is important that prior to a change being implemented a method of measurement be agreed on. Verification of quantities may take time and effort that the owner does not want to invest. Any kind of a quantitative-based change order should be verified in proportion to its value.

> *Omissions and additions within the same change order may be priced on a different basis.* It is not uncommon to price additions and deletions using different methods. In some cases, this may be correct; for example, adding doors and deleting doors can be charged different prices. However, this is not always the case, so care should be taken when different pricing methods are applied. This is also another reason to agree on methods in the contract.

▶ *Materials may be overpriced by using list prices, that is, by ignoring discounts.* Often, pricing for change orders will be based on list prices, especially those from published sources. In fact, list prices are seldom paid because contractors will almost always receive substantial discounts. Therefore, it is important to verify pricing from several different suppliers. This is particularly common in mechanical/electrical systems.

▶ *Overhead and profit may be overcharged both at a lower-level subcontractor level all the way up to the prime.* This should be addressed in the contract, as previously pointed out.

▶ *Labor productivity for change may be estimated as substantially lower than for labor productivity overall.* In some situations, this is absolutely correct, but not always. In all cases, labor productivity should be carefully reviewed. For example, a premium may be associated with a change that will be actually put in place directly with the standard conduct of the work in hand, meaning that no adjustment for productivity is required.

▶ *A change order may include billing for site overhead costs that are already covered under general conditions, such as job superintendents, engineers, and other field staff.* Any labor billing that is not directly associated with the work should be clearly identified.

▶ *Work may be billed on a time and materials basis when unit prices are already in the contract.* Any time and materials-based pricing should be agreed to by both parties before work is started. If existing pricing from the contract or from a previous change can govern the work, then that pricing should be utilized. In some situations, unit pricing may be advantageous to the owner, and it is possible to receive a unit price lower than the contract amount. However, it is not advisable to use this technique when the basic contract pricing is not fair.

▸ *Adequate backup information may not be provided to substantiate changes.* Adequate backup information should always be required to accompany any contract change. Certainly, in the case of urgent circumstance, the change may have to be submitted without complete backup, but backup should be submitted when it is available, stating that further negotiation may be required. In all circumstances, adequate backup should be submitted for record-keeping purposes.

▸ *There is a failure to solicit competitive bids when required.* Certain changes are of such significance, or require special expertise, and simply negotiating with an existing subcontractor is not adequate. In these cases, the general contractor should be required to solicit competitive proposals from more than one qualified subcontractor. Likewise, it should be understood that mobilizing a new contractor on the project may incur additional costs that could outweigh simply negotiating with a contractor already on-site.

Understanding the Impact of Delivery Methods on Cost Management

When construction management (CM) evolved in the 1970s, the construction industry experienced its first major shift away from traditional design-bid-

> ### Claims
>
> Claims and the appropriate processing of claims is a very complex subject. Numerous reference publications are available that treat claims in detail and that can serve as guidance in dealing with claims. The Construction Management Association of America (CMAA) is one good source. Obviously, the preferred way to deal with claims is to manage projects so as to minimize or eliminate them in the first place; however, this is not always possible, so it is advisable to be prepared for dealing with this expensive and difficult aspect of the industry.

build delivery, which subsequently impacted contract and project management. More recently, design-build has emerged as a viable option, and today's owner can select from a variety of different procurement methods, known by equally variant names, including CM at Risk, "agency" CM, "pure" design-build, "bridging" design-build, "fast-tracking," "guaranteed maximum price (GMP)," and "best value" procurement.

All of these options and suboptions have built-in advantages and disadvantages from the perspectives of time, quality, cost, risk, and management control. To help to sort them out, this section describes key aspects of each delivery approach, explores advantages and disadvantages of competing systems on cost management, and examines concepts for more effectively delivering projects to the owner.

Historical Background

The need for management and oversight of the construction process has existed in one form or another since the dawn of the industry. Everyone has always agreed on the necessity of *managing* the process; what has proven more difficult is deciding *who* should provide the management and *how* the management should be provided.

In the period leading up to the Industrial Revolution, the so-called "master builder" exercised total control of the process, while relying on the trades to perform the actual work. During the Industrial Revolution, general contracting became the primary method of project construction, and until the 1960s, competitive bidding to general contractors was the primary means of project delivery. It was also during the 1960s that new tools were introduced to the construction industry; these included critical path scheduling, value engineering, and economic analysis.

When inflation soared in the 1970s, owners' dissatisfaction over spiraling construction costs gave rise to the formal establishment of construction management, especially in conjunction with "fast-tracked" overlapping of design and construction.

In the 1980s and early 1990s, new trends linked construction management with a fixed-price delivery system, referred to as a "guaranteed maximum price" or GMP. The current dramatic rise in popularity of other delivery systems, especially design-build in several forms, has added even more options for the owner.

A concurrent trend since the 1970s has been the diminishing size and capability of the owner's technical and management staff. Previously, these professionals represented a storehouse of knowledge, expertise, and experience; more recently, such broad-based knowledge has been replaced with a focus on project management alone. Concomitantly, that means the remaining staff are overloaded and undersupported; hence, "outsourcing" has become a way of life.

Design and construction professionals and cost managers now have to interact in a process with many and varied players and participants, numerous delivery options, and an owner's staff who are often only marginally capable of managing the overall process. Thus, increased care and attention are required to properly manage costs throughout the process and for the benefit of the owner.

Procurement Terminology

The process of planning, programming, designing, and constructing facilities is complex and fraught with potential conflict. To help prevent conflict and to promote effective communication, a consistent terminology is essential. Important terms are defined in the following subsections.

Phases of the Construction Process

This book has divided the construction process into three phases:

1. *Planning/Programming.* During this phase, scope, objectives, expectations, budget, schedule, and approach are identified.

2. *Design.* During design, which is usually divided into three subphases—schematic design, design development, and construction documents—the eventual products are completed plans and specifications for the project.

3. *Construction.* During the construction phase, *shop drawings and submittals* are processed, and *as-built* documents are prepared. Construction can be divided into several activities that usually proceed sequentially but may proceed in

parallel. *Procurement* activities, including scheduling, purchasing, bidding, negotiating, and award, usually precede *construction* activities, which include fabrication, delivery, assembly, erection, site construction, and field administration.

Procurement/Contractual Relationship

Owners procure services and products through a variety of methods and contract arrangements. *Services* are typically procured using an approach based primarily on qualifications. Price is always an issue but tends to be secondary to qualifications. Services to owners are generally provided by *agents,* and are directed at the owner's best interests through a *fiduciary* relationship (i.e., one based primarily on trust). *Products* are typically purchased against a set of specifications and are provided by a *vendor.* In a bidding environment, price tends to be the primary determinant; however, procurement techniques based on "best value" allow for qualifications to be considered along with price.

It is very difficult, if not impossible, to develop and maintain an *agency* relationship while maintaining a *vendor* relationship, and vice versa, as serious conflicts of interest may arise. It is possible to transition from one to the other, but it is difficult to be both at the same time.

Payment Approach

Construction contracts can be either *lump sum* or *reimbursable.* When conditions are clearly laid out and details are well understood, lump sum is generally preferred. When scope and conditions are unknown or prone to rapid change, the reimbursable, or *cost-plus,* approach may be the only viable choice.

Construction contracts can be lump sum, reimbursable, or vary in between. Contracts with known conditions are generally *bid*, with award going to the lowest responsive bidder. Other contracts are *negotiated* to either a lump sum price or to a given set of pricing conditions. *Unit price* contracts are one method of defining a *fixed price* by simulating a probable contract scope with predetermined pricing.

Award of Construction Contract

The award of a construction contract can occur at almost any point in the procurement process. The primary decision is whether the owner desires to award a construction contract in advance of the completion of documents. As a general rule, pricing on the basis of only *preliminary construction documents* requires a negotiated approach, whereas use of *final construction documents* allows for a lump sum bid.

Locking in a contract price before design work is complete can be accommodated using one of two basic approaches:

1. *Some form of initial design and documentation can be developed.* This may consist of as little as a preliminary scope and conditions, or the design may be advanced to as much as 65 percent complete. When a contract is solicited in this fashion, it is often referred to as the aforementioned guaranteed maximum price or GMP. If minimal documentation has been developed for the initial GMP, the process will often lead to a final negotiation at some future point, fixing a firm price for the contract or a *final GMP*. In some circumstances, as a means of finalizing the price, the owner may choose to have individual trade subcontracts openly bid and assigned to the construction manager.

2. *Subdivide the project into definable subprojects, which can be independently bid and priced as lump sums on the basis of completed documents for that scope of work.* These *packages* can represent sequential elements of work (e.g., sitework, foundations, structure, etc.) or they may be trade groupings. In some cases (and in certain states and municipalities), the packages may represent complete major trades and subtrades. Regardless, the final cost will not be complete until all subprojects have been bid.

Project Delivery Options

Where project delivery options are concerned, no universal agreement has been reached on terms or concepts, and definitions vary widely, with numerous variations and twists even on individual systems. The basic options can generally be described by the relationships between participants. For the purpose of highlighting impacts on cost management, the following basic options will be addressed: traditional design-bid-build, construction management at risk, and design-build. Subsequently, we will address the advantages and disadvantages of each.

Traditional Design-Bid-Build

This, the "classical" approach, maintains a design architect/engineer (A/E) in an agency relationship and a general contractor in a vendor relationship. Cost management is primarily the responsibility of the A/E team, although the owner may secure additional outside advice. Throughout the majority of this book, the traditional design-bid-build approach was used as a reference for a baseline for methodology. It is presented here in Figure 5.27.

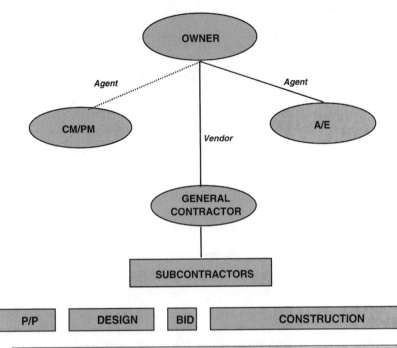

Fundamental Approach

- Prime contracts directly with owner.
- A/E selected by qualifications or qualifications/price.
- A/E prepares design to 100%.
- Open bidding to general contractors (may be prequalified).
- Award of contract to lowest responsive bidder.
- Construction start after award of contract.

Variations

- General contractor can be brought in during design for advice.
    - ▶ Can lead to negotiated contract with general contractor.
    - ▶ Or bidding can also remain open.
- Subcontracts (trades) can be bid separately.
    - ▶ Assigned to general contractor.
    - ▶ Assigned to general contractor or the owner can hold multiple prime contracts (as in New York, Pennsylvania, North Carolina).
- A CM/PM can be retained in an agency relationship to coordinate the process.

Figure 5.27 Traditional design-bid-build delivery approach.

Construction Management at Risk

Using this approach, a CM is selected, who initially acts as an agent then converts to a vendor relationship after a GMP is issued. Cost management is generally the joint responsibility of the A/E team and the CM until the GMP is issued. After the GMP, the A/E team usually retains cost management oversight responsibility. The CM at risk approach is presented in Figure 5.28.

Design-Build

The design-build family of options maintains a single entity for the procurement (design-builder). Cost management responsibility depends initially on who the owner retains to prepare an RFP, and subsequently whether the owner retains oversight service after selection of a design-builder. The design-build approach is essentially a one-step procurement from a single entity that provides both design and construction. Figure 5.29 details the design-build approach.

Summary of Approaches

In addition to the definitions of these approaches, the following points are important because they explain how an owner typically utilizes the services of the A/E, CM/PM, contractors, and the cost manager:

> ► Using any of these three approaches, the owner can retain the services of an A/E team in an agency relationship (as a prime designer or as an advisor) and may add the services of an overall construction or project manager (CM/PM) to act as an owner's representative. These services, regardless of source, are provided as an extension of the owner's staff and are a direct result

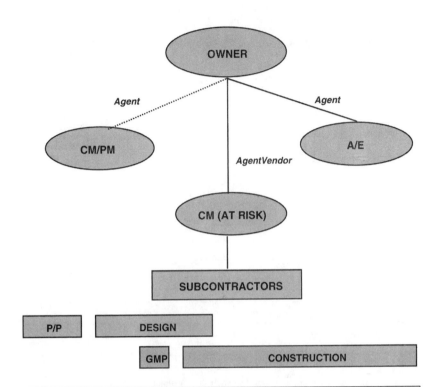

Approach
• CM (at risk) has direct contract with owner, as does A/E.
• A/E selected by qualifications or qualifications/price.
• CM (at risk) selected on qualifications or qualifications and fee for general conditions and profit.
• CM (at risk) responsible for work scheduling and means/methods.
• Construction can start prior to design completion with early packages.

Variations
• CM (PM) can be retained in an agency relationship to coordinate process.
• GMP can be followed with CM (at risk) open bidding to subcontractors.
► Final price can "float" up to GMP.
► Or "shared savings" up to GMP with owner.
► Or a firm fixed price can be negotiated.

Figure 5.28 Construction manager at risk delivery approach.

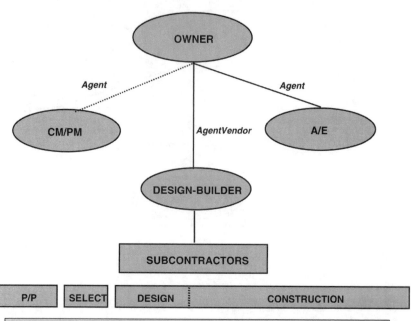

P/P	SELECT	DESIGN	CONSTRUCTION

Fundamental Approach
• Prime contract directly with owner.
• Planning/programming prepared by owner or consultant.
• Owner issues RFP with scope and performance specifications.
• Design-builder selected by qualifications and price.
• Design-builder may initially act as an agent during planning/programming.

Variations
• CM/PM and/or A/E may be retained as agents to assist in preparing RFP and overseeing process.
• Design may be advanced to approximately design development for bidding to design-builders ("bridging").
• Design-builder may include financing and complete up-front services ("turnkey").
• Land costs may also be part of package.
• Design-build package may be complete "build-to-suit" with a lease-back or lease-to-own.
• May include full operations including staffing ("design-build-operate").

Figure 5.29 Design-build delivery approach.

of the need to "outsource" what was historically an "in-house" role.

▶ The role of a cost manager under the traditional design-bid-build scenario is as presented in the body of the book. Cost management is usually provided by/through the A/E team, whose members are responsible for overseeing changes throughout design and during construction.

▶ Under the CM at risk approach, cost management is provided jointly during design, usually with some form of formal estimate reconciliation between the A/E team cost manager and the CM. After the GMP is issued, the A/E team plays an oversight role during the completion of design that is similar to the A/E team's role during construction—that is, oversight and negotiation of changes. The CM will also have an internal responsibility to "manage" design interpretation as the project proceeds from GMP through final design, procurement, and price finalization. This role is similar to internal contractor cost management under traditional design-bid-build, except that the design is not finalized.

▶ Under design-build, the design-builder may retain all major cost management functions, especially if a price guarantee is provided early in the process. The owner will generally retain some form of cost management oversight and capacity to negotiate changes and any final pricing. Using a "bridging" form of design-build, through the development of "bridging" documents, the A/E team retains traditional cost management responsibilities until the design-builder is selected and a price is reached.

Thereafter, the A/E team may continue in an oversight capacity or the owner may select a separate team, such as the PM/CM, to oversee costs.

Advantages and Disadvantages of Each Delivery Method on Cost Management

Which approach is superior for cost management? Each approach has certain built-in benefits and deficits; moreover, in some cases, because of procurement law or corporate preference, choices may be limited. Some owners avoid the use of certain delivery methods no matter what the circumstances, while others use one method exclusively—and many owners disapprove of *all* three methods!

Evaluating the advantages and disadvantages of the various approaches in a fair and reasonable way is difficult, at best. To date, the "analytical" assessments of delivery methods have represented collections of opinions—opinions of knowledgeable and capable people, to be sure, but opinions nonetheless. A completely fair analysis has yet to be conducted.

Figure 5.30 outlines the advantages and disadvantages for each of the systems discussed, all from the perspective of the owner. It becomes obvious that, under certain circumstances and for certain owners, one method will tend to perform better than others but that no one method is superior for all.

And what about performance? Does any one approach result in a better cost performance? To answer this question, risk transfer and the effects of risk transfer should be evaluated. Each approach will adjust and assess risk in some proportion to each party's willingness to accept risk. This also raises a question regarding the relationship between initial

Traditional Design-Bid-Build		
ISSUES	ADVANTAGES	DISADVANTAGES
Cost and Budget Management	• "Best price" potential. • Perception of "best price."	• Cost not finalized until bids. • Cost overruns after bid require expensive redesign. • Bidders may seek to "get low" by omitting work not clearly shown.
Schedule Impact and Management	• Delivery schedule stipulated in contract.	• Construction difficult to start before design is finished. • Extended/compressed schedules may add cost and not be evident. • Schedule changes after award difficult to implement.

Construction Manager at Risk		
ISSUES	ADVANTAGES	DISADVANTAGES
Cost and Budget Management	• Cost "guarantee" prior to design completion. • Improved perception of control. • Cost saving incentives are feasible.	• After GMP, costs may increase due to detailing not correctly reflected in the GMP. • CM may "expand" budget to create opportunity for future "savings."
Schedule Impact and Management	• Construction can start before design is complete. • Cost impact of extended/compressed schedule can be addressed prior to GMP.	• Schedule changes during construction difficult to implement.

Design-Build		
ISSUES	ADVANTAGES	DISADVANTAGES
Cost and Budget Management	• Early cost guarantee. • Price tends to match quality. • Can obtain best price for performance.	• Fair price competition difficult to verify. • Cost impact of risk issues may not be evident in initial pricing. • Owner overemphasis on price as a selection criterion may force the design-builder to compromise quality to reduce price.
Schedule Impact and Management	• Construction can start after very preliminary design. • Generally considered as most beneficial schedule approach.	• Schedule changes at any point after pricing difficult to implement. • Use of "bridging" type approach may expand schedule.

Figure 5.30 Advantages and disadvantages of each approach.

cost and final cost for a project, reflecting the impact of changes and the cost of implementing those changes. In short, there is no simple answer to which approach offers best cost performance, but it is probably fair to say that any well-managed method will produce an acceptable and cost-effective result. Conversely, any poorly managed method will undoubtedly produce an unacceptable result.

Cost Management Methodology

Cost Management Requirements

Regardless of the delivery method, the owner's need for cost management services remains. In some cases, oversight services are available from the owner's staff, but more frequently, as the result of widespread "downsizing," the owner's capabilities in this regard are limited. Few owners have facility staffs anywhere near the levels they did during the 1960s and 1970s. Furthermore, many owners simply cannot afford to hire full-time technical staff, and expecting other staff members to fill these roles is unreasonable. This situation tends to be true in both the public and private sectors.

The owner may seek services from the "designer of record," but under several delivery options the designer of record may not be in an agency position or may no longer be under contract, making it necessary for the owner to add a professional design or CM/PM consultant, as discussed previously.

The choices for project delivery have expanded and been refined significantly over the past 30 years. In particular, professional and trade associations have promoted better communications and have developed much-improved forms of agreement, general conditions, and supporting documents. At the same time, laws, rules, and regulations affecting the public sector have been changed and expanded to allow much greater flexibility and choice. Large private organizations, too, have expanded and better defined their choices.

There is no doubt that, given the wide choice of delivery methods, the owner can improve many aspects of the ultimate delivery. Better control of schedule and cost are direct results of implementing a variety of delivery methods. On the other hand, the use of CM at risk and design-build have stressed and strained an industry that is still entrenched in the traditional design and contract administration process. Many aspects of project delivery and contract management can be substantially improved and better attuned to nontraditional approaches. Areas for consideration include:

Better and More Effective Documents

➤ *Producing better documents that clarify the process of design and construction is an advantage for any delivery system.* This industry has a great deal of experience developing documents for traditional delivery, but has struggled when it comes to defining appropriate standards and approaches for nontraditional systems. While eliminating or minimizing errors and omissions remain a goal throughout the industry, documents should better communicate design intent, especially in preliminary phases.

➤ *Preparing more refined and efficient GMP pricing documents.* Using standards appropriate to traditional design-bid-build (design development level to 60 percent construction documents) is not necessarily sufficient for GMP pricing. This is particularly true in the mechanical and electrical areas, where typical design development documents are completely insufficient for pricing. As a general rule, under the GMP approach, mechanical and electrical development would have to be substantially advanced, nearly to the point of architectural and structural development. This approach is not convenient for the design process and will require more time and effort on the part of the designers to reach effective conclusion. This is a fee issue for both the designer and the owner.

▶ *Developing improved specification procedures for early-stage pricing.* In the past several years, much has been done to define methods for preliminary project descriptions and outline specifications. Performance specifications likewise have numerous advantages over prescriptive specifications, but are, in general, much more difficult to price because very little design is available. Methods are needed not only to help define design intent, but to also help those responsible for pricing. Reasonable methods are also needed to reconcile multiple estimates and to allow for reasonable tracking of changes.

Clarified Change and Change Order Procedures

▶ *Understanding the difference between an actual change and a clarification of the natural development process, in particular with CM at risk and design-build.* To that end, the industry requires standards and procedures that more rigorously define conceptual and schematic project development and that clarify when a change is actually a change.

▶ *Developing models for certain facility types would aid in this overall process, in conjunction with improved documents referenced above.* Models of this sort could help in the definition of initial project cost and provide a better benchmark for future changes.

▶ *Using past projects as a reference point can also assist in the clarification of design intent and expectation of system performance.*

Improved Selection Techniques for Construction Managers and Design-Builders

▶ *Factoring price, quality, performance, and long-term operations without the initial price dominating.* Essentially, in the selection process, the owner has to be sure that low price doesn't mean cheap.

▶ *In the traditional design-bid-build process, using a standard invitation for bid requires that the lowest responsible bidder be awarded the project regardless of history or past performance if that past performance isn't directly applicable to the ability to produce the work.* For example, the history of change orders and the aggressiveness by which the contractor pursues change orders would not be factorable in a standard invitation for bid. The objective of bidding is to *be low* in order to be awarded the project. Unfortunately, the pattern of bidders (especially in the federal government) is to concentrate on missing elements and conflicts in the documents that can be omitted from the initial bid (to get low) and to pursue them later as a change order at perhaps a significant premium.

▶ *Using a "best value," or source selection, process requires that all selection factors be defined up-front and used as the exclusive basis of selection.* Over the last decade, especially in the federal government, more and more procurements have been conducted using this process. Price can be one of the factors, but because other factors can be considered, the desire to "be low" can be offset by the desire to perform well against the other factors. Many in the industry feel that source selection produces better results.

Cost Management Methodology   291

▶ *Using long-term life-cycle performance as a factor for selection*. Because design-build selection can be based on as little as conceptual documents and performance specifications, owners want to protect themselves by incorporating life-cycle performance along with potentially long-term guarantees. In some cases, these guarantees can proceed through a design-build-operating agreement. Needless to say, this type of selection process requires some form of best value procurement.

Future Efforts

Design and construction professionals, professional societies, and trade organizations involved in cost management can do a great deal to improve the delivery of projects and overall cost management. The variety of choices available to the owner, coupled with the continuing reductions in size and capabilities of the owner's staff, are making the necessity for these improvements more evident. But regardless of the commitment of the service side of the industry, owners should take a much more aggressive position in demanding that changes and improvements be implemented; concomitantly, they should recognize that change takes time, resources, and money. Furthermore, the investment and improved standards for price determination and reconciliation in negotiation appears essential.

Conclusions

This chapter presented an organized approach to coordinating and applying the tools and techniques presented in earlier chapters, all as part of an overall cost management approach. Particular attention was focused on the early planning and conceptual/schematic phases of the development of a project, but the entire design and construction process was addressed. The necessity of integrating and coordinating cost management into the overall project delivery process is a key aspect of the book.

The author encourages readers to aggressively apply the processes and techniques presented in this book with the aim of improving cost management. Applying these techniques will help assure that scope, expectations, and budget become aligned and remain aligned throughout the life of the project and that owner demands for more effective cost management will be satisfied.

References

Books

Bull, John W., ed. *Life-Cycle Costing for Construction*. Glasgow: Blackie Academic & Professional, an imprint of Chapman & Hall, 1993.

Civitello, Andrew M., Jr. *Contractor's Guide to Change Orders*. Upper Saddle River, NJ: Prentice-Hall, Inc., 1988.

Dell'Isola, Alphonse J. *Value Engineering: Practical Applications for Design, Construction Maintenance & Operations*. Kingston, MA: R. S. Means Company, Inc., 1997.

Fatzinger, James A. S. *Basic Estimating for Construction*. Upper Saddle River, NJ: Prentice-Hall, Inc., 1997.

Kirk, Stephen J., and Alphonse J. Dell'Isola. *Life Cycle Costing for Design Professionals*, 2nd ed. New York: McGraw-Hill, 1995.

Levy, Sydney M. *Construction Databook*. New York: McGraw-Hill, 1999.

Mendler, Sandra, and William Odell. *The HOK Guidebook to Sustainable Design*. New York: John Wiley & Sons, Inc., 2000.

Parker, Donald E., and Alphonse J. Dell'Isola. *Project Budgeting for Buildings*. New York: Van Nostrand Reinhold, 1991.

Pena, William M., and Steven A. Parshall. *Problem Seeking*, 4th ed. New York: John Wiley & Sons, Inc., 2001.

Swinburne, Herbert. *Design Cost Analysis for Architects and Engineers*. New York: McGraw-Hill, 1980.

Articles, Reports, and Workbooks

American Society for Testing and Materials. "ASTM Standards on Building Economics," 4th ed. West Conshohocken, PA: American Society for Testing and Materials, 1999.

——. ASTM E 1557-97: "UNIFORMAT II: Standard Classification for Building Elements and Related Sitework," 4th ed. West Conshohocken, PA: American Society for Testing and Materials, 1999.

Bowen, Brian. "Construction Cost Management," in *The Architect's Handbook of Professional Practice*. Washington, DC: The American Institute of Architects, 1998.

——. "Building a Better Bottom-Line Course Workbook." University Park, PA: The American Institute of Architects, and Pennsylvania State University, 1988.

Bowen, Brian, and Michael D. Dell'Isola. "Cost Management Applications Workshop Workbook," prepared for the American Institute of Architects Convention, 2000.

Committee on Budget Estimating Techniques, Building Research Board. "Improving the Accuracy of Early Cost Estimates for Federal Projects." Washington, DC: National Research Council National Academy Press, 1990.

Construction Industry Institute. "Improving Early Estimates," in *Best Practices Guide,* Austin, TX: Construction Industry Institute, 1998.

——. "Alignment during Pre-Project Planning," A Key to Success Workbook, 1997.

Construction Management Association of America. "Cost Management Procedures." Washington, DC: Construction Management Association of America, 2000.

——. "Contract Administration Procedures," 2000.

Dell'Isola, Michael D. "Cost Estimating for Land Development Professionals," Presentation Workbook. Chantilly, VA: Engineers and Surveyors Institute, 2000.

——. "Professional Management Services Applied to Different Contracting Methods," report given at Construction Management Association of America Annual Conference, Washington, DC, 1997.

———. "Impact of Delivery Systems on Contract Management," *Construction Specifier Magazine,* September 2001, pp. 18–35.

———. "Conceptual Estimating for Design-Build Projects," Course Workbook. Washington, DC: Design-Build Institute of America, 2001.

Dell'Isola, Michael, and Beatriz Pita and Thomas Wiggins. "Learning How to Control Building Costs," Course Workbook. Atlanta, GA: Georgia Tech College of Architecture, 2000.

General Services Administration and Hanscomb Associates Inc. "Value Engineering Program Guide for Design and Construction," Washington, DC: General Services Administration, 1992.

———. "Cost Estimating Guide," Draft, Washington, DC: General Services Administration, 1999.

———. "UNIFORMAT: Cost Control & Estimating System Database," Database and Report. Washington, DC: General Services Administration, 1975.

Hanscomb Roy Associates Inc. "MASTERCOST: A National Building Cost Data File System Report." Washington, DC: American Institute of Architects, 1974.

Horsley, F. Willliam. "Means Scheduling Manual." Kingston, MA: R. S. Means Company, Inc., 1998.

Marshall, Harold E. "Techniques for Treating Uncertainty and Risk in Economic Evaluation of Building Investments." Gaithersburg, MD: National Institute of Standards and Technology, 1988.

Marshall, Harold E., and Robert P. Charette. "UNIFORMAT II: Elemental Classification for Building Specifications, Cost Estimating, and Cost Analysis." Gaithersburg, MD: National Institute of Standards and Technology, 1999.

Pierce, David R., Jr. "Project Planning & Control for Construction." Kingston, MA: R. S. Means Company, Inc., 1988.

References

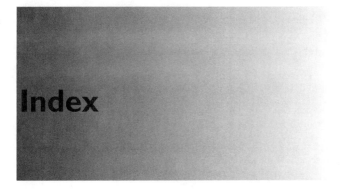

Index